DR IAN GREEN Hon. Doc. RSAMD was born ⟨⟩e son of a Highland piper and head gardener. ⟨⟩ resulted in many moves until the family fin⟨⟩e Ian completed his education. He followed h⟨⟩ ⟨⟩an an apprenticeship.

When National Service beckoned, Ian signed for three years in the army, serving as a vehicle mechanic in the REME, including two years in Korea and Japan. He was demobbed in 1955 holding the rank of full corporal.

Another change of direction saw Ian join Edinburgh City Police, later Lothian and Borders Police, in which he served 30 years. During this time, he married his wife June and raised three children. Ian gained wide police experience in various specialised departments before being promoted to sergeant and latterly inspector, retiring in 1985.

During his service Ian pursued an interest in folk music and was involved in many aspects of the music – as organiser of the Police Folk Club ('Fuzzfolk'), co-editor of *Sandy Bell's Broadsheet*, co-founder of the Edinburgh Folk Club, concert promoter and assistant to Dr John Barrow, director of the Edinburgh Folk Festival.

In between times, Ian found time to grow and exhibit award-winning chrysanthemums, and represent Scotland in the Annual International Angling Match.

In 1986, Ian launched Greentrax Recordings which has become one of the most successful independent record labels in the UK. Many awards have been bestowed upon Ian, including the Hamish Henderson Award for services to traditional music, entry into the Scots Trad Awards Hall of Fame, and culminating in an honorary doctorate from the RSAMD in 2006.

This autobiography looks at Ian's active, varied and interesting life as he turned 76 years of age.

Since first meeting Ian Green at the Edinburgh police folk club ('Fuzzfolk') during my early teens, I've watched a man who has worked tirelessly to turn his passion in to a profession, a dedicated, caring individual who has frequently risked all to promote the music and musicians he believes in. The Greentrax Empire has grown, but it's not really an empire it's more like one huge, happy family with a proud and beaming father figure watching over it.
DR PHIL CUNNINGHAM MBE

You know he would put his hand in the fire for you – that's Ian Green.
BRIAN MCNEILL, Musician, Composer and Author

A man whose personal integrity and passion for the music are only two of the reasons why I admire him tremendously.
ERIC BOGLE, Singer/Songwriter

fuzz to folk

Trax of My Life

IAN GREEN

Luath Press Limited

EDINBURGH

www.luath.co.uk

First published 2011

ISBN: 978-1-906817-69-5

The publisher acknowledges subsidy from

ALBA | CHRUTHACHAIL

towards the publication of this book.

The paper used in this book is recyclable. It is elemental chlorine free (ECF)
and manufactured from sustainable wood pulp forests. This paper and its
manufacture are approved by the National Association of Paper Merchants
(NAPM), working towards a more sustainable future.

Printed and bound by
Thomson Litho, East Kilbride

Typeset in 11pt Sabon by
3btype.com

contents

appenöices

acknowledgements

N WRITING THIS autobiography I depended principally on my memory so please excuse the lack of specific dates in places, although to be honest I am sure many get bored with such exact detail, so perhaps the chapters benefit on occasions from these omissions. I also apologise to anyone who finds some minor discrepancy or worse even, but please do remember that events in a 76 year life may well become distorted by the passage of time. The memory does play tricks on you. That is for sure.

I was greatly helped by a diary I found in our loft which spanned the years 1953 and 1954. Oh, that I had kept a diary all my life. I was also able to refer to various documents, scrapbooks, photos and notes I have kept for years. I am a bit of a hoarder you see. I was also greatly helped by friends. What would we do without friends?

The person who contributed most was my good friend Kate Ward, and I owe her a great debt. When she heard that I was writing my autobiography, she volunteered to proofread and correct my draft, making very useful suggestions as I presented each chapter to her. If the truth be known, Kate additionally greatly improved my grammar and helped me choose a few photographs from many. Kate was always a great source of encouragement to me when I seemed to have lost my way or confidence was ebbing. To be honest, at times I thought I was wasting my time! She was also solely responsible for me completing it in a relatively short period of time. I actually started the book in 2006, but was writing it at home where there were too many distractions, and I was using a laptop, which I never really mastered. I stopped midway through the first chapter and did not return to the book again until late in 2008 when Kate volunteered to help me. She didn't know then what she had let herself in for! Thanks Kate. Thanks also to Tom Ward for his helpful comments.

There were several people who willingly provided information and I particularly wish to thank Mary Duff, a lovely lady from Forres, who heard me on The Reel Blend. She wrote to Robbie Shepherd who kindly passed her address on to me. We both attended Fornighty School at Lethen and, while I don't think our paths ever crossed, we have many things in common. We regularly communicate and June and I have visited her home.

Mary readily passed on information about Lethen Estate and names of people whose identity I had forgotten. With the help of Willie Chisholm and Pat Smart, who both remembered me, she was able to elicit even more information on my behalf. I also met Willie, a real gem, and what a knowledge he has of Lethen and the surrounding area. It was also Mary who finally ended my search for a wind-up gramophone when she tracked one down in Forres in 2009. Thanks on both counts Mary.

Others who were of great assistance are Judith Sleigh and Dr John Barrow who helped fill in my memory blanks on the early Edinburgh Folk Festival years. I am also most indebted to John for writing the foreword.

Both Cath Mack and Elaine Sunter were always willing to rummage on websites to confirm historical and other details for me (I am lacking this kind of computer expertise) and they never tired of my cries for help. Cath, in committing my words to CD for Kate, read chapter by chapter, made favourable comments, and I was often aware of enthusiastic chuckles, providing further encouragement. She also came up with a very good suggestion for a title: 'Diction of Doc Green'. Maybe too obscure for a book shelf?

My thanks to ex-colleague Tom Fergusson for permitting me to include some of the humorous stories from his book *Capital Coppers – The Lighter Side of Edinburgh's Finest*, some of which I had contributed.

I have included many photos and memorabilia such as newspaper clippings, mainly from the *Edinburgh Evening News* I think. The photos are from many sources, long forgotten, but thanks to Louis Di Carlo (for a stage picture of myself), Brian Aris (for the Barbara Dickson photo), The Scottish Parliament Broadcasting Unit for the Sheena Wellington image, Katzel Henderson for use of the Hamish photo, my wife June for a variety of photos, Douglas McCalman, the RSAMD and the artists who allowed me to use their publicity photos. Tash MacLeod drew the wonderful cartoon of the three *Sandy Bell's Broadsheet* editors and Malky McCormick (a genius) allowed me to include his wonderful sketches.

My wife June also provided much useful information, even although her memory is supposed to be worse than mine! I am also most grateful to her for allowing me to disclose so much of our private life. We must have got some things right though, as we have been together for 54 years, and still love each other – even after this book! June read the draft and surprisingly only asked for a couple of minor amendments which I was pleased to make. She also kindly remarked that it was a really good read.

I have taken the liberty of mentioning many people by name in this autobiography. I hope they forgive me, and thanks for not suing! Where I considered it necessary I did not disclose the identify of individuals, to protect the innocent and not-so-innocent!

This book is dedicated to my daughter Linda Brown whom I love dearly.

Ian Green

FOREWORD

HIS BOOK READS, unfolds even, like possibly the longest curriculum vitae ever – school, employment as a young gardener, cycle-speedway rider, drafted into the British Army for the Korean War (and demobbed as a corporal), a mechanic, footballer, 30 years as a policeman (including promotion to inspector), angler, music organiser, concert promoter, record seller, and latterly, and finally, owner of the most successful small record label in the UK – and not so small now either. And perhaps not even finally yet!

Ian seems to be the epitome of the Scots 'lad o' pairts' for, although going to university never entered his life 'plan' (or perhaps more correctly, his life ramble), he ended up with a degree anyway: the honorary degree conferred by RSAMD for his tireless work on behalf of Scottish traditional music and the musicians who sing and play it. And thoroughly well-deserved it was too.

I was befriended by Ian and his indefatigable wife, June, a long time ago now towards the end of the 1960s, a decade which turned the western world on its cultural head in many ways. Certainly, as far as popular culture was concerned, the 1960s provided a watershed after which there was no going back. We entered the decade after years of deprivation for many as a result of WWII, soon followed by the Cold War and the Korean War. Society was changing rapidly after the minor advent of skiffle music; but then came rock 'n' roll in the mid 1950s, and young (and sometimes not so young) musicians caught rebellious youthful imaginations as never before with their free-wheelin' take on culture.

Against this background arises our hero in the far north of Scotland, in the beautiful but hard-as-nails rurality of Morayshire. Born shortly before the outbreak of WWII, Ian's young life took a major turn when the family relocated to Edinburgh in the 1950s as his father sought employment after life in the countryside changed irreversibly.

From then on, as the young Green grew, matured, married and gained employment of various kinds, he found pleasure in doing things for which school had ill-prepared him – like simply surviving and indeed succeeding – in a competitive world where hard work brought rewards and not a few knocks along the way. In fact, this is the story of an ordinary Joe like many, many other people through the ages, who simply had to face up to life with a degree of native wit and intelligence, and make his luck rather than wait for things to drop into his lap.

Ian has chronicled his life openly and honestly here and I hope other readers will find as much enjoyment, at least, as I did in its unfolding twists and turns, and perhaps even draw some inspiration from a life fully and well lived – and far from complete yet.

Dr John Barrow

part 1

A Wee Mistake.

CHAPTER ONE

the early years – always on the move

I WAS BORN ON the 29 January 1934 at the Greshop on the banks of the River Findhorn, Forres, Morayshire – I was a mistake! It didn't bother me at that precise moment, although I bawled the house down about something! Being a mistake did, however, cause me some grief when I did eventually find this out and was, I believe, responsible for a bit of an inferiority complex I laboured under in later years. That complex also left me with an obsessive need to succeed above all else, in whatever I turned my hand to and, while this determination has tended to get in the way of relationships during my life, it has also resulted in me being able to accomplish things I lacked confidence for in the first place! But I'm getting ahead of myself.

According to my birth certificate I was born the son of John Whitecross Green, head gardener, and Mary Anne Bonnyman, domestic servant. I should have been named Iain, but I understand that my father met some friends for a dram or two on the way to the Registrar's Office and he spelled my Christian name as Ian! I was the youngest of three 'Greenies' – my elder sister Elizabeth, six years older, and brother James ('Jimmy' or 'Sonny' as he was strangely nicknamed in his early years) who was three years my senior and always able to kick the living daylights out of me when we were growing up – and did! Elizabeth and I had a somewhat closer relationship until it was soured by events when I was in my teens. Like most families we had to play the 'happy families' game from time to time.

My father was head gardener on the modest Greshop Estate, but had served his apprenticeship on the much bigger estate and walled garden of Burgie Estate in Morayshire, where he underwent rigorous training. He had to stand to attention with his 'bunnet' doffed when the laird passed by! His first position as head gardener was apparently on an estate near Forfar but that was a short-stay venture, as were so many of Dad's positions in the '30s and '40s. This was due, in no small way, to the forced closure of Scottish estates and the decline of the many wonderful walled gardens – caused by post First World War death duties, plus rising labour and other costs. Despite improvements in working conditions, the wages of a head gardener of those times still only provided a meagre existence and, even in later years when we were assured by the politicians that we had 'never had it so good', my parents remained close to the poverty line for much of their lives. They deserved much more but I never heard either complain about their lot and their philosophy throughout their lives remained – 'there are many far worse off than us'.

Moray enjoys a wonderfully mild climate – something to do with the Gulf Stream – or so Dad assured me, although I was never really convinced by that one. No denying, however, the Moray Firth always enjoys more pleasant climatic conditions than other parts of Scotland, helping those highly skilled gardeners of the 19th and 20th centuries to produce high quality and often quite exotic fruit, flowers and vegetables within their high-walled, sheltered gardens. These were mainly to supply the estate house, always known to us on every estate we lived on as 'the big house'. Dad was one of the best gardeners of his time and while his thorough training was based on practical experience, he had a natural gift, with gentle 'green fingers' and a love of the soil. Strangely his burning ambition as a young boy had been to learn the trade of saddler, but he was forced to abandon that notion because no apprenticeship was available. He had to turn to apprentice gardener to earn a meagre wage which was, nevertheless, desperately needed by his mother, Granny Green, who was eventually to give birth to a total of 13 children. I was privileged

Dad (back row, fourth from right) when he was a member of the Seaforth Highlanders Territorial Pipe Band, Forres.

and proud to admire Dad's gardening efforts, and saw him win many prizes at horticulture shows, especially in post WWII years. I was fortunate to learn some of his remarkable gardening skills in later years. Dad was also a pretty good Highland bagpipe player and for a while was a member of the Seaforth Highlanders Territorial Pipe Band in Forres, along with my Uncle Bill (Duncan).

'Mam', funny it was never Mum, was a great mother, even though it fell to her to administer the occasional (but always well deserved) dose of corporal punishment, believing as she did that to 'spare the rod is to spoil the child'. This was referred to as a 'leathering' and in later life we jokingly teased Mam that Friday was bath night but also the night for a leathering whether we needed it or not (not true of course). The minor but effective physical punishment I was exposed to at home caused me no physical injury or any mental damage, but resulted in a relatively well-behaved child, with a good sense of discipline and consideration for others – something not always evident in the 21st century. Some of the badly-behaved children I come across nowadays leave me in no doubt that the pendulum has swung too far in the wrong direction.

Mam totally devoted herself to looking after her beloved John, three children and the organisation of her home. She never spared herself in these pursuits and was particularly adept at managing the purse strings. We never went hungry or lacked the necessities of life, being always cleanly turned out, even in hand-me-downs, while enjoying a clean, warm home – even in difficult times. Mam was a wonderful cook of homely Scottish food, and one of the best bakers I have ever known. Her griddle scones, pancakes and many delights from the oven were something to behold. Her 'clooty dumplings' were a work of art and for years the sole but exciting birthday present the 'Greenies' received – if you found the silver three-penny piece in your slice, then even better! No expensive Christmas presents for us either, just one of Dad's socks, hung up on the mantelpiece and filled by Santa with an apple, an orange, a few nuts (if available), a penny and maybe snakes and ladders or some similar simple game or toy. The strange thing is that these small gifts gave us immeasurable pleasure. This and the very commercial aspect of modern day Christmas were, I think, what eventually left me cold about this religious festival, although being an atheist may have contributed towards my desire to eventually dissociate myself from something I really do not believe in!

Yes, we were lucky children to be born to John and Mary Green and I feel fortunate to have been brought up by two such generous, honest and decent people, loved by everyone who knew them. They died within a few years of each other in the '70s/'80s, and I miss them terribly to this day. I frequently dream that they are alive and back with us.

My first recollection as a child is of sitting on top of a cartload of swedes, pulled by one of those monstrous, but ever so gentle, Clydesdales so common on Scottish farms prior to the farm tractor revolution. Why that small incident should have stuck in my memory, I really don't know, but it remains a vivid picture to this day. Dad had by then upped stakes from the Greshop, which I believe was put up for sale and later became part of an industrial estate, and was gardening on the Pluscarden Estate near Elgin. The only other recollection I have of Pluscarden is of a very stupid woman, a neighbour probably, who took me on a hunting expedition for, of all things, poisonous adders. These she proceeded to push and prod into various receptacles to be sold on, probably for medical experimentation. The snakes scared the living daylights out of me but, even worse, on the journey to and from Adder Hill, as it was known locally, I was forced to walk along the parapet of a bridge which seemed very high to me. I recall becoming hysterical and pleading to go home to Mam. I have no doubt that horrendous experience contributed to my subsequent uncontrollable fear of heights and severe vertigo. It also resulted in recurring snake-filled nightmares which continue to this day. That was my first introduction to an insensitive human being.

After a short stay at Pluscarden we were on the move again, this time to an estate near Rhynie in Aberdeenshire. Before all the packing boxes had been emptied, Dad had fallen out with the laird and we were off again to the Glen of Rothes, a shooting lodge set in that lovely valley between Rothes and Elgin. The lodge had yet another beautiful and prolific walled garden which produced all the usual fruits, flowers and vegetables. That was where I first tasted fresh apricots and nectarines. The conditions of employment for head gardeners always included free fruit and vegetables from the garden and fire logs and coal to heat the rent-free, 'tied' house. This did provide us with a very healthy fruit and veg diet. In addition, were the occasional hare, rabbit, pheasant, grouse, pigeon, haunch of venison and fresh salmon supplied by the estate gamekeeper, who presumably benefited from Dad's gifts of vegetables.

Some of these unusual ingredients left me with a lifelong adventurous taste in food. But nothing really tastes as good as 'stolen fruit', and the young Greenies, often in the company of visiting cousins, would carry out commando-style raids on the succulent fruit locked so temptingly behind those garden doors. These thefts would surely have cost Dad his job had the laird caught us in the act. I like to believe it was not serious crime though, just a bit of innocent fun and adventure, since we left with only a pocketful of apples, pears or whatever was in season at the time. I was the youngest and was only tolerated on these raids because I might 'spill the beans' (excuse the pun) if left behind. To gain entry into the garden it was necessary for the culprits to climb the high garden wall. This was totally beyond my capabilities, so I was invariably left outside as lookout. I had the last laugh on one occasion though. While the others struggled to the top of the wall, leaving me complaining bitterly at the bottom, I tried the handle of the usually locked and bolted garden door which magically opened at my touch. I was in paradise and sampling my first tasty apple before the others had managed to scramble down the inner wall.

The Glen of Rothes years were a glorious period of my young life, despite the fact that the Second World War broke out just as I was about to enter the exciting, but slightly intimidating, world of strict Highland schooling. My first day at Rothes Primary School did not go well and when Elizabeth dropped me off at Primary One I was not a happy chap.

Ian being interviewed by Robbie Shepherd for 'Summer Roads', with producer Jennifer Forrest, at Rothes Primary School.

Apparently I screamed and bawled the place down for the major part of that first fearful day – I wanted my Mam! I gradually settled into school routine however, even though this entailed a trek of several miles on foot some days. On winter mornings, the long, cold and sometimes stormy walk ended with a visit to the Rothes bakery shop where we were welcomed by the generous owner (who seemed in my young mind always covered in flour) with a hot 'buttery' (a kind of morning roll with high butter content) liberally spread with fresh butter. Why do only bakers in the north-east of Scotland know how to make butteries?

The primary school in Rothes holds no other nightmares for me, so I must have enjoyed my spell there. We always found things of interest at lunchtime or after school, such as a visit to the 'smiddy' (blacksmith's shop) where you could watch big Clydesdale horses being shod. The smell of burning horse hoof, when the smithy stuck the newly-made, red-hot shoe onto the mighty hoof to check for size, is a smell I will remember always. One unusual caper by us schoolboys comes to mind though. The boys' toilet (urinal) was not covered overhead, but the facing wall was fairly high in relation to small boys. The aspiration of all the boys in my class was to 'pee' over this wall, while the girls stood at a safe distance and watched for a stream emerging over the top. They seemed very impressed on such occasions, I have to say!

School summer holidays are imprinted indelibly on my mind because it was always sunny, or so it seemed, and we ran about in bare feet with the gamekeeper's son (James Roy, I think) and visiting cousins – Betty and Alastair McIntyre, and Gertrude and Jack Tevendale – and the Smith family children, friends of Mam and Dad from the Greshop, I think. It seemed that we spent days on end building a raft (or was it a bridge?) to reach an island in a pond situated in the field opposite our house. We never reached the island but we certainly had great fun trying. Mam must have been fed up washing the mud out of our clothes, but strangely I don't recall us getting into bother for what was probably a fairly risky escapade. No one drowned and none of us ever sustained more than a cut or bruise.

I did suffer a nasty accident a year or two earlier though, prior to attending school. My father was using a pick to dig a hole for some purpose and I was dangerously close to his rear when I saw something of interest being unearthed. I ran forward just as Dad brought the pick back over his shoulder to have another whack, when the blunt end of the pick met my forehead. I was knocked out and bled like a stuck pig, but apparently bounced back after a good bawl and without needing to be hospitalised. I assume by then I had earned the reputation for having a good pair of lungs! The scar was still visible when I subsequently joined the army, and was recorded as a 'distinguishing mark'.

I remember clearly the day war was declared against Germany in 1939 because Mam's sister, Aunty Jess (McIntyre), was visiting us. Quite an eccentric person in my view, she started wailing and moaning as the news came through on our old wet-and-dry battery-operated wireless, and pronounced, 'We'll a' be deid soon.' It all seemed hellishly exciting to me but, at that time, I did not have a clue as to the reality of war. Shortly after the declaration the Glen of Rothes Shooting Lodge and the extensive estate were requisitioned by the army for the duration of the war, as happened to many of the Highland estates. We found ourselves in the middle of a huge army training camp, which was very exciting for my brother Jimmy and me, but was the death knell of the lovely walled garden and the end of the shooting lodge. Dad was conscripted, joined the Army Catering Corps and was sent off for training as a cook, only to be involved in a bad shooting accident which caused him to be invalided out of the army.

Grandad Bonnyman came to stay in the small 'bothy' adjoining our house. He was recovering from a broken back, sustained in an almost fatal farming accident – he was thrown off the top of a cartload of corn sheaves when his Clydesdale horse suddenly moved forward. He was employed by the laird as the solitary caretaker/gardener. Dad had to take temporary employment at the local Glen Grant Whisky Distillery at Rothes while he recovered from his shotgun wounds and sought a new head gardener position. With few gardening skills, Grandad basically filled the walled garden with potatoes as part of the war effort ('digging for victory' as Winston Churchill described it). The decay of the greenhouses, flower borders and fruit trees began and, by the end of the war, the garden was an overgrown wilderness. Years later I revisited the Glen of Rothes to find the remains of the garden had been bulldozed aside. Gravel was being quarried from below, revealing the secret that this natural drainage had provided an essential ingredient for the fertile garden which flourished on an otherwise peat-covered Highland hillside.

Jimmy and I quickly made friends with the soldiers. Some were Dunkirk survivors and part of the 51st Highland Division, far from home and their families. Understandably we were almost adopted by these homesick souls with a vacuum to fill. We frequently hung about the cookhouse next door to our house for tasty handouts. We were spoiled rotten with treats of chocolate, already rationed and difficult to buy even if you had the necessary ration coupons, plus army slab fruitcake and more. Our new-found friends also introduced us to the bawdy language and crude jokes of the British soldier, much to Mam's chagrin. One unforgettable highlight occurred when two soldier buddies gave me a lift to school in their Bren-gun carrier (complete with mounted machine gun) and deposited me at the school gates. I climbed out of that carrier in front of my school pals as proud as punch and, to further elevate my school standing, the teacher called me to the front of the class to give a blow-by-blow account of the journey. It was the proudest moment of my young life up to then and I was class hero for a long time!

Jimmy and I had other exploits which we undertook quite fearlessly from time to time – of which poor Mam knew nothing. One was to creep unnoticed onto the army firing range, which accommodated both small arms and artillery, often with bullets and shells flying towards the various targets. Not satisfied with this hugely dangerous prank, we'd then await the end of the firing exercises and departure of the soldiers when we'd search for discarded live ammunition. We'd then jam the .303 bullets into fence posts or dykes and 'fire' the rounds by placing a nail against the firing cap and whacking it with a stone. Where the bullet was likely to go without first passing down a rifle barrel was anyone's guess, but fortunately no one was ever struck by the stray bullets. Occasionally we'd come across a live Thunderflash, used by the army to provide realistic battlefield explosions. These we would then hurl at each other until one day, inevitably, one ignited and exploded close to my face, causing a burn which we had great difficulty explaining away to Mam. How we were never seriously injured, or worse, is now a marvel to me. It all seemed like fun at the time – and certainly gave us a tale to tell at school.

Air raid warnings occurred from time to time and the soldiers would rush to machine-gun emplacements and, under the cover of the blackout, we'd creep up on a position and throw stones at them. Often we had to run for our lives when we scored a hit. To include all the exciting incidents and events of 'life in an army training camp' could fill another book but, suffice to say, the war was welcomed with open arms by two country 'loons' who would otherwise have grown up in a quiet rural environment.

Grandad Bonnyman was an incredible old character. Well over six feet tall with a back as straight as a rod, a white moustache and a shocking temper, he owned a wind-up gramophone and a substantial collection of

Jimmy Shand and other 78rpm recordings. The gramophone made him a popular visitor to neighbours in the Glen, where even the battery-operated 'wireless' was still a novelty. Grandad would strap his gramophone and a few 78s onto his back, leap onto his old fashioned, high, upright bicycle and pedal off into the night to entertain some far-flung neighbour or 'girlfriend' (yes, he was a bit of a lad!) with this relatively new form of entertainment. When Jimmy or I were in his favour, which varied from week to week if not day to day, the favoured one would be invited into the sanctum of Grandad's bothy to be plied with apples and other goodies, while being entertained by Jimmy Shand on the gramophone. I think his 78 collection was my very first introduction to Scotland's traditional music and I vowed then that one day I'd have my own wind-up gramophone and record collection. It was to be 2009 before I purchased the wind-up, but the other half of that dream was achieved much more quickly, and I now have a huge collection of traditional music recordings on 78s, LPs, cassettes and CDs.

The first big journey I recall going on was one Saturday when Mam and Dad dressed us all up for a trip by bus to Elgin. This was an amazing journey for a wee guy like me – I actually believed Elgin was where the world ended (some people might agree!). I remember we were taken to the matinee at the 'pictures' (cinema) for the first time, but I have absolutely no idea what we saw. However, I do recall that we were then taken to a fish and chip shop for my first fish and chip tea. If you have never had a fish and chip tea you must do this soon before such places are no more. This was a grand day out and I remember falling asleep on the bus journey home – a happy and contented loon who had gone to the edge of the world and back!

During this period my entrepreneurship came to the surface and my first business enterprises were undertaken – picking and bunching snowdrops and daffodils off the estate and selling them on to Rothes florists earned the family a few pence; gathering the eggs of seagulls nesting on the nearby hillsides, which was also part of the war effort; tattie-howking; polishing soldiers' boots, shining their uniform buttons or performing any task for a few pennies. Gathering seagull eggs off the hillside was fun but slightly dangerous because the seagulls did not take kindly to the theft of their forthcoming chicks and frequently dive-bombed us in an attempt to frighten us off. We must have had a sixth sense about which would be 'good' eggs (edible) as opposed to eggs that were close to hatching (inedible, of course) because, when we got them home and put them through the 'water test', we invariably had it right. I cannot recall now how it worked, but I think that if the egg sank it was close to hatching and if it floated it was okay. Strange that many years later I should join the Royal Society for the Protection of Birds – probably my conscience from the '40s.

It was also at the Glen of Rothes that Jimmy and I tried our hands for the first time at smoking. The war was on and tobacco was scarce and, while Mam and Dad both smoked Woodbine, we resorted to rolled-up brown paper – absolutely disgusting. Anyway, we hid ourselves away in a wee shed to try out this adult caper and had a good fug (or fag) going when the door burst open and we met the full anger of Dad, not a man who roused easily. He gave us both a kick up the arse as we bolted for cover. Dad never held grudges for long though. I remember, during a really heavy fall of snow, he spent the day in his potting shed making sledges for us all, and arrived home in the evening with three of them. What enormous fun we had on a nearby slope with these home-made wooden sledges.

Glen of Rothes was the first place I tried my hand at fishing for trout. I fished in the nearby burn, armed with a worm on a hook at the end of a line attached to a bamboo cane. In a relatively short time I caught a wee trout which I carried home as proud as punch to Mam who promptly fried it for my tea.

As the war progressed Dad continued to work at Glen Grant Distillery, but on occasions he was coming home from night shift very drunk and one morning was found lying in a ditch beside his bicycle. The workers didn't get drunk on whisky though. The Customs and Excise men ensured workers got only their then regulation 'dram' at their break and end of shift. The workers, including Dad, were drinking 'ale' – the malt mixture brewing in open vats before distillation began. This stuff had the potency of beer and, when taken regularly throughout the night when there was less supervision, plus the two free drams during the shift, was a recipe for disaster. The 'free distillery dram' was outlawed some years later for safety reasons.

This could not go on and fortunately Dad found a position as head gardener on the Lethen Estate near Auldearn. Once again the boxes were packed, the linoleum was rolled up, the paper stripped off the walls (only kidding) and we were on the move again. Lethen was another glorious place for a child to grow up and I settled down quickly. With one exception, I absolutely loved Lethen Estate and the surrounding area.

The exception was the headmaster of the local Fornighty School, Mr Fyffe. He was a fairly tall, straight man with a haircut which was 'down to the bone', penetrating and frightening eyes, exaggerated by very thick 'bottle-bottom' glasses and the most evil temper I have ever known in a man. The school had only two classrooms. One teacher, a lovely gentle girl named Pearl Campbell, taught the very young children, while he taught the classes up to the qualifying stage for secondary school. As I recall there were four rows of desks and each row in Fyffe's room represented a different year. So, at any one time during the day he would be covering four different subjects – one class writing an essay maybe, another doing sums, another studying a history book and one class out at the blackboard having a geography lesson or such like.

We had only been at Fornighty School a day or two, and I was in the younger class, when I first suffered Fyffe's brutality. We arrived at school one morning to learn that a telephone kiosk close to our home had been slightly damaged the previous afternoon, and the suspects were school kids. Jimmy and I had passed the telephone box and had seen some of our classmates in the kiosk, but had walked on. When interrogation began Fyffe immediately settled on us as the prime suspects but, after quizzing Jimmy briefly, for some unknown reason, he was released and I became the sole suspect – and as far as Fyffe was concerned I was guilty! But he wanted a confession and he resorted to violence to get it. (Remember the belt or tawse?) I got two of the belt and was then locked in a dark cupboard for ten minutes or so, with the threat that should I not admit causing the damage then punishment with the belt would be increased. I came out of the cupboard still unable to admit to something I hadn't done. Four of the belt followed, then back into the dark cupboard for another ten minutes. Out of the cupboard to six more of the belt, still no admission, and back into the cupboard again. Now remember, this was happening to a young boy not even ten years of age, so what did I do when I was back in total darkness? Well, self-preservation must have taken over and, when I again emerged, petrified and with my hands now stinging badly, I could only blurt out – 'It was me that done it sir.' I was then marched in front of both classrooms and made to confess again to each.

You might ask, why did I not go home and report this assault to my parents and have this madman, because that is what I thought he was, removed from the teaching profession? Well, this was the '40s when corporal punishment was still administered in schools. More importantly I suppose, in those days, the head teacher, the doctor, the local minister, the laird and the local 'bobby' were all regarded as pillars of society who could do no wrong. (We know better now.) I did go home that afternoon and tried to explain, but the predictable parental reply in those days was, 'If you got the belt at school, you must have deserved it.' End of story. It taught me one very important lesson though, which stood me in good stead in later years as a police officer: that forcing an admission out of a suspect is no guarantee you have the actual culprit, and quite rightly the law demands proof!

By the time I went into Fyffe's class Jimmy had moved on to Nairn Academy some six miles away. Rattling pupils' heads severely against the blackboard or wall was another of Fyffe's delights. One day he grabbed my classmate Mary (who I was already having romantic notions about) and rattled her so severely that poor Mary peed herself in front of the entire classroom, while I stood rigid as urine splashed against my bare legs. My romantic notions died in that terrible moment! Few days passed without someone in our classroom, especially me, suffering the belt at his hands. Not for misbehaving, I hasten to add, as was the intended use of the tawse in the educational system of that time, but for spelling or sum errors which could not be instantly corrected. In my memory, no one ever misbehaved in that classroom. Fear ensured that.

One last incident relating to Fyffe before I move on to all the good things about Lethen, is one which, in retrospect, brings a smile (black humour, I suppose). During the war all schools were encouraged by the government to grow vegetables on school land as part of the dig for victory campaign, and he was enthusiastic – although it was us poor kids who had to do all the work, while he and the school kitchen benefited from the fresh vegetables. Fyffe also moved his beehives into the school garden and, as you can imagine, children and bees do not mix well. One day, when all the kids were out weeding in the garden, bee-stings became more frequent as we neared the front of the hives. An impromptu meeting of my fellow pupils was held and they unanimously elected Ian Green, as the oldest boy (and having surprisingly survived a year or two of Fyffe's brutality), to report the excessive bee problem. I need hardly say his reaction was extreme, and the entire class was threatened with the belt. I did not utter another word, ran from the classroom and, for the next half-hour, any passer-by was treated to the hilarious sight of one kid at a time racing to the front of the hives, grabbing a handful of weeds and then racing out, with the free hand flailing at the angry bees. Humorous to imagine perhaps but, for my classmates, it was a straight choice of bee-stings or Fyffe's belt. The bees won hands down. The highest number of stings that day to one pupil was, as I recall, six!

Near the end of my time at Fornighty School, Fyffe moved to Elgin to take up the position of headmaster of Elgin Academy. (Somebody must have thought highly of him.) I would like to think he was from then on deskbound and far less likely to be in daily physical contact with kids. By contrast, his replacement was an absolute gentleman, brought out of retirement to help the war effort and, for the first time, we actually had a school sports day. I always found it difficult when Fyffe called on my father, presumably to scrounge spring bedding and vegetable plants. The sight of Dad and this monster chatting and laughing was something I could not reconcile in my head. To this day, every time I pass Fornighty School, now converted into houses, I get out of my car and shout to the sky, 'Fyffe you are a bastard!' – to the eternal embarrassment of my wife June.

Thankfully Lethen was not all violence and I have wonderful memories of our neighbours the countryside with its bountiful supply of hazelnuts and wild fruit trout and sea-trout to catch in the Muckle Burn cattle we herded for miles along country roads to new grazing and riding on the back of the estate's beautiful Clydesdale horse, which would walk

Ian being interviewed by Robbie Shepherd for 'Summer Roads', with producer Jennifer Forrest, at Lethen Estate.

miles back home to its own stable while the estate forester, Alan Grant, stopped to chat to friends. Helping the mole-catcher and the gamekeeper to catch moles and rabbits respectively was very exciting, often resulting in a rabbit to take home for Mam to make a sumptuous rabbit stew.

Some of our other neighbours included the Smart family – son Pat and daughters Jean and Mary – farming the nearby Burnside Farm where I first 'picked tatties' (gathered potatoes), backbreaking stuff, but great when Mr Smart came to pay us. Jocky Taylor was the estate joiner and Geordie Mackie the blacksmith. They were all lovely people.

As his part of the war effort, Dad would buy a wee piglet from time to time. It was kept in a wooden shelter in the wood behind our house where it was fattened up with Dad's excess potatoes and vegetables. Every new pig became a pet. (Did you know that they love having their backs scratched with a Dutch hoe?) It was a terrible experience when the butcher arrived on the day of slaughter. We were chased away, but always crawled back through the bushes to witness the kill – even though we cried our hearts out seeing our pet meet its end with a whack over the head and its throat cut. All illegal, I'd imagine. I believe the arrangement was that the butcher kept half the pig and the other half was returned to Dad, all cured and ready to augment what was already a good diet, despite rationing.

Mam, for her part, kept chickens, ducks and turkeys in a hen run which was supposed to be hen-proof, but Jimmy and I spent a lot of time rounding the little buggers up after they had escaped to the freedom of the woods. Our diet was also varied by the occasional catch of trout or a sea-trout, caught or even poached by the Greenie brothers. Jimmy was invariably the ringleader and the expert but both of us were paraded by Dad in front of the Auldearn bobby and given our first 'Police Warning' for spearing a couple of sea-trout locked in a pool during a drought. We were spotted by a passing motorist (few and far between in those days) who reported the two 'big-time poachers'. The same policeman was rumoured to be a bit of a poacher himself. It was certainly confirmed that, when he went fishing legally, his favourite bait was maggots (you know, these horrible wee white things you get in rotten meat). His method of placing these onto his hook was to pop half a dozen into his mouth and then, one at time, impale these disgusting creatures on his hook!

We roamed the country far and wide, occasionally chasing wild ponies which we never caught. For lunch, we'd collect pheasant eggs, which we would boil on a wee fire and then consume – the gamekeeper must have wondered where his pheasant eggs were going. It might seem as if we had no conscience, but that was not entirely true. Not far from our house, there was a small camp of Italian prisoners of war whom we befriended. They worked on local farms and were unguarded, free to come and go as they pleased in their easily identifiable jackets and trousers with coloured diamond and other shaped patches. To augment their meagre rations, the prisoners trapped wild birds, such as blackbirds and thrushes, and kept them in cages until they wanted a couple for dinner. We thought it was cruel. So we regularly sneaked up on their huts and released the birds from the cages, to the fury of the prisoners.

We had a pal, Robbie MacKenzie, who lived close to the Italian prisoners. He had what looked like a real Colt revolver in a holster, and we were so jealous of this. I do believe it was a real weapon which had been altered, and the barrel blocked so that it could not be fired, but for two cowboy fanatics Robbie was a hero.

Just across the small valley from our house at Lethen, there was a small farm – Mill Croft – managed by Jimmy and Mamie Urquhart. They were lovely, generous people but the house and croft were just a muddle. Jimmy never spent enough time working the fields and was 'always behind, like the coo's tail' – as people used to say. They had generously taken into their home a man called Alec who had been released into their care from a mental institution. I understand the arrangement was that they supplied him with all his needs, plus some fags, and in return he did some manual work on the croft. He was, apparently, a well-educated businessman who had suffered a severe nervous breakdown and never recovered. Alec was a lovely, gentle man but had little conversation, other than sentences, such as, 'Nice lads, aye nice lads,' which he repeated over and over again. Alec seemed to live in a wee world of his own. He was able to clean out the cow-shed and even thin neeps (turnip seedlings) with a hoe in the field, plus other fairly simple tasks. Jimmy and I would often help him with these tasks because everyone in the district tried to help Mamie and Jimmy. Alec was cared for pretty well by the Urquharts, but I always had the feeling he was treated no better or no worse than most people would treat their pet. It just seemed so sad that an intelligent man had come to this.

Dad encouraged his sons to become involved in gardening and gave each of us a small plot of ground in the back garden. We both entered into gardening with great gusto and produced some good vegetables, although Mam's hens often wreaked havoc when they escaped, especially on the seedlings. This interest in gardening led again to raids on the superb Lethen Estate walled garden, laid out on a south-facing slope and full of rich pickings. Dad reckoned the Lethen garden was one of the best he had ever worked. He had several under-gardeners, including Willie Chisholm and two of the famous 'land girls' (formed by Winston Churchill during the war) – Bunty Glashan and Barbara Manson. The garden certainly provided the most wonderful apples and other fruit trained to the walls, including the largest 'greenhouse-grown' peaches I have ever seen in my life. One Saturday, while Dad and Mam were off to Nairn shopping, we scaled the wall and were gobbling up strawberries and rasps when female voices indicated that Mrs Diana Brodie (a beautiful and kind lady) was taking an afternoon stroll in the garden with friends. We hid ourselves amongst the raspberry canes and lay there shaking for fear of discovery. The danger passed and we escaped unseen – a close shave that one! It was much safer stealing Dad's bee sugar ration (for winter feeding) to make tablet, which sadly was never truly successful.

Dad had by then purchased a very old 'Baby' Austin motor car, a wee box on wheels. Not only did it get us into Nairn sometimes, we also had the hilarious experience of riding around Lethen as Dad learned to drive – with crunching gears, wheels mounting the grass verges and narrow misses with gateposts etc. Mam, for some reason, insisted on being in the car during Dad's learner-driver forays, and she often screamed in terror at his narrow misses, while we sat in the back having a ball. There were no driving instructors in those days and no driving tests. Thankfully, a car was a rarity around Lethen but, by gosh, Dad frightened the life out of the hens, ducks and other livestock. How he managed to afford this wee car in the first place is beyond me, but I suspect he got it for a song and I am not being unkind when I say it ran well on the petrol supplied for the estate grass mowers! It was illegal to drive into Nairn during the war without having some legitimate reason for the journey. As far as I could fathom, Dad just heaved a bag of turnips or cabbages onto the luggage-rack attached to the back bumper and off we went, with the foolproof excuse that he was delivering vegetables to hotels in Nairn.

I had by then acquired an old bicycle (with a lady's frame – i.e. no crossbar) and would boldly set off most Saturdays to Nairn for the film matinee in the Regal Cinema, first depositing my faithful old bike at Aunty Nell's house. She was one of Dad's sisters and was married to a hugely popular Nairn character, our Uncle Sandy, known locally as 'Sannie Fraser the Milkman', just as Dad was known as 'Jock Green the Gairdner'.

Entry to the cinema was three old pennies or the appropriate number of jam jars – an extra penny got you in to the balcony. The films were frequently stopped by the projectionist while order was restored by the usherettes. Not serious bad behaviour, just overexcitement among the audience. After seeing yet another Roy Rogers or Gene Autry cowboy film, it was back to Aunty Nell who would fuss over me and set out the most enormous tea. She would frequently pat me on the head and tell me I was 'a right good loon'. My abiding memory of Nell and Sandy's tiny house was that it absolutely gleamed from top to bottom, and two kinder people you could not find. Sandy and a pal often came up to Lethen on Saturday to fish all night when the sea-trout were running. Jimmy and I dug the worms and, in return, got a few fishing hooks. I have no recollection of good sea-trout catches, but Sandy and his pal were often 'well-oiled' when they cycled back to Nairn in the morning.

Sometimes I'd stop off at Auldearn on the way home from Nairn to see my cousins, Alastair and Betty McIntyre, but I was always a bit apprehensive of both Aunty Jessie and Uncle Sandy McIntyre, after spending a holiday with them some years earlier. Shortage of beds had resulted in me sleeping with grumpy old Sandy, known locally as 'Hairy Wull' – he was covered from head to toe with rampant hair and, like Jessie, totally eccentric. Is that where I got it from?

It was at Lethen that I first learned I was a 'mistake' during an argument between Mam and Dad, arising out of Mam thinking she was pregnant again. This was her constant fear, which later became a phobia during a very long and difficult menopause. In this argument, reference was made about me having been a 'family-planning error', and Mam was apparently adamant 'never again'. It did not trouble me greatly but later when we left Lethen after the war, I was to experience more of Mam's absolute horror of pregnancy, as well as constant reminders that I was a mistake – and it's then that it began to have an effect on me.

Regular visitors to Lethen were my Aunty Peg (Dad's sister) and Uncle Bill. On these visits, it was not uncommon on a warm evening for Dad and Bill to tune up their pipes and march up and down the lawn at the side of our house, playing tunes for most of the evening. The house was a lovely stone-built, two-storey building, with beautiful diamond-shaped panes of glass set in lead-framed windows. It was situated at the entrance to the driveway leading to the big house, with two large wooden gates which in the 'old days' were no doubt closed at night. In common with all the houses we had lived in up to that point, there was only cold running water and an outside loo, but no electricity or gas. Bath night was Friday, when Mam hauled in a big zinc tub, boiled up pots and kettles of water on the big black kitchen range and, with a big bar of carbolic soap, scrubbed each of us in turn – in the same tub of water. The taste of carbolic soap in my mouth and up my nose is another lasting memory of those years. I've no idea when Mam and Dad had their weekly bath but I suspect it was after we were all packed off to bed, so that we were not confronted with naked bodies in the kitchen. Incidentally, Mam was a fine figure of a woman and Dad was a strong, wiry and quite handsome devil in his day.

One day when I was at school, a platoon of infantry soldiers on route-march stopped outside our house and asked Mam to fill their water bottles. After a rest they moved off, leaving behind a wee grey Cairn terrier that had presumably followed them for miles. When I got home from school there was this cracking wee dog which took to us immediately. To my horror, Dad reported it to the local police, but no owner ever came forward and, in due course, we were allowed to keep the Cairn permanently – after taking out a dog licence. Mam gave this poor wee dog the most awful name – Toodles! Where she got that name from I cannot imagine, but it stuck. We enjoyed his companionship for many years.

Toodles was the greatest rat killer any of the local farmers had ever

The only photo of faithful Toodles.

seen and we were invited to all the local corn threshings. A wire-netting fence was erected around the stacks of corn and threshing with those wonderful old steam engines and threshing machines would commence. Almost immediately, rats emerged from the corn stacks and as the farmer got to the bottom of each stack the rats raced out in greater and greater numbers. We killed a few with clubs, but Toodles had a great time, pouncing on one after another by grabbing each rat at the back of the neck, sinking his teeth in and breaking its neck, before casting it aside and on to the next one. He was a very efficient rat-killing machine. He was also a 'randy' little bugger. Every now and then, he would take off on some romantic pursuit and we'd not see him for two or three days until some farmer a few miles away would report that Toodles had turned up on his doorstep. Jimmy and I would then head off on our bikes to pick him up – usually, a very dirty wee dog. He would be unceremoniously dumped into the bicycle's message basket and taken home where he would be plonked into a bath.

Regrettably, Lethen was also the scene of our first family crisis when my sister Elizabeth got into some bother over money. To save the family name, very important in a rural environment, recompense was necessary. Dad and Mam had no alternative but to use all our individual savings to repay the debt. Such an event is unsettling in the family circle but life has to go on. Elizabeth, who was courting a young, Polish soldier against Dad and Mam's wishes, was packed off to Edinburgh to live with Aunty Mackie to allow the dust to settle. (She was not really our aunt but a cousin from another relationship in this tangled web that was the Green family tree.)

When WWII ended (I have no recollection of any big celebration at Lethen) the laird, Major David James Brodie, returned home from an army commission and immediately threw himself overzealously into the running of the estate. This was despite having a factor, forester, game-keeper, joiner, maintenance man and gardeners doing all this for him. He seriously interfered with each and every one. Dad was not the type to sit back and be told how he should do his job and so discontent set in. It was strange that the laird was such a pain in the backside while his wife was such a charming woman. The highlight of every year was Mrs Brodie's Christmas party for all the local children when she decorated the hall above the game store. A tall spruce tree from the woods was deco-rated with real candles burning brightly at the ends of the branches – probably a serious fire risk in today's world, but we were mesmerised.

Anyway, Dad started applying for the position of head gardener elsewhere. Disaster struck when one of his prospective employers phoned the factor, Mr Gourlay, for a reference. The Major was at Dad's throat a moment later in an uncontrollable rage. Dad was sacked on the spot and given one week to get out of the tied house – no tenant's rights then. Fortunately, he found a small house for rent in Auldearn and was soon in demand as a temporary jobbing gardener around the hotels in Nairn.

I was finishing my last year at Fornighty, cycling there and back daily on the trusty steed. After the summer holidays I started my first year of secondary education at Auldearn School where the headmaster was a veteran of WWI and suffered from shell shock (now known as post-traumatic stress disorder). The poor man would go into spasm, and stand rock-still and unseeing for a moment or two at his desk, while some of the pupils would behave very unkindly, I'm sorry to say. He was regarded with affection locally and nicknamed 'Willie Woodbine' after the brand of cigarettes he smoked incessantly. I could never feel anything but sympathy for the poor man. He was a kind soul, but my secondary education did not get off to a great start.

I remember being involved in a mighty punch-up with another schoolboy at Auldearn School. I think it was in defence of my cousin, Alastair McIntyre. The school bell ended the fight, but I was warned to be ready for 'round two' after school ended. I worried about this all afternoon but turned up for the clash, only to find the 'bully' was apparently even more apprehensive than me and had gone home. I was declared the winner and, for a few weeks, was 'champion'. Stupid really!

Not long, however, before we were on the road yet again, this time a somewhat longer road, as Dad had found a new head gardener's position at Bower House near Dunbar in East Lothian. The stay was to be of less than two years' duration due to the owner selling up and moving on. He had a high position in the cement works just outside Dunbar and was taking control of another plant elsewhere within the company. The new owner was bringing his own gardener.

Bower House was a pleasant place and I loved Dunbar Secondary School but having not long been released from the clutches of Fyffe, I sat in the classrooms like a mouse and made no sound. This prompted one teacher to ask me to stay behind one day. He asked why I was so introverted during lessons. I told him the tale of Mr Fyffe and he was astonished and dismayed. From then on he did succeed in getting me to relax in class and education became interesting for a while. My self-confidence had taken a knock though. Not much else happened at Dunbar except that I got my photo in a newspaper for the first time. A freight ship ran onto the rocks and its entire cargo of pit-props came ashore close to the school. We were given permission to go to the rocks with many local people to help salvage them, and the press arrived in force. I always thought there was salvage money for such work but I never saw a penny.

One Saturday evening at Bower House, there was a knock on the door and, when Dad answered it, there was stunned silence as Elizabeth and her young Polish husband, Johnny Swiercz, stood on the doorstep and blurted out news of their recent marriage. There was much weeping and wailing, but in the end the newlyweds were accommodated in the family home and continued to live with us for some time.

At Dunbar I tried my next business venture when I bought a couple of Angora rabbits with my tattie-howking money. (Male and female, of course, because I had learned about the birds and the bees, especially the bees – and had even heard about how rabbits breed, well you know, like rabbits!) I sold the young Angoras to schoolmates and did a roaring trade. Tattie-howking also continued to provide annual income. A treat at that time was the occasional trip into Edinburgh in the old Austin. Edinburgh seemed such an exciting place in those days. Little did we know that soon we would be residing there!

I had a crush on a young girl, daughter of the handyman and chauffeur at Bower House, Mr Rankine. She was still at primary school but we became really good friends. There were no boys in the Bower House community, so we shared a lot of time together. Of all bloody things, she taught me to knit, a skill that has proved to be of absolutely no use to me to date! Maybe one day? I do recall a sad parting from young Miss Rankine when we finally moved on.

The final Green family move was to Edinburgh where Dad had secured another head gardener position at Craiglockhart Convent of the Sacred Heart/Craiglockhart Training College, despite the fact that he was a declared Freemason. The nun who interviewed him took the view that if he had been a Catholic he would be expected to attend a lot of prayers and, if he was doing that, he wouldn't be working – so why not employ a Protestant? Good sound business sense but something of a surprise to Dad. Another furniture van, now complete with rabbits, a dog and a budgie, rolled into Glenlockhart Road, Edinburgh. Many years later, after all the 'chicks had flown the nest', Mam and Dad would make one last retirement move to a council house in Stenhouse but, for

Craiglockhart Training College/Convent of the Sacred Heart.

the time being, we settled into No.1 The Cottages, Glenlockhart Road. These cottages were demolished many years later.

A few days later, to my embarrassment, Mam accompanied me to the local Tynecastle School and into the headmaster's room. With all the upheaval of my education, the headmaster had difficulty in deciding where to place me. After a few basic questions, including: 'Repeat the 12 times table,' and 'Where is London?', it was decided that I should go into the 'technical' class – a terrible mistake on the headmaster's part because I considered I was never going to work successfully with wood or metal, and technical drawing was a nightmare that I'd had a few skirmishes with at Dunbar. I could have told him this at the outset but was not asked, and I had already learned to keep my mouth shut in front of headmasters.

I loathed Tynecastle School and, to be frank, I learned little there. The pupils, in the main, behaved abominably in class and discipline in most classes was nonexistent. There was one poor teacher – a young girl not long out of teacher training college – quite unable to control this class of near morons who refused to take the belt from her. As punishment she would send a boy to stand in the corridor, followed by another and yet another until half of the class was supposed to be on punishment in the corridor, but were round the back of the boys' toilets, either smoking fags or playing football. This poor girl was frequently reduced to tears in front of this rabble while I sat there in utter amazement at the chaos around me. Clearly, there was no control at the top and how anyone received a decent education is beyond me. (Funnily enough, my wife-to-be, June McLennan, was a year behind me at Tynecastle and her experience in the girls' class was the direct opposite.)

I found myself at the hands of a couple of bully-boys because of my Morayshire accent and I quickly had to change the way I spoke. I began to speak something which is now difficult to quantify, but is my own brand of English with little or no accent. It seemed to satisfy the bullies who then turned to annoy some other poor sod. Strangers, however, still hear traces of my Highland accent especially when I'm on the phone.

The teachers all had nicknames – 'Wee Nell' was the gym-master and 'Boris Karloff' was the English teacher. He was a decent, considerate man, although not very handsome as the nickname suggests. He also took an interest in the quiet 'country loon' and on one occasion he commented to me that, if he had a classroom of pupils like me, teaching would be a pleasure. I was actually chuffed about that and I did better in English and also history and geography, than I was ever able to do in the technical classes where I turned wood into shavings and sawdust, and metal into unrecognisable scrap. My technical drawings always ended up with the virgin roll of white paper ruined by excessive use of an eraser or 'rubber'.

A wasted education? Ian at Tynecastle Secondary School. Ian is 2nd from right on back row.

In addition, I arrived at Tynecastle horribly out of kilter with mathematics and algebra and never really got up to speed with the other pupils or the teachers. The most enjoyable part of my time there was going out at lunchtime to chat to the Hearts football players as they left the training ground. So began an interest in football – a year or two later I joined the Edinburgh branch of the Rangers Supporters' Club. The other release from the grim daily grind of school was when we were excused school to go off to the tattie-howking. It was great to get on the bus in the morning with the other volunteers and set off to some East Lothian farm where the backbreaking but financially rewarding work began. I was in my element in the country and became 'top dog' when it came to rooting about the farmsteads for eggs and explaining the workings of a farm to my schoolmates. If I knew nothing of algebra, I certainly knew the workings of the countryside!

At the earliest possible opportunity, after sitting my Lower Leaving Certificate exams which, on the whole I did pretty badly in, I walked out of Tynecastle for the last time. I did get some sort of certificate but no one was ever very impressed by it, least of all me. Before my 15th birthday and before the end of the term, with no concerns about what was in reality a failed education, I started my gardening apprenticeship under my father at the Convent of the Sacred Heart. An exciting new life opened up for me, despite the fact that Dad was a hard taskmaster as a boss.

CHAPTER TWO

teens to manhood

he convent of the Sacred Heart/Craiglockhart Training College/ Girls' Catholic Day School (currently Napier University) is situated on Colinton Road, Edinburgh, at its junction with Glenlockhart Road. It was built originally as a hydropathic hotel, but during WWI was requisitioned by the army. It became a hospital for the treatment of officers suffering from mental breakdown resulting from the bloody conflict in France and Belgium (1914–1918). The two great WWI poets, Siegfried Sassoon and Wilfred Owen, both recuperated there.

After WWI the Convent of the Sacred Heart purchased the buildings and grounds of the old hotel, and later opened its doors as a Catholic teacher-training college and day school for Catholic girls. How nuns and romance-seeking, nubile females in their teens and early '20s coexisted was a wonder to all of us living in the tied houses. It was not an uncommon sight to see students sneaking back into the college grounds late at night, well after 'curfew'. The resident engineer, Mr Marsden, had a story or two about some of the sights he saw as he went about his maintenance work inside the convent, not to mention the various items he found secreted behind bedroom radiators and other places. I suspect the nuns would have been pretty shocked by some of the high jinks – but then, maybe not. People loved to tell 'nun jokes' to convent workers! There is the story of two nuns returning to a convent late at night and, as they climbed the outer wall, one said to the other, 'Sister, I feel like a commando,' and the other retorted, 'So do I but where can we get one at this time of night?'

The huge original building of red sandstone sits in quite spacious grounds on Glenlockhart Road with a group of workers' cottages, known locally as The Convent Cottages. The convent and grounds are overlooked by the lofty Craiglockhart Crags to the east. The crags attracted the occasional pervert who felt a need to show his 'assets' to nuns and girls – the local police were regular visitors! Extensions to accommodate the college and school had already occurred when we arrived but, years later, the building (apart from its front) became a jumble of extensions, none very pretty in comparison to the original building. The gardens comprised a fairly large vegetable, fruit and flower garden with greenhouses, plus lawns, tennis courts and other sports and leisure facilities. Mature trees fringed the grounds on the Colinton Road boundary.

A huge sycamore tree stood beside Convent Cottages, reputed to have been planted by Bonnie Prince Charlie but if he planted all the trees credited to him in Scotland, then it is hardly surprising he finally lost at Culloden. He was so busy planting bloody trees! It was a bonny sycamore though and the Green family spent many happy hours under its protective branches on summer Sunday afternoons, with many a 'drink' consumed in its shade. The nuns had a surprisingly liberal attitude to alcohol and, many years later when Dad retired, they laid on a great party within the convent for friends and family. I recall the drink flowing freely, although I think they underestimated our consumption!

When I started my apprenticeship at the convent, there was Dad (head gardener), 'Mack' MacKay (the under-gardener) and a labourer. (The labourers never stayed long, so there was a stream of them.) Work started at seven in the morning, there was a lunch-break of an hour, and we finished work at five o'clock. On Saturday, we worked from seven until twelve-thirty. Wages were poor, especially for the apprentice, and the work was hard. There was no union representation. But it was just great to be free of school, and there was also the added attraction of good-looking young girls running around in PT attire!

Ian serving his apprenticeship as a gardener.

Mack was an interesting character who had served with the Royal Artillery in the Desert and Italian Campaigns during the WWII, and was a real gem of a man. I wish I had told him! He told me many tales of his escapades, and my knowledge of the opposite sex was dramatically increased. There was no sex education at school, and it was too embarrassing a subject for Mam or Dad – so most of what I learned was from the experiences of others, and crude male humour.

I learned so much about gardening under Dad's guidance. While he expected a lot more from me than the other gardeners it was probably no bad thing and I learned more as a result. We had our disagreements but, in the main, working with Dad went well. I enjoyed working in the open air and life was good. I was adding new interests to my life and also attended night school to increase my theoretical knowledge in horticulture.

The garden labourers came and went before I could get to know most of them, but one, Davie Gordon, a few years older than me, stayed longer. He was a tall, fair-haired, good-looking lad who had an eye for the girls and they for him. We became pals but it was a strange relationship. He was a more cavalier type and I kind of trailed along because I suppose he impressed me. He got us into a couple of scrapes which could have ended far worse than they did. The relationship came to an end when Davie made a date with one of the convent day-school girls who must have let this fact slip at home. He was reported to the convent secretary, Mother Dillon. A bit of a tyrant, she had overall responsibility for all the convent workers, and Dad frequently had quite serious disagreements with her, which led to him threatening to leave a few times. But I suspect he was tired of always being on the move and a compromise was always reached.

Mother Dillon instantly threatened Davie with the 'sack' (dismissal). An alternative was for him to join the armed services – he chose the Royal Navy, and was soon on the high seas. This relieved the convent of an embarrassment and, to be honest, was no bad thing for me because, amongst various other bad influences in my life, Davie was an inveterate liar. His treatment at the hands of Mother Dillon was extreme however and her behaviour would certainly not be acceptable today. Later, I too would suffer from Mother Dillon's unchristian behaviour.

Davie introduced me to the world of ice-skating, which ultimately led me to my first serious girlfriend, Aileen Turnbull and later to the girl who was to become my wife, June McLennan. Aileen was a lovely girl with a quiet personality, and we courted on and off for well over a year. I grew very fond of her, but I suspect the relationship was always doomed because her father was the 'Turnbull' in the draper's firm, Turnbull and Wilson of South Bridge in Edinburgh. We were from a different social class of that time and I suspect her father was against the relationship, although Aileen's mother apparently thought I was a 'nice lad'. For a long time, I went to the pictures with Aileen, midweek and then met her at Haymarket Ice Rink on Saturday. The relationship never blossomed beyond holding hands and a few kisses, due to the shyness of both of us and our inexperience in romantic matters and it all but ended when I went into the army at 18. I had one last date with Aileen when on leave, but it was obvious to us both that the relationship had run its course. I met her again many years later while on police duty. She had married and had her young son with her. We chatted for a few moments and I felt a twinge of regret for what might have been. Young love, eh?

In this happy period at the convent, Dad again gave me a bit of land to crop vegetables in my spare time, and the extra income gained by selling vegetables to neighbours helped spread the financial load of all my interests – romantic and sporting. By this time I was no longer breeding Angora rabbits. The last female had sadly died and I was quite upset. I gave her a respectful burial close to the sycamore tree.

Jimmy had finished his apprenticeship as a joiner in Nairn and was back in the family home. We shared the same bedroom which led to niggling and arguing. It was a sad part of our relationship that my brother Jimmy was inclined to 'push me around', especially when we were young. I recall one occasion we fell out when Mam and Dad were out for the evening. Jimmy completely lost it and gave me a sound beating – whether I deserved it or not I am unsure. He hit me so severely that I bled quite badly from my nose and mouth. There was so much blood on the walls in the back lobby of the house that when tempers settled, we had to set to and clean away all traces before Mam and Dad came home. It was a strange relationship Jimmy and I had, with lots of ups and downs during our lives – sometimes we were on really good terms and at other times there was friction. I could never say we were really close and age did not seem to mellow us. Also, Jimmy sadly seemed to be jealous of my achievements in life.

As a member of the Edinburgh branch of the Rangers Supporters' Club, I travelled all over Scotland. My choice of Rangers was simple – I followed my father's favourite team – like father, like son, in so many things! The great Willie Woodburn (who was to be banned *sine die* from football for repeated fouling) often travelled back in the supporters' coach with us to Edinburgh where he lived. I got to know him quite well, and maintain to this day that Willie was not a dirty player, but simply committed himself 100 per cent to every tackle. I was pleased when, some years

A section of the huge crowd attending the Hibernians-Rangers match at Easter Road to-day. (" Dispatch " picture.)

Ian (on the wall, third from left), around 15 years old, at a Hibs versus Rangers match.

later, after his playing career had ended, Willie's ban was finally lifted. I obtained many Rangers players' autographs – great names like Bobby Brown, Jock Shaw ('The Tiger'), Geordie Young, Ian McColl, Willie Waddell, Willie Thornton, Tory Gillick and more. This was a great period for the 'Gers', although one thing I disliked, and could never come to terms with, was the religious bigotry so evident in those days, especially at 'old firm' matches. Even after all these years of so-called enlightenment, it still rears its ugly head from time to time. A great shame.

About this time, I also developed a fanatical interest in speedway, and every Saturday evening saw me at Meadowbank Stadium to support Edinburgh Monarchs. My heroes were Jack Young and Bill Maddern (both Australians as many of the riders were back then). The roar of motor cycle engines and the smell of burnt high octane fuel excited me. There was huge interest in speedway in that era and very soon a miniature version of the sport, cycle speedway, began to develop. I decided I had to have a piece of this action and started turning up at informal racetracks across the city. The determination to succeed at anything I turned my hand to immediately showed itself and soon I was invited to join one of the Edinburgh league teams – Lothian Speedbirds.

At first we rode only slightly modified bicycles but, as the sport developed, the machines gradually became more sophisticated – with

Ian at a Festival of Sport in the Waverley Market.

specially designed handlebars to give more purchase, low seats used only when cornering, and, importantly, the right gearing ratios between the crankshaft and rear wheel. All excess pieces of equipment, such as mudguards, lights and brakes, were discarded! The lack of the latter two got me and most other cycle speedway riders into confrontations with the constabulary who, quite rightly, took a dim view of lads riding to and from racetracks without brakes or lights. There was one policeman who caught me several times on Colinton Road, but continued to give me only verbal warnings long after his patience must have run out. When I later joined the police, I met the same officer and we laughed about these heinous crimes.

Dad was at first totally against this 'silly nonsense on bikes', and Mam worried constantly that I would get hurt. One Sunday I had a bad crash in a practice race which necessitated me having treatment and stitches to one hand from a local doctor. I was warned by Dad that there would be no more cycle speedway if I was not at my work on Monday. I gritted my teeth and went to work on Monday and, despite the pain each time I knocked the heavily bandaged hand, I was determined not to give in. Dad eventually became my staunchest supporter and attended many of our matches, roaring his head off in support. Not always a predictable man, I have to say.

My determination to succeed in this new sport knew no bounds – I ran for miles to get myself fit, practised 'starts' for hours on end, and rode my cycle speedway bike up hill and down dale in an effort to be at peak fitness in races. I also maintained my bike in immaculate condition. It worked and I raced my way into being a top scorer and captain of the Speedbirds. I befriended a cycle dealer in Fountainbridge after my first bike collapsed under me in a race. He was of great expert assistance in providing me with the right replacement cycle frame, advised on gears and, when eventually special tyres were developed for the sport by Dunlop, it was this good man who introduced me to these and gave me a free rear tyre to experiment with. Another of those really genuine and generous people you bump into every so often as you travel through life.

Cycle speedway tracks were laid out all over Edinburgh by the corporation (council) but in addition, we raced in special matches in Princes Street Gardens (on the area often used to accommodate dancers) and in the old Waverley Market during sports exhibitions. One highlight was when I was chosen to captain an Edinburgh team against a Lanarkshire team in the central arena in the Waverley Market. Jack Young was invited along with his speedway bike, and gave a display of 'wheelies' before being introduced to both teams. Battle commenced in front of a capacity audience of several hundred, including my family, friends and relations – plus girlfriend, Aileen.

It was an exciting match. I finished up with maximum points after overcoming a big lad from Lanark who had made his mind up to sort me out. In the race where I came up against him, there was a crash on the first bend and the race was restarted – without any of the four contestants being eliminated for causing the crash. In the restart, I was beaten into

Cycle speedway at Festival of Sport, Waverley Market.

Ian scores a maximum against a Lanark select.

the first bend by the big Lanark lad but, a bend or two later, he went a wee bit wide, and I sneaked and jostled my way through the inside to win the race. No disqualification! Edinburgh won the match, and I had a maximum of 15 points. At the end, we were all busy signing autographs – yes, it was taken that seriously – when the mother of the Lanark lad approached and started to scream at me, describing me as a 'dirty racer'. But not for long! My sister Elizabeth, a fair-sized woman, arrived on the scene and sorted her out in no uncertain terms. What a night! Although there were many other exciting matches and displays to follow in various towns in Scotland that night was a bit special. Having our photos and reports in local and national newspapers became commonplace. At one point, I was selected for a Scotland versus England match, but only as third reserve. The match was in London and, regrettably, the third reserve did not travel, so I never won a Scottish Cap. My cycle speedway career was all too soon cut short anyway by army call-up.

Cycle speedway introduced me to many good pals, including one Jimmy Duff from Bathgate. We became real good buddies, racing in the same team and ice-skating most weekends. We kept in touch over the years, even after he and his wife emigrated to Canada. Jimmy was a coal miner but became disillusioned when the mines were nationalised and no one seemed to take pride in their work any more. He started a new life in a car factory near Toronto where he did very well. Another of the lovely people I have the pleasure to call my friend.

My days as an apprentice gardener at the convent came to an end just over a year before I was called up. I wanted a rise and, like all other employees, I had to make my first approach through Dad who then presented my case to Mother Dillon. Back came the reply that she had refused any wage increase, so I told Dad I was giving a fortnight's notice. Mother Dillon was outraged, refused to speak to me and advised Dad that he should turn me out of the family home (the tied house) – seriously! He was unsurprisingly astonished by this response and announced that, if I were to leave the house, he would do likewise. Much negotiation ensued.

Dad stayed on at the convent and I was allowed to remain in the family home. I have to say, that incident left me shocked.

I left the convent garden a week or two later and started work at the Astley Ainslie Hospital in Morningside. The gardens there were extensive and included several houses and large gardens that had been gobbled up as the hospital expanded. I really enjoyed the new challenge and was soon being allocated skilled work since most of the other employees were garden labourers. It was there I met Andy Henderson, greenhouse under-gardener. I was often sent to work in the greenhouses with him, and we quickly developed a friendship and respect for each other. Andy attended my marriage to June several years later, and we remained friends until his premature death. Andy had served in Burma in WWII with the famous Chindits, a volunteer force that went behind enemy lines wreaking havoc on communications and supply lines. One rule in the Chindits was that any soldier who was so badly wounded that he could not walk out was left behind, simply because they had to move quickly to keep one step ahead of the pursuing Japanese. One day, Andy's group ran into a Japanese ambush. He was hit by machine-gun bullets in both legs and went down. A pal dragged him back into the jungle and was making him comfortable before leaving him, when a donkey emerged from the jungle. Where this 'miracle' appeared from no one knew but 'never look a gift-horse (or donkey) in the mouth'. Andy was quickly thrown onto its back and transported safely out of the jungle into British lines and hospital. He made a full recovery, but had some mighty scars on his legs. Andy was a lovely man, with an absolutely charming wife and young son.

The head gardener at Astley Ainslie was a strange man who rarely left his office except to sow seeds and, occasionally, to cycle around the gardens and grounds. I recall that he had a big smelly dog, a spaniel. The assistant head gardener, Mr Cardownie, was very eccentric and he stood no nonsense. He ruled with an iron hand, but I always thought fairly. Working at Astley Ainslie Hospital was very rewarding and the wages were good. I learned additional gardening skills and the characters who worked there gave me a great insight into life. Some of the advice Andy Henderson gave me about coping with army life stood me in very good stead when call-up came.

My sister Elizabeth and Johnny were living with us at Convent Cottages and it was there that Elizabeth gave birth to their son, David. Not long after, they found a tied top-flat house in Thistle Street. In lieu of rent, Elizabeth and Johnny carried out the duties of cleaners for the firm of solicitors who

A newspaper plea for witness to a fatal road accident.

occupied the two lower flats and ground floor. They settled into their new life and seemed happy. I visited them a lot and became close to Elizabeth, as well as a really good friend of Johnny who spoke an almost comical style of Polish/Scots. No one in the family knew what was in store though.

I received my call-up papers for national service duty just as I reached the age of 18, but I had been invited to be part of a big cycle speedway event taking place, again in the Waverley Market, during the following month. I cheekily wrote to the Ministry of Defence for a delay to call-up and 'glory be', they accepted my request, delaying my joining date for over a month. The inevitable day arrived though and I attended the Army Medical and Selection Board offices in Queensferry Road, Edinburgh. I passed the medical no bother, although I wasn't keen on stripping naked in front of the other lads, and then being asked to cough while my testicles were held by an ancient bloody doctor! Once in the army though, it became common practice for doctors to peer up your rear end, examine your 'willy' and hold your testicles.

No accounting for other people's tastes, eh!

Having satisfactorily proved my manhood, I was allowed to join others who were volunteering to sign up as regular soldiers. My intention was to do three years 'in the colours' (serving soldier) and four years in the 'reserves' (you could be called up at any time of emergency) instead of the two years' national service. My reason for doing this was purely financial – national servicemen earned a mere pittance, while the regular soldier was paid a substantial wage and received a sort of retainer payment during reserve service.

The selection officer set me a series of tests to assess my ability for selection to the most appropriate regiment. I wanted to be a dispatch rider in the Royal Signals (the speedway craze I suppose), but that was brushed aside. The tests consisted of putting round blocks of wood into

round holes and square blocks of wood into square holes, which I succeeded in doing, although I saw one poor lad not coping with this at all.
I am not sure if he ever managed to get the round block into the square
hole, but he seemed a determined boy! Having put the right things in the
right places, I was then asked to assemble a bicycle pump. This was a
piece of cake for an ex-cycle-speedway rider – I told Dad my cycle speedway experiences would come in handy one day!

There were other tests, but why the army bothered I'm not sure
because once I was in uniform I discovered it was quite common for the
army to turn excellent motor mechanics into cooks and cooks into lorry
drivers, and so on – apparently refusing to take advantage of skilled and
time-served tradesmen. Anyway, I clearly got some of the tests right because
on 31 March 1952, I was accepted for the 'elite' regiment, the REME
(Royal Electrical and Mechanical Engineers) to be trained as a motor
mechanic. Could it be that the headmaster of Tynecastle School saw in
me the same signs of a tradesman that the Army Selection Board also
'cleverly' spotted – or was it just another of the army's monumental
cock-ups? After three years' service, I was left wondering how we ever
won wars and came to the eventual conclusion that it was all down to
the squaddies (soldiers) and not the hierarchy, certainly not the selection
boards. Anyway the REME it was and again the determination to succeed
in all things surfaced. After a slow start as a motor mechanic I came
away strongly, and in time became a pretty good one, although I say it
myself. I reached the dizzy rank of full corporal – with an offer of promotion to sergeant if I stayed on for another term. I decided that three
years was enough.

Basic training for the REME was at Blandford Camp in Dorset, which
meant an overnight train journey to London and then on to the camp. I
had never been out of Scotland in my entire life, not even across the
English border, so it was all a bit daunting but also exciting. Dad accompanied me to Waverley Station, bought me a drink on the way and
warned me as I boarded the train to keep my nose clean.

Arrival at Blandford Camp on 2 April was a shock. As soon as I and
the other recruits stepped through the gates, 'khaki people' started screaming at us and, once assembled, this latest rabble was marched to the billets
allocated to us. We were then issued with full army kit at the quartermaster's stores, where your height and shape were estimated by a glance
and the equipment thrown at you. There was no use complaining that it
did not fit. Exchanges had to take place in the barrack rooms until

everyone had uniforms and boots that were close to a fit. A quick change into fatigue uniform (a sort of denim-type material) and then off to the army barbers. These were notorious people, with little skill and even less conscience. A young lad with a huge crop of ginger hair in the fashion of the day had been advised that if you offered the barber a ten-shilling note, he would be 'gentle'. The barber snatched the 'ten bob', stuck it in his pocket and proceeded to run the electric clippers from the back of the lad's neck, right across the top of his head to his forehead, eventually leaving him with a 'baldy'. The rest of us had short back and sides, right to the bone of course, but we escaped with some hair on top.

It was then straight to the medical officer where all the required 'jags' were administered – with 'blunt needles' of course! Big tough-looking lads from Liverpool, Manchester and Glasgow fainted on the spot or later on. It was like a battlefield!

Next day, it all started in earnest – up at the crack of dawn and down to the cookhouse for breakfast. I foolishly told one of the cooks that I did not take milk or sugar in my tea and was told, 'The tea, milk and sugar are all in the one bucket. If you are not happy, remove the bloody things you don't like!' The cooks were cynical buggers! When serving food on to your tray (which had sections for the various courses), they took great delight in letting your sweet slop into your mince or your marmalade spill over into the bacon and egg. I have never been a fussy eater but in the army I grew to intensely dislike margarine, marmalade and later when I went abroad, dried potato mixture. To this day, I won't eat them.

The training was intense, but much of it was interesting and exciting, like feeling the kick of a .303 Lee Enfield rifle or firing bursts on the amazing Bren gun (the light machine gun or LMG). Parade ground drilling was hard, made worse by the fear of getting anything wrong and being punished – e.g. running around the parade ground with your rifle above your head. That really hurt! An hour or two of intense drilling on the parade ground could be followed by physical training, with only a second or two allowed in which to change from army uniform into PT kit, accompanied by screaming, shouting and threats of punishment for the last man out from the drill corporal. When I look back, it seems comical, but at the time it was fearful stuff.

'Bulling' boots was a tedious but essential part of training. The boots supplied were of real leather and all 'pimply' and rough. The toecaps and heels had to be smoothed right down, and then a shine produced that you could see your reflection in. This meant hours of smoothing down the leather with the handle of a bone-handled knife and rubbing black boot polish on with added spittle. Hard work, but the end result was astonishing – God help anyone who stood on your bulled boots.

The particular sergeant and corporal assigned to our intake were real hard buggers. The sergeant was ex-Scots Guards, tall and like a rod of steel – he simply gleamed. He set himself as an example for us to follow but, although we all tried, few succeeded – I have to say he was the smartest soldier I ever met. He would not tolerate anything but the very best from us. He claimed that he always won the 'best platoon' award at every passing out parade, and God help us if we were to let him down! He duly won, and of course by then the army had succeeded in breaking us down. It then instilled a sense of pride and team spirit into us, the real strength of the British Army. We were quite proud of ourselves when we passed out top dogs.

You have probably heard the expression: 'in the army you are just a number'. It's true. You had to learn your army serial number in quick time and be able to scream it out when ordered. My number is embedded in my brain forever – 22798573, sir!

The corporal was an evil bloody man who took great delight in inflicting punishment on recruits. He relished watching us suffer. He had many punishments up his sleeve, but for some minor omission he gave me the task of searching the entire camp for a hundred used matchsticks, which I then had to scrub clean and cut all to the same length before tying them into bundles of 20 (exactly) – each bundle tied with a different colour of wool or thread. When I presented my efforts to him in his room, a boxed cubicle within our billet, he took the bundles, counted them and then threw them about the room. He roared at me to pick up every one. I had to crawl about the floor searching for each matchstick while he gloated above me. Extra evening drilling or running until you dropped were some of his other punishments – this could be individual punishment or involve the entire platoon!

We were not allowed out of the camp for the first six weeks, but Easter weekend followed and we were allowed to go home for a couple of days. The Scots lads hired a bus and we travelled home overnight. The pride on the faces of Mam and Dad, when they saw this smart young soldier who had replaced the boy who'd left home some weeks earlier, shone in their eyes. Brother Jimmy, who had been deferred until he served his joiner apprenticeship, had also been called up about the same time. I think this was the only time the two of us were ever seen in army uniform together.

The 'Greenies' – Ian, Elizabeth and Jimmy.

Soon it was back to Blandford and the rest of our initial training. We had a massive 'piss-up' after we passed out, and drinking was something I had really not indulged in much up to that point. Something else the army successfully taught me. One sad thing about that night though was having to watch the real 'crawlers' fawning around the sergeant and corporal, buying them drinks, while the rest of us were muttering 'bastards' and worse into our beer. It never surprised me to learn that more than one hated officer/sergeant/corporal died of a bullet from the 'opposite' direction during war.

Next day, it was into trucks and off to the Army Driving School near Winchester where we met another weird corporal. On arrival at our new camp, he welcomed us in the most friendly and charming manner, informing us that this was a great camp. He said the food was good, with a choice of dishes at every meal. (He was right – the food was good.) He totally lulled us into a false sense of security when he said, 'Remember you are here to learn to drive and there will be no kit inspections or drill, and very little discipline.' We all thought, what a nice guy, and off we went to enjoy a good meal. We were back in our billet for only a moment when this raging tornado entered – yes, the same corporal we had been fooled by earlier. He demanded a full kit inspection in half an hour and, when he returned, he systematically went round our beds hurling most of our equipment out of the windows into the wet night. Another inspection followed later, and boy did we get it right the second time! So much for 'mister nice guy'!

Initially, I found driving a bit difficult, possibly because I was slow on the uptake. But I think also because the instructor, another corporal, was quite impatient and often lost his temper, which did nothing for my confidence. I had to undertake extra driving tuition in the evenings with another instructor who was thankfully the opposite – a gentle, patient soldier who did wonders for my driving. I subsequently passed my driving test in Winchester along with everyone else on the course.

The Basic Training Squad at Blandford Camp. The 'smart sergeant' is holding the pace stick and the 'mad corporal' is on his left. Ian is 4th from the left at the rear.

We bade farewell to the driving school and the crazy corporal, and travelled to the Army Trades Training School at Ellesmere, close to the north Welsh border, to be trained as motor mechanics etc. Discipline was more relaxed there and, after only a few days, the company sergeant major selected me as the smartest soldier in our platoon. My reward was to act as his 'batman', excusing me from morning parades and other thankless duties. After morning parade, it was off to the classroom for the rest of the day for theoretical and practical work. I struggled a bit with the theory, but strangely I really enjoyed working on engines and, eventually, army trucks. I was delighted at the end of what was a very intensive course to attain my Grade 3 motor mechanic qualification which allowed me to be posted to an army Light Aid Detachment (LAD). I was also 'promoted' from private to craftsman. It was another very proud day for this steadily maturing country loon.

While at the Army Trades School, we were allowed every weekend off, so a Welsh pal and I used to hitchhike into Manchester, book into the servicemen's club and have a night or two on the town. My love-life developed somewhat during this time because 'Taffy' (all Welshmen were 'Taffy' and Scotsmen 'Jock') was an experienced wee devil in the ways of women. He said I was too timid with girls and offered me some advice. What I needed to do was show a sense of purpose and be bolder. I put this advice into practice one night when a crowd of us went to Manchester to see the great American singer, Frankie Lane. We met a bunch of girls, paired off, and after the concert we all disappeared into doorways for a bit of 'sport'. I took my advice from Taffy to heart, and after a couple of kisses I felt it was time to 'explore'. Well, seemingly I read the signs all wrong because the girl let out a scream, told me she was 'not that sort of girl', and I got an almighty whack across the face. Apologies were ignored and she stormed off. Thanks for the advice Taffy!

I had more success a week or two later when I first met a nurse and then a WAAF, Margaret Barbery, who I started to date – one on the Friday and the other on the Saturday each week in Manchester. The romance with the nurse soon faded. We were discovered in a 'compromising' situation in a back lane by a constable, and were warned! But I became very attracted to Margaret, and a gentle relationship developed, to be ended when I was posted to Troon in Ayrshire. New relationships got in the way and of course 'out of sight out of mind' took its toll. I maybe made a mistake though, because her family had loads of 'lolly'.

I was beginning to have my eyes opened by some of the strange people who inhabit this planet, some of whom served alongside me. In our billet at Ellesmere, we had a real 'wanker' who did so with remarkable frequency every evening – and boasted about it! Strangely, the same lad could not march in step at all, despite every threat from sergeants and corporals. That probably explained a lot! Less strange, but nevertheless remarkable, was my pal Taffy. He was an Al Jolson fanatic and had seen 'The Jolson Story' and 'Jolson Sings Again' in excess of fifty times each, or so he estimated. He persuaded me to go along with him to a nearby cinema to see 'The Jolson Story'. I wish I hadn't because we were damned near thrown out. Taffy sang every song with gusto and prepared me for every new scene with a running commentary, to the total annoyance of other film-goers around us. A warning from the usherette only made him lower his voice slightly. I was so embarrassed and pleased to exit the cinema before the credits had finished.

For the one and only time in my life I was actually propositioned by a homosexual in Manchester when I visited a pub for a pint one Friday. I had broken off with the nurse by then, so had Fridays free. I was so naïve that I did not realise what was happening initially, as this adult male offered me free pints and asked me about army life. It was only when he started telling me what he'd like to do to and with me that I ran for my life, shaking with fear! Close shave, but another lesson learned.

Finally, it was time to move on and say goodbye to what had been happy times at Ellesmere, including my enjoyable weekly visits to Manchester and my WAAF girlfriend. On the great day all the postings were placed on the camp notice board, and there was a clamour to see where we were all going. Some lucky buggers were off to sunny climes in Egypt, Aden, Singapore and Hong Kong. For myself, I was off alone to the LAD (Light Aid Detachment) with 50th Heavy Ack Ack Regiment Royal Artillery at Dundonald Camp near Troon in Ayrshire – 'home posting', as some of the guys scornfully 'took the piss'. I have to say I was disappointed, not only at what seemed a bad posting, but having to say cheerio to some great pals – some I had been with since basic training. Strong bonds are formed in the army, and Taffy, who I was never to see again, and I were both upset to part. The company sergeant major, whose batman I had been, was very generous in his praise of my efforts, shook my hand and wished me well in the future. It's not often the CSM shakes your hand.

On arrival at Dundonald Camp, I found the LAD to be a mixture of both regular soldiers and national servicemen. We all shared one billet in the spider-type barrack blocks which were standard in all the camps I had been in. I quickly found out that my comrades were a real good bunch of lads who bonded well and looked out for each other. There was a feeling of elitism within the REME LAD – we kept pretty much to ourselves, which also added to the close bond we had. We were excused from all parades and guard duties etc. because our function was to maintain the many huge gun-towing Matadors, Bedford and Ford 15-hundredweight and three-ton trucks, plus other small vehicles and motor cycles. Initially I found it difficult to put the theory of the Army Trades School into everyday practice, but the other lads were always there to lend a hand or give advice, and I began to enjoy the work – up to my elbows in oil and grease. I wonder what my metalwork teacher at Tynecastle School would have said if he had seen me. He rightly thought I was the most useless student in the world.

We worked in army-issue boiler suits which, in the course of a week, got really filthy. In this scruffy condition, each morning we would amble down to the NAAFI mobile van and buy a cup of tea or coffee and a doughnut at our break. We'd then straggle back to the workshops and get on with what was invariably a heavy day's work. As we sauntered back one morning, a young artillery officer came upon us and he went berserk, describing us as 'disgusting soldiers with a sloppy attitude'. He formed us up, marched us back to the workshops and reported us to the artillery commanding officer. As punishment, we were to appear in full marching order at the weekly company parade, along with the Royal Artillery personnel. The LAD commanding officer, a real gentleman, had some sympathy because he knew we worked hard, but of course he could do nothing about the requirement to attend this parade. His advice to us was to really 'spit and polish' our uniforms and equipment, go out there and win the 'best platoon on parade' award. We worked our socks off in the evenings, marched out onto the parade ground with a swagger, and totally blew away the artillery lads – and won the award. Our own CO was elated. There was never again another mention of 'these scruffy mechanics' by any artillery officer.

There was one 'Fifer' in our LAD (George Williamson was his name I think) who was excellent at every sport he turned his hand to and, at some point, he befriended an airman from the American airbase at Prestwick. Americans, of course, love basketball and the airman had formed a team at Prestwick. But he was absolutely fed up playing the same two or three teams from American bases. He asked our lad to form a team to provide fresh opposition. Explanations from the Fifer to the effect that the British kick the ball, we don't pick it up and throw it about, were to no avail. We were surprised by the challenge, but even more astonished when our own Fifer said, 'Right, we are going to form a team and play the Yanks.' He bullied us all into volunteering for this crazy venture and actually taught us the sport from scratch. He shouted and bullied us for nights on end in the Dundonald gymnasium until slowly he thrashed us into some sort of basketball team. A pretty poor one, I have to admit, with most of us on match night floundering around waving our arms in front of these bloody big Yanks, not with any hope of winning but in the desperate and forlorn hope we could keep the score down. I don't recall the final score, but it was no points for us while the Yanks were in three figures. Later in the billet, we all said to the Fifer, 'Well so much for that bloody idea – there will be no more of that humiliation,' or words to that effect, e.g. 'Fuck you.' No way though, the tough wee lad had already booked a return match and wouldn't take no (or resignations) for an answer. We went on to play several more matches against the Yanks. We never beat them, but eventually we managed to hold the scores to less embarrassing figures and often popped the ball into the Yanks' basket. Great social events though, and we were at least able to show them how to drink pints!

As at Ellesmere, we had every weekend off at Dundonald and those in the LAD who could make it would head for home. It meant a quick change and a dash late Friday afternoon, but every second weekend we got away at lunchtime on Friday and did not have to be back in camp until eleven o'clock on Sunday night. I went home most weekends and invariably resorted to hitchhiking on the way to Edinburgh to keep costs down. Hitching was a piece of cake in army uniform and, while every lorry driver would stop, this meant a slow, ponderous journey compared to a fast Jaguar. I would sometimes hide as a lorry went past and get the thumb up for the first car that came along. My best 'home-run', according to my diary, was 1 hour and 20 minutes!

I used to visit friends of Mam and Dad – 'The Mackenzies' as they were always referred to. They lived in Manor Place but were originally from Auldearn. The Mackenzies were the salt of the earth and had a very bonny daughter, Varrie. On visits to the house, we used to share an interest in pencil drawing – she was bloody good and I was pretty awful. An attraction developed and I asked her out a few times, but I suspect I was Varrie's first boyfriend. She was so shy that, when I first put an arm around her shoulder at the pictures, she nearly jumped out of her skin. I was also very shy at this time and that probably did not help matters. We had quite a few dates and maybe it needed time to develop, but I was already attracted in another direction. I was very fond of Varrie though and have many happy memories of visiting her and her parents at their home in Manor Place.

It was during my weekend leaves late in 1952 that I met June at Murrayfield Ice Rink. She was skating around with her friend Margaret and, as I skated past, I pinched a sweetie out of her hand. I then 'chatted her up' and tried to talk her into letting me walk her home to Balgreen Park, but she was not up for it. I had to resort to the sympathy tactic – 'young lonely soldier in the army in need of female company, blah, blah, blah'. It worked, and I met June again next day for a walk. I saw her quite a lot and I think a strong relationship was developing, but soon I was to be in foreign lands.

I spent Christmas of 1952 at Dundonald Camp with the other Scottish lads. Our English pals were given leave for Christmas, and the arrangement was that they would return in time for the Scottish contingent to get home for Hogmanay. Christmas in the army is quite an experience. As is the tradition, the other ranks are wakened in the morning by the sergeants who serve the soldiers in bed with tea or coffee (heavily laced with rum). Christmas lunch is later served by the sergeants and the officers and, for one day of the year, the soldiers can take liberties with their 'waiters' and get away with it! Good healthy fun.

Hogmanay 1952/53 was a great experience. My pal, Jimmy Duff, came to Edinburgh and we went to the Tron to take in the then traditional

New Year celebrations. The street was jam-packed. There were street entertainers and all sorts of things going on. When the bells rang in the New Year we received swigs out of the bottles of complete strangers and, of course, returned the compliment. Being in uniform, I was hugely popular with the girls that night. I lost count of the number of girls I kissed or was kissed by! Jimmy and I had an amazing Hogmanay.

I had two weeks leave in February 1953 and went directly up to Morayshire from Dundonald. I stayed for a few days with Granny Green in Tolbooth Street in Forres, and she spoiled me rotten. Apparently she adored me. I took her along with me to visit a number of other relatives in Moray and Nairn, and then took a nostalgic cycle trip up to Lethen to see all our old friends there. It was just so good to see so many friends from my earlier years, plus relatives I had seen less of since the Greenies moved to Edinburgh. After a week or so, I went back home and finished my leave in Edinburgh before reporting back to Dundonald Camp.

At this time poor Mam was in the throes of her difficult menopause, with the fear of pregnancy consuming her life. She was in and out of hospital for treatment, including electric shock treatment. Nothing appeared to work and, when she was at home, she was doped up with all sorts of prescribed drugs. Often when I arrived home on a Friday, I would find her in tears, sitting by the fire smoking one Woodbine after another. I am sorry to say she often looked in a terrible condition. She was seriously neglecting her appearance and nothing around her seemed to matter. Dad was at his wits' end, working a full day and then trying to do some household duties, including cooking. Mam ate next to nothing. She was eventually admitted to a psychiatric hospital for a lengthy stay. It was just so sad.

To compound the matter at this time, my sister Elizabeth packed a bag one day, left a note and her young son David behind, and travelled to Bristol to join Emile, a Polish friend of Johnny's. The saddest thing was that Emile had visited Johnny and Elizabeth at Thistle Street, and it was there that a relationship developed between them, presumably behind Johnny's back. It was all pretty sordid really. Dad travelled to Bristol to try and make Elizabeth see sense, but her mind was made up. Eventually Elizabeth and Johnny divorced. Elizabeth married Emile, and Johnny also remarried – a nice girl from Edinburgh, Chris. They went on to raise two girls, but Elizabeth had no more children. Elizabeth's son David was a sad example of a disturbed child from a broken marriage. He went on to develop what I can only describe as a really evil streak in his personality, which was to have serious consequences for all of us in later years. Elizabeth's behaviour outraged and disgusted me and for several years I had no further contact with her.

Between having to deal with Mam's condition at weekends and the selfish fact that I wanted to see more of the world than Dundonald Camp, I spoke to Dad one weekend. I told him I had applied for a foreign posting with the army. He said, 'Ian, quite frankly I'm not surprised and, while this will not help your Mam, I can understand the effect this is having on you each time you come home. Good luck. Go and enjoy your young life.' It was totally selfish of me and very generous of him to take this attitude. In retrospect, I suspect Dad needed all the support he could get but was not the type to ask for it. I think I failed him in that moment of need.

Jimmy was serving in Germany and came home on leave only occasionally, so Dad was left to deal with the situation on his own. When I was clearing out the family home years later, I came across a letter written by Dad to Mam about this period of time, in which he pleads with her to get herself well and not to give up the ghost. He also referred to how proud of me they should both be, which made me positively humble. I kept the letter and still cannot read it without crying.

Dad was to stick with it on his own, although he had some good friends. While the many doctors attending Mam were successful in returning her to her home environment and some kind of normality, she was never the same again. She was not able to deal with life without the help of prescribed drugs, and the illness left her a bag of nerves. What a shame for a warm, loving and generous woman.

I was in the workshop one day at Dundonald when my posting came through. The co came to me very excited: 'Your posting is here Ian and you are going to Korea. This will be the most amazing experience, going to a war zone.' I was totally thunderstruck because I had actually applied for a posting to Singapore or Hong Kong and never expected to be sent to Korea. How bloody naïve of me yet again?

The excitement began to build up, however, as I contemplated this trip more than halfway round the world – any thought of danger was pushed aside. Also, I had just learned that I had passed my Grade 2 exams as an army vehicle mechanic. This had earlier entailed attending the Army Engineering Examination Centre at Stirling for trade exams. These were intense and wide-ranging, including a further driving test. I passed with flying colours, I believe. I was totally chuffed. I also passed an army education exam about this time, so all was looking good. A few weeks later I was instructed to report to Arbourfield Embarkation Camp in the south of England and, after a great sendoff from my REME pals at Dundonald, and with more than a hint of sadness, I travelled down overnight on 29 July 1953. Arbourfield was a big, impersonal camp where I seemed to be in 'hot water' from the moment I entered the main gate until I left on embarkation leave the following day.

I was given two weeks' embarkation leave, and packed a lot into that time, including consolidating my romance with June. I also had the satisfaction of racing for Lothian Speedbirds in three cycle speedway matches and found I had not lost my touch. Ian Laing, the Speedbirds' manager, a really nice guy I had always been friends with, was most complimentary in his praise and insisted I make contact on my return from Korea. He reckoned I had a huge influence on the team, which was really nice.

One weekend, I went off on a camping and fishing trip with my good pal, Jimmy Duff. We travelled by bus on the Galashiels road and camped on the banks of the Gala Water. We had a fabulous weekend, caught quite a few trout, ate all our food between Friday afternoon and noon on Saturday and had to hitchhike into Galashiels to stock up again. Jimmy was such an easy lad to get on with. I really enjoyed his company. I will always cherish that weekend.

All too soon, however, it was time to say a last, sad farewell to June, when we made all sorts of promises including waiting for each other. By this time I was forming a very strong attachment to this very bonny girl and getting to a point when I would have walked through fire for her. They say when you fall in love it is immediately apparent to you and I do believe there is a lot of truth in that statement. The feelings I had for June were far stronger than I ever had for any other girl. It was the wrong time to be heading off to the other side of the world, that's for sure.

Saying cheerio to Mam was just hellish. She cried her heart out and made me feel rightly very guilty. I also felt real sadness leaving our wee dog, Toodles. Dad once again accompanied me to Waverley Station, took me to the pub, for a couple of drinks this time, and for a second time told me to keep my nose clean. For the first time in my life I could see Dad was close to tears. It was a very sad Ian that travelled south overnight to Arbourfield Embarkation Camp. I was absolutely devastated by the various partings and I don't think I have ever felt so bloody lonely in my entire life. But the world was about to become a bigger and more exciting place for the country loon, and there certainly could be no turning back. I was on my way to Korea, more of a man than a boy now though.

CHAPTER THREE

KOREA

brief history of the Korean War:

After WWII and the departure of the Japanese, Korea was divided into North, under the Democratic People's Republic of Korea, and South Korea, under the Republic of Korea (President Syngman Rhee). The two countries were divided roughly by the 38th Parallel. War broke out on the 28 June 1950, when North Korea invaded South Korea. The Communist north quickly overran the South Korean Army (Republic of Korea or ROK) which was poorly equipped and weak. The local conflict became an international one as America sent forces on 1 July from Japan to try and bolster the ROK Army. The retreat could not be halted, however, until the ROK Army and US forces finally stopped the North Koreans on the 'Pusan Perimeter'. The conflict then became a matter for the United Nations, and very quickly British and Commonwealth forces, plus contingents from other UN countries, were sent into Korea, while the Americans, under the command of General Douglas MacArthur, were reinforced.

The tide was then turned by the UN forces and General MacArthur quickly sent the North Koreans homeward in a disorderly retreat. The USA and UN forces crossed the 38th Parallel in early October 1950, but surprisingly continued northwards towards the Chinese border and the Yalu River. There followed a big rumpus between General MacArthur and the US president, resulting in MacArthur being replaced as UN Commander by General Mathew Ridgeway.

Towards the end of October, the Chinese entered the war on the side of North Korea and poured thousands of troops into North Korea, endangering world peace. This sent the UN forces into full retreat back to the 38th Parallel. The Chinese and North Koreans were finally stopped by the UN forces at the end of January 1951. The war then became a vicious stalemate around the 38th Parallel. Armistice talks began, but struggled on and on. Not until 27 July 1953 was an armistice signed in Panmunjon and Munsan. To this day there is only an armistice between North and South Korea and the two lines of defence suspiciously watch each other's movements.

When I arrived at the embarkation camp at Arbourfield it was all hustle and bustle. There were more inoculations (and more big tough soldiers fainting); overseas (tropical) kit to collect from the quartermaster's stores; wills to be written; health checks (with bum and 'willy' inspections of course!) and so on. I loved the army's descriptions of kit – for example: boots, soldier's combat – pairs one; or underpants, jungle green – pairs two, and so on. Once all these things were in order, it was route-marches every day to get us fit and prepare us for the long sea passage by troopship – six to seven weeks for the Korean contingent. I remember one particular route-march commanded by a very cheerful corporal who gave the order to left turn at a nice wee country pub. (They were not all bastards!) He ordered us to halt, dismiss and go in. A couple of pints later, we formed up again and marched off, feeling all the better for it.

On the 27 August 1953 the day of embarkation arrived, we boarded trains and 'chuffed' our way up to Liverpool Docks where we boarded Her Majesty's troopship HT *Lancashire*. She was an old vessel, well past her decommissioning date and clearly suffering from too many sea voyages. I had never seen a ship close up, and I was taken aback by her size. (Why is a ship always female?) We were allocated hammock-style bunks, in tiers of three, on massive troop decks. It was chaos for an hour or so while everyone settled in. There was little space, and we were on one of several troop decks. Soon there was a call to the mess deck, in relays. The food proved to be okay on the old Lancashire.

At 6.30 pm HT *Lancashire* put to sea and, as the lights of Liverpool disappeared into the night, I felt a bit alone and homesick. It would be a year and a half before I returned to Liverpool Docks. Soon those feelings faded and it was a real voyage of discovery as the ship steamed a course towards the Mediterranean. The first day at sea was taken up with lectures about ship routine and our behaviour whilst aboard. The top deck of the ship was assigned to officers and officers' wives on their way to join husbands already serving in foreign parts. A total ban was placed on all 'other ranks' from entering the out-of-bounds top deck area, or from having any contact with the women.

The daily onboard 'fatigues' (duties) were then allocated, and I was really fortunate in being placed on the 'cinema party'. This job entailed setting out chairs on deck in the evening for the 'moviegoers', and clearing the chairs away at the end of the film. Not exactly a taxing detail when you consider that some poor sods were consigned to potato peeling and washing the kitchen's pots and pans. There can be nothing more demoralising in the army than peeling spuds, especially when it is for the whole camp or, in this case, a whole boatload of soldiers. I was once placed on a 'tatty-peeling' fatigue at Blandford Camp and loathed it.

It was hellish sleeping on these huge troop decks even in the best of conditions, but when we hit a storm in the Bay of Biscay, everyone was throwing up from their bunk beds onto the deck. The poor guy on the bottom bunk got covered in the mess, and by morning the stench was unbearable. I suffered from seasickness continuously except when in good sea conditions. We were urged to eat, but as soon as I got near the mess deck, the smell of food set me off again. It was common to see the ship's rail lined with guys 'calling for Hughie', as it was laughingly described. It was not a laughing matter though, as some of you may know.

Once we reached warmer climes there was a race each night to grab sleeping space on the open deck. It was hard on the bones, but so much better than the troop decks, which became as hot as ovens and 'reeked'. I had joined a group of other REME lads, and we took it in turns to go to the open deck early to 'reserve' space.

There were lots of interesting things to see as we passed through the Straits of Gibraltar and into the more sheltered Mediterranean where life became easier for the seasickness sufferers. The first port of call was Port Said at the north end of the Suez Canal and, whilst we were not allowed ashore, hundreds of 'bumboats' – small rowing boats laden with leather and other cheap goods – surrounded the ship, and bargaining commenced. Many a soldier let his money go down to the bumboat first and, to his dismay, got nothing in return. Silly boys! On the other hand, some soldiers got the goods but didn't send down the cash. So 'war was declared' and by the time we left Port Said buckets of water, and even slop pails, were being emptied onto these 'rogue traders'. Some of these Arab 'gentlemen' had quite an uncanny ability to swear and insult us in Scottish, Irish, Birmingham and Geordie accents. The language was especially uncomplimentary when reference was made to our mothers and sisters! The officers' wives from above let out screams of horror, but worse than that was to come.

After refuelling and taking on fresh supplies, we were on our way down the Suez Canal – an amazing sight, with a freshwater canal, railway line, telephone line, palm trees and a road all running parallel for many straight miles. Sailing majestically along this narrow strip of water, with the canal banks so close you felt you could almost touch them, was something never to be forgotten. British Army trucks thundered up and down the road, close enough for us to shout insults such as, 'Got a nice home posting, eh?' The response was invariably,' 'Get your fucking knees browned!' The sight that often greeted us, and offended the sophisticated ladies above, was something else though. As the troopship slowly passed the Arab labourers, fighting the never-ending battle against silting, they downed tools, lifted their clothing to expose themselves and gleefully waved their sometimes erect 'private members' at the women, to their extreme embarrassment, while we all roared with glee! These guys had absolutely no shame, and little regard for the feelings of the British women. Taunts and insults were hurled at the soldiers, only to be returned, of course, by crude racist insults of which the British soldier of those days was master. I began to realise that British soldiers were, back then anyway, only tolerated in most parts of the world and absolutely loathed in others.

The delicate armistice in Korea included the release of prisoners on both sides of the conflict. We passed a troopship while we waited in a Suez Canal 'lay-by' – the HT *Asturias* – loaded with recently released prisoners of war. We gave three huge 'hip-hip hoorays' to send these poor lads on their way home to their loved ones. Many of them were national service-men, and all had suffered badly at the hands of their North Korean and Chinese guards.

Soon we were in the Red Sea and had our first shore leave at Aden. The sights, sounds and smells were utterly fascinating. We wandered about amongst beggars, camels and donkeys being led along pavements, and bazaars, where stall holders made the most almighty din to attract buyers – especially soldiers who they presumed had a lot of money to spend. We drank lots of beer (beer was rationed on board), went to a restaurant and I ate a horse steak for the first time – it was delicious, I must say. We then bought up as many bananas, coconuts and pineapples as we could carry back to the ship. An hour or two later we were on the high seas again. Flying fish became a common sight and were often found dead on the deck in the mornings. Dolphins escorted us for hours and we occasionally saw sea snakes on the surface. Shipping was heavy, including warships from various countries. It was great fun guessing to which port and country the merchant ships were registered. A British ship would be greeted with a huge cheer.

Our next stop was Colombo in Ceylon, now Sri Lanka, which was still very British and much cleaner than Aden. We did a bit of sightseeing, went for a meal and again washed it down with loads of beer. I was starting to get used to palm trees and other exotic flora, it was all so exciting.

Numerous photos were taken by my pals, and fortunately I was able to get copies – I did not own a camera at that time. Colombo was the first time I became aware of some lads sloping off to find local 'available' female company. They reappeared later with smiles on their faces which suggested they had been both successful and satisfied! Then it was back on board again, loaded with more fruit, and on to our next port of call.

When we were well out at sea, we were encouraged to attend at the stern (the blunt end for non-sailors!) of the troopship to improve our aim with the Lee Enfield and Bren gun, firing off .303 rounds to our hearts' content at targets – usually balloons – thrown overboard. Lectures were given daily by officers on all aspects of warfare, plus how to escape if taken prisoner by living off the land etc. The medical officer subjected us to the most horrific films on the cost of being infected with one or all of the various horrible venereal diseases. It should have put us off any association with 'girls of the night' (or any sexual intercourse!) but surprisingly did not. The days passed quickly and it was a pretty lazy existence really.

One of the lads I befriended was Alex Boyes from Edinburgh. He was a painter and decorator by trade, and one of the few tradesmen the army made use of – as a paint sprayer. Alex was a 'randy' wee bugger who could not be trusted with any woman. In the weeks of the sea voyage we became good friends and, although we were given separate postings in Korea, it was a friendship which would continue when we were both back in Edinburgh.

When we arrived in Singapore, we went ashore in the evening and headed immediately for the Britannia Club, a wonderful, old colonial establishment near the Raffles Hotel, with an open-air swimming pool and garden. We sat by the pool and had several beers before Alex 'dragged me screaming' to the red-light district which was, of course, totally out of bounds to soldiers. Alex did all the negotiation and headed off to one room. I headed off to another room with the most beautiful, very dark-skinned Asian girl you could imagine. I was not used to the business aspect, and an argument ensued as to whether I should pay before or after 'services' were provided. This made the girl very angry and I was thrown out of the establishment. By sheer bad luck, I found myself in front of two Redcaps (Military Policemen). I was bundled into their Jeep and driven to the 'in-bounds' area. Having ascertained that I was on shore leave from the Lancashire, I was clearly too much trouble for the Redcaps, so I was dropped off with a warning and told to get back to the ship. I couldn't leave without Alex. Somehow I found my way to the street and house by sheer bloody luck, just as Alex was emerging with a smile on his face. We grabbed a rickshaw and headed for the docks as we were almost late for boarding. Not only did we harass this poor man to pedal faster and ever faster but, when we reached the docks, I am ashamed to say we leapt from the rickshaw (by prior agreement) and bolted through the dock gates. We left a very irate rickshaw man screaming the usual obscenities kept for British soldiers. It was shameful behaviour on our part.

Back on board, I went to bed still a 'virgin', but kind of thankful that I had not been successful when visions of the medical officer's films flashed before me. Alex was none the worse for wear. That beautiful Asian girl's face (and figure) stayed with me for a few days though.

Many years later, I revisited Singapore and made straight to (not the red-light district) the Britannia Club. It hadn't changed a bit on the outside, but was by then the Singapore Police Officers' Club. I asked if I could visit, and was made most welcome. I was not surprised to learn that they had a regular stream of ex-British servicemen visiting. I went out to the rear of the club and, to my utter astonishment it was like walking into a time warp. There was the same swimming pool, ringed with palm trees, with tables and chairs around it. The place had not changed one iota, and I would not have been surprised if Alex and a few of my other buddies had appeared. It really was spooky!

Next day, it was back to the daily ship routine and on to Hong Kong. We were now entering much busier shipping lanes and passing islands galore. Small fishing boats, junks and all sorts of small vessels created new interest for us. Once again, we had a few hours' shore leave in Kowloon, Hong Kong – enough time to do a bit of shopping, have more beers and then back to the ship. No time to search for women this time! Hong Kong, even in those days, was a really busy place, with what seemed like millions of people and rickshaws galore – all muddling together with motor traffic. Another place I made a mental note to visit in the future, and did.

Our final stage of the voyage was Hong Kong to Kure in Japan. On arrival on 4 October we got into full marching order, collected our kitbags which had been stored in the hold and bade farewell to the old HT Lancashire. Once ashore, we boarded Bedford QL three-ton trucks and were transported to the Army Battle Training Camp on the outskirts of Kure. These were old Japanese Army barracks built close to some hills which we were to run up and down a lot as part of our pre-Korea training. In addition we did all the usual stuff – running obstacle courses, physical training and firing range practice – all designed to get us fit and ready for possible action in Korea. We were issued with the most incredible army 'winter' kit which included 'commando' boots (pairs one, of course), string vests (yes, the same as Rab C Nesbit), three-quarter length parka coats, cracking khaki crew-neck woollen jerseys and trousers of man-made fibres of about three or so layers thick. We were also issued with excellent sleeping bags. Most of this equipment was, we were informed, on army experimental trials and, I have to say, it was the very best. When we reached Korea, I was to learn that a pair of these boots or a parka could be bartered with the American soldiers for all sorts of more valuable things. The problem proved to be laying your hands on extra boots and parkas. For once we and our extraordinary kit. were the envy of the Yanks.

It was in Kure that I finally lost my 'cherry', as the Japanese girls called it. Alex once again dragged me against my will into town where there were hundreds of beautiful, young Japanese girls trying to meet the needs of thousands of troops either returning from or about to go to Korea. The girls were so bold that they would approach you in the main street and slide their hands down inside your trousers, with the inevitable reaction (of which they were well aware). They were available young girls and it doesn't require much imagination to guess what happened when all these sex-starved and over-sexed young soldiers (some married) were exposed to such temptation far from home. I didn't know a soldier who did not yield to temptation, despite army threats. Alex and I were tempted! I won't go into details, of course, but it is vividly imprinted in my memory that the beautiful young Japanese girl I was 'with' was singing, in broken English as she undressed, 'If you've got the money honey, I've got the time'; The army seriously frowned on this but, at the same time, encouraged us to pick up what was described as prophylactic packs before leaving camp. I suppose their attitude was: If you can't stop them, then at least give them the necessary medication and condoms (strangely called a French letter then) to minimise the risk.

I had played some recreational football in Scotland, although nothing serious, but while in Kure a match between The Royal Scots and All Other Regiments was arranged, and I was chosen as goalkeeper for the latter. I think we beat the Royal Scots 4–2, but it was a great match any-way, with a lot of soldiers cheering on the two teams. It was played on a gravel pitch and I came off at the end with masses of cuts and 'burns', but proud as punch for having made a few great saves.

Soon all the hard training (and fun) was over and once again we boarded a ship – this time a small, filthy thing which leaped about in the sea as if demented. Fortunately, it was a fairly short overnight trip, and we disembarked in Pusan, Korea. Whilst Japan was a fairly modern country, Korea proved to be the opposite, appearing to be a hundred or so years behind most of the rest of the world. From the outset, it became obvious that the country had been through the meat grinder of modern war, which had flowed up and down Korea until there were few buildings above single-storey level remaining. The place looked totally devastated. It also became obvious that the Korean people were war weary and extremely poor.

After helping unload supplies from our ship, we boarded trains in Pusan to travel north overnight towards the 38th Parallel (which was roughly where the opposing forces faced each other) to join the 1st (and only) Commonwealth Division. The carriages were not exactly cattle trucks, but they had few refinements, and were cold and uncomfortable. We came to a halt while it was still dark and gladly got off the train, stiff, sore and freezing bloody cold. Once again, we boarded the faithful old Bedford QL 3-tonners (I was soon to see a lot of the working parts of these work-horses of the British Army.) One of the first sights that greeted us, which has stuck in my memory, was a British soldier on guard. He was outlined against the morning light, all wrapped up in his parka, his rifle and fixed bayonet over his shoulder. It seemed a very warlike scene somehow!

The Bedford Model QL army truck was used throughout WWII, and still going strong during the Korean campaign, but was gradually phased out after that. Not a particularly bonny vehicle, it was a tough machine which would 'go where no other truck had gone before'. The Yanks often ridiculed our Bedford QLs but, in extreme weather conditions, the old Bedford was still churning through the mud in its lowest gear, with four-wheel drive engaged, while the American equivalent was stuck in the mire. In my period in Korea, I became quite attached to this vehicle. I suppose it was a love/hate relationship. Sometimes I would swear loudly and continuously at one of them, and at other times I was in heaven when driving a well-tuned and sweetly running one. I still see the occasional QL on television, so there are still a few about after all these years. If anyone knows where I can find a Bedford QL truck and arrange one last drive for me, I would be over the moon.

A few other REME buddies and I were posted to 57 Company RASC (Royal Army Service Corps) LAD. This was another very happy posting and I made some great friends, both in the LAD and the RASC. On arrival

HQ in Korea.

we were assigned beds in the standard 12-man army tents. The guys already in the LAD laid on a barbecue for us and we were made to feel really welcome in our new surroundings. I remember getting very drunk, and when I went outside for a 'pee', I fell down and went to sleep on the frozen ground. Snow began to fall heavily. It was only when another lad going to relieve himself fell over me that I was found. I was hauled back into the tent, half frozen. I remained on this attachment for the rest of my service in Korea.

There was not a lot of snow in Korea but the cold was extreme. It was not uncommon to wake up in the morning with the top blanket frozen. It was so much worse than anything we have in the UK, at sea level anyway. I recall instances where drivers were pouring water into their trucks first thing in the morning and the water spilling over the front of the radiator was actually freezing as it ran down. All new arrivals were warned not to pick up cold spanners in the morning but I think we all did so at least once without thinking. The metal spanner stuck to the skin and could only be removed by tearing away some skin or by submerging the hand and spanner in warm water for a moment or two.

The summers were very hot, but there was also a monsoon season which brought chaos to the roads which disintegrated in the downpours.

Our tents were fairly tough but eventually moisture came through – all our daily clothes got soaked, until everything, including our bedding, was wet. It was a pretty miserable period.

The tents were all fitted with what were called 'space-heaters', pretty basic heating appliances consisting of a round burner, into which dripped pure petrol which ignited and produced the heat. A chimney went up through the top of the tent. The only control for this potentially dangerous piece of equipment was a regulator which adjusted the flow of petrol into the burner. If the weather was at its worst then the regulator would be at 'full' and very quickly the space-heater would become red-hot. (We could make great toast and cook a tin of beans on it when it was running red-hot!) There was the odd accident when a tent went up in flames, but surprisingly few occurred. During the winter, the last person to bed placed a basin of water on the space-heater which was then turned off. The first person up in the morning lit the space-heater, and the basin of ice was heated. I leave it to your imagination what condition the water was in by the time the last, or laziest tent occupant washed in the one and only basin of unfrozen water!

We gradually settled into a routine of working on the maintenance of fleets of Bedford QLs (which had four-wheeled drive), as well as Bedford and Ford 15-hundredweight trucks used by the platoons of 57 Company. We also had American Willys Jeeps which were robust little machines, also with four-wheeled drive, that allowed them to go almost anywhere. They were capable of being tipped up onto their sides when maintenance had to be carried out on the underside. These amazing little vehicles were also used widely in WWII, and were adapted and heavily armed for use by the Long Range Desert Group and other Special Services operations.

Not long after my arrival at the LAD in Korea, we had to move camp. It was a bit of an upheaval, breaking down tents, loading up all our equipment and moving to a new location where tents had to be re-erected etc. We were quickly back to full operation. Some months later a move was executed again.

Toilet facilities in Korea were very basic. The lavatory was a hole in the ground with a wooden construction over it, planking with holes cut out every three feet to form the 'seating'. A rough canvas shelter surrounded this stinking Heath Robinson affair. New arrivals in Korea would be seen hanging about the lavatories until they thought everyone had left, and then nipping quickly in and out again, but after a while it became a very communal meeting place! The latrines amounted to old shell cases with

The tough Willys Jeep.

the bottoms removed then sunk into the ground close to the barbed-wire entanglements around the camp. Not very efficient because, if over-used, or in very wet or frosty conditions, they rapidly filled up.

When full it was pretty pointless peeing into the shell case so, in common with others, one day I went a little to one side and relieved myself into the barbed wire. Not a good idea because I was spotted by the officer commanding the LAD, a captain by rank, and I was dragged before him and punished. My punishment was to dig a new lavatory on the nearby hillside on the extreme limits of the camp. This I had to do in the evenings after work was ended. The captain was a tiny little bugger and, like so many of his size, he felt a need to compensate for his lack of inches – he could be a wee 'shite'. He gave me the exact width, length and depth of the lavatory excavation, warning me that if it was an inch out in any of the measurements I would have to fill it in and dig another to the correct dimensions. I stuck at the job manfully evening after evening, but it was hard, lonely work and, with only a couple of lanterns to see by, not easy to get the dimensions absolutely spot on. At first I could throw the excavated soil out of the trench with my shovel but as it got deeper I had to fill a couple of buckets, climb out of the trench, empty them and then climb back into the bloody hole. That slowed it all down, I tell you. I continued with this over Christmas and into Hogmanay that first year in Korea.

On Hogmanay I finished my digging about 11pm, and went over to the mess tent, because I knew the lads had bought in some beers (Asahi beer from Japan – the same stuff that got me pissed at the welcoming party). When I got there, a party was in full swing, and who was sitting holding court but the 'poisoned dwarf' (the captain) who had conde- scended to join the other ranks for Hogmanay! As I entered, filthy and freezing, he commented, 'Oh, here's the shit-hole digger – have a drink on me Green.' I was pretty pissed off one way and another, so I said, 'No thank you. I'll buy my own fucking drink, SIR.' I turned on my heel and went to my tent, where I poured out a large dram that Dad had sent me in one of Mam's many fine food parcels, and went to sleep. Oh, by the way, the 'shit-hole' proved to be of the exact dimensions and was accepted by the captain. I cannot remember if there was an official handing-over cer- emony or who had the first 'crap' in my work of art, but it was 'good luck to all who shit in her' from me!

Apparently my work as a mechanic was greatly appreciated by the captain, or maybe he wanted rid of a troublemaker, but not long after completing the 'hole' I was promoted to lance corporal and attached directly to one of the RASC platoons to work on the daily maintenance of their trucks. In other words, I did the daily running repairs. Anything major went to the LAD, and anything they could not tackle went back to Base Workshops in Seoul. This was just great for me and I really enjoyed the work. I put in long hours, often into the early hours of the morning, but it was very rewarding to see 'sick' trucks that had struggled into camp late afternoon purring out the gate next morning, as a result of my efforts. I also relished being my own boss and being left to get on with my work.

The captain wasn't quite finished with me yet though! One morning I had to go to the nearby LAD to pick up spare parts. We were having a bad run of breakdowns, burst radiators, broken springs etc. To get much- needed trucks on the road again, I worked for two days and two nights non-stop until I was exhausted. I admit I was filthy, unshaven and not looking my best! The captain spotted me at the LAD and sent for me because of my appearance. He seriously bawled me out, giving me no chance to explain. When he had finished I asked for permission to speak, explaining that I had not been to bed for two days and two nights. He muttered something under his breath and told me to get out. He then phoned the 'B' Platoon RASC commander who thought highly of me – time and time again he would ask me to get the maximum amount of trucks on the road for the following day and, time and time again, I did so. I believe the RASC officer gave the REME captain a pretty hard time on the phone, praising me to the heavens. The captain got the message. Later, when he occasionally visited me or bumped into me at the LAD, he would enquire if I was managing to get enough sleep. He also made the occasional complimentary comment: 'Well done, Green. You are doing a bloody good job for the REME.' Or something like that.

The commander of the RASC 'B' Platoon was a lieutenant and a really decent bloke. When things were quiet for me, he would sometimes invite me into his caravan (the officers did not live in tents!), give me a beer, or sometimes something stronger, and blether with me for ages. We had a lot in common and could have been pals but for the rank barrier. He had bought a beautiful Voigtlander Vito II 35mm camera through the NAAFI, and he occasionally loaned it when I was out on the road on convoy duty. I eventually bought an identical camera for myself. On occasions he would appear by a truck in the middle of the night and ask if I could have it ready for the morning. He would then pass the spanners to me as I completed the repair. He was a very grateful man who, although under pressure from above, knew that the way to get the best out of a soldier was not to bully him but to give encouragement. A cracking officer!

The 'B' Platoon's trucks were used mainly for supplying petrol to the various regiments and groups that made up the 1st Commonwealth Division. The petrol came in 48-gallon drums and was collected from the huge American supply dumps. Our trucks were loaded up until they were, in my opinion, quite unstable. The drivers delivered to various locations around the Division. The work for these tough old Bedford QLs was brutal, and the cost in radiators, springs and engines was high. The hard-packed gravel roads were

The indestructable Bedford QL three tonner.

appalling. They were extremely dusty during the summer, with speed restrictions close to the 38th Parallel down to about 15 miles an hour in an attempt to prevent the dust clouds being spotted by the Chinese/ North Koreans on the 'other side'. In both summer and winter the roads developed huge potholes which wreaked havoc on springs and radiators. In the monsoon season the roads simply disintegrated, and only emergency traffic was allowed to move. The six-cylinder Bedford engine took a severe hammering because of the workload and the atrocious road conditions, and engine wear was excessive. Trucks frequently had to be fitted with reconditioned engines from Japan where, I suspect, not a lot of expertise was available in the Japanese workshops.

When an engine was badly worn and burning excessive oil it would be taken out of service. When we had a few of these at the LAD, on a Sunday when we were usually off, the engines on these trucks would be changed. Each REME mechanic, assisted by one RASC driver, would line up beside a truck. The staff sergeant would shout, 'Go!' and we would race to see who could change a Bedford engine quickest. The engine was considered 'changed' when it had been fitted, filled with water and oil (in different orifices of course) and the engine running. Competition was fierce but in good spirits. The prize for the winners was a couple of crates of Asahi beer, which was shared by everyone anyway. Great fun and a grand way to spend a Sunday morning!

In bad weather crashes were inevitable, with trucks sliding into ditches at the side of the roads or drivers failing to negotiate bends, resulting in trucks tipping over and even sometimes rolling. Strangely, injuries were minor – nothing serious that I can recall. Accidents should have been more frequent because it was not uncommon for drivers, including myself, to race each other. In attempting to overtake another platoon truck, one might get alongside but not have the steam to overtake quickly. An approaching blind summit would be no deterrent, and the two drivers would 'play chicken' to the brow of the hill where, thankfully, there never seemed to be an oncoming truck. Another game was when we were on the Seoul run to collect reconditioned trucks. There would be a duty driver and maybe six other drivers to bring back the replacement trucks, plus myself (in case of any breakdowns). At some point, the driver would put the throttle onto a fixed setting, disappear out the offside window and clamber into the rear of the truck, while the front-seat passenger had to scramble across to take control before the truck crashed. This crazy manoeuvre would be executed several times

Changing a Bedford engine in Korea.

The 'not so indestructable' Bedford QL.

Ian (back row, far right) and RASC drivers in front of a Bedford QL.

before we reached Seoul. Total and utter madness! And while I, as lance corporal in charge, would tell them to pack it in, the daft buggers played their crazy game anyway!

One so-called bit of fun on such a run was for some of the more evil guys to load up with stones and hurl these at the outdoor shop displays in Korean villages as we hurtled through at breakneck speed. Another was to drive slowly alongside a Korean farmer with a huge bundle of brushwood or straw on his 'A-frame' (a fairly basic piece of equipment worn on the farmer's back and used to carry quite astonishing loads). The driver would light a match and drop it into the dry material, with the resulting alarming sight of the poor bloody farmer having to rapidly extricate himself from the burning A-frame. Remember, these poor people were supposed to be our allies!

The South Koreans were not all angels, of course, and frequently raided our camps at night. All camps were surrounded by heavy barbed-wire entanglements, with sentries patrolling the perimeter all night. However, many raids were successful. I awoke one night to a hail of bullets whistling through the canvas of our tent as a couple of male Koreans slashed the side of the tent then exited rapidly. The sentry 'lost the plot' on seeing the Korean invaders enter our tent and just fired off in their direction, without regard for his sleeping comrades. Tales of tents being emptied of all movable equipment resulted in us having to sleep with our heads on our kitbags, and our boots under two legs of the metal beds which had replaced the earlier camp beds.

The Koreans loved to eat dogs. A bitch (we named her Peggy) which had sought refuge in our camp and befriended us had to be guarded day and night. Eventually she gave birth to half a dozen puppies, lovely wee things, but sadly they were picked off one by one by the Korean camp workers for 'Sunday lunch'.

As part of the LAD equipment we had a huge Scammel recovery vehicle. These were amazingly powerful, and when in the very lowest of numerous gears, movement was barely perceptible – but what power there was in this low gear! I recall our Scammel driver, who was a bit of a nutcase, being sent out to recover a tank that had gone off the road into a paddy field. He arrived at the scene at the same moment as an American recovery vehicle and an argument ensued between the respective drivers as to which one was the more powerful. To solve the argument, the two vehicles were set back-to-back and linked with a strong chain. All the while the tank crew were sitting patiently in their tank waiting to be rescued. At a given signal, both drivers took up the strain and the contest was on, with both engines roaring, to see which truck could pull the other – backwards. The REME Scammel won hands down and, not content with pulling the American recovery vehicle a couple of yards, our REME nutcase pulled the American truck 50 or so yards along the road before stopping. The British 1 – Yanks 0. Did we enjoy that!

Every so often there would be army manoeuvres or alerts and warnings that the Chinese/North Koreans were preparing to advance. Our trucks would be loaded up with supplies or infantry to be moved up to the British front lines, usually in the middle of the night. I always accompanied our platoon convoy in case of breakdowns, and would be 'tail-end Charlie' of the convoy. On one such alert, one of the trucks broke down and the other trucks in the convoy moved off, leaving me to try to make the offending truck serviceable again. I was unsuccessful and had to take it in tow, in total darkness. We got horribly lost, so I stopped to get my bearings. We heard voices fairly close by – and they were not speaking English or Scottish. Fortunately, there was an area where we could turn around. Having done so, I switched on the headlights and left the area at a speed which left the driver of the towed truck in a panic. It got us back quickly to a road junction where a Redcap was on duty. He told us to, 'Get those f——-g lights out!' and wanted to know why we were coming from the enemy lines. It was a great laugh next day but, bloody hell, were my legs shaking at the time.

Another 'hairy' trip was when myself and an RASC driver were sent to Seoul for spare parts and, on the journey back in the dark, the petrol supply to the engine got blocked – a common occurrence because of the filthy petrol. I had no lights to work under the truck and we could not leave it by the side of the road with valuable stores in the back, so what to do? Well, we improvised – and how! I removed the engine cover of the QL, which was inside the cabin, disconnected the air intake from the carburettor and, while the driver 'drove' this leaping, bucking monster, I poured petrol into the neck of the carburettor using a tin cigarette box, with a bigger can of petrol balanced between my knees. Needless to say, the flow of petrol was neither the right strength nor a regular flow, but somehow we struggled the last miles to camp – with me screaming at the driver to avoid potholes, and him screaming at me to keep an even flow of petrol as he tried to regulate the air intake with the accelerator. I can hear motor mechanics saying, 'Can't be done.' Well, I told you they were amazing machines these old Bedford QLs. Adaptable is the word!

Our camp was fairly close to a valley which had been named 'Gloster Valley' after the heroic action of the Gloucester Regiment during fighting. They fought an incredible holding action to allow other outfits to withdraw and, when they finally started to pull out from their positions, the Chinese were everywhere. As the 'Glorious Glosters' retreated through the valley, the Chinese on the surrounding hillsides threw everything at them. Many were killed, wounded or captured, but it was a very brave action. Discarded weapons and bodies were still being recovered during my time in Korea. Just north of Gloster Valley was the Imjin River and towards the end of my tour of duty, swimming parties were organised. I could not swim at that time, so I gave it a miss. However, one poor lad from another regiment lost his life when swimming in the Imjin which had some serious currents.

We became very friendly with a New Zealand transport regiment camped a few miles from us, and took it in turn to host parties with the mainly Maori soldiers. They were amongst the warmest and most gentle people I have met in my entire life and some great friendships flourished. (I had an invite from one lad to visit him in New Zealand but, by the time I got home, I had somehow lost the address.) We did not have an 'Other Ranks Bar' or anything like that. So when we were the hosts, one lad would get the use of a truck, visit the NAAFI and purchase crates of beer (we were not allowed anything stronger) from a 'kitty'. The party would be held in the mess tent. The Asahi beer was powerful stuff, or so it seemed, and fairly got the parties going. Soon a great singsong would develop. The Maoris would sing their traditional songs using the most wonderful harmonies and we, in turn, would sing whatever songs we'd been brought up with. The Maoris beat us hands down though. As the drink flowed and everyone got a bit drunk, the ribald army songs would start:

'Oh, we're fighting for that bastard Syngman Rhee,
Syngman Rhee, Syngman Rhee.
Oh, we're fighting for that bastard Syngman Rhee.'

or

'Drinking rum and coca-cola
Working for the Yankee Dollar'

and so on.

Regrettably, I am unable to recall any of these songs in full. Years later, when I had a letter published in the British Korean Veterans' Association magazine, requesting words for the songs, I strangely got no response.

The countryside where we were camped was a mix of hills and flat paddy fields. In spring, the hillsides were covered with azaleas which burst into glorious colour. (Unfortunately, there were no colour photos in those days.) I was intrigued by the scene when the Korean people planted their rice. It involved both men, and women who often had small babies strapped to their backs. The paddy fields, flooded by the monsoon rains, were just a sea of mud, and into this the young rice plants, grown in nursery fields, were thrust. The Koreans worked in lines, moving backwards as each straight line was planted by hand. It must have been back-breaking work, but it was a great spectacle. In due course, the paddy fields would dry out, the rice would grow tall, and the ears of the rice appear and ripen. The crop was cut with small hand tools.

On the lower slopes of the hills and better drained pieces of land, crops such as beans, chillies, marrows, green peppers and other assorted vegetables grew. On the upper slopes of some of the hills were Korean graveyards, marked by individual gravestones. I was assured that the rich people were buried on the upper slopes while the poor were lower down. A funeral was an extraordinary sight and seemed more like a wedding procession. The Koreans danced and jigged their way along the road to the nearby hill, singing what sounded like happy songs, banging drums and playing other instruments. It was just a cacophony of noise to our ears.

Despite the bromide, alleged to be put in our tea to inhibit our sexual desires, night-time forays out of the camps and into the Korean villages were common. This meant making 'an arrangement' with the duty guards in our camp to ensure they knew we were going 'over the wire' as it was known. This was crucial because, on a couple of occasions, returning soldiers were mistakenly shot at by trigger-happy guards – one soldier in our camp suffered a nasty bullet injury to his backside as he struggled in the barbed wire.

These forays were usually made by a couple of pals. The plan was to get to a Korean village unseen, knock at doors and then pose the question – 'Habba any sexies?' Pretty pathetic pidgin English, but usually understood by the Koreans. Entry was gained or the door slammed in your face. Payment could be in money or kind – food scrounged from the cook, clothing or whatever. The Koreans were very poor, and many of the women providing services were married with babies in the house. They quite simply needed the money to subsist.

One night I was making my way back to camp when suddenly I was illuminated by headlights, accompanied by the call 'Halt or I'll fire!' – Redcaps again! I bolted and dived under some old corrugated iron, only to find myself in a ditch of foul-smelling liquid. I moved slightly to get my face out of this stuff, banged the corrugated iron and was immediately hauled out by two Redcaps. I think it would be accurate to say I was 'in the shite' twice that night! I was hauled off to a nearby Jeep and my pay-book (a soldier's identification papers) seized. We were about to move off when another 'out of bounds' soldier was spotted and arrested. He was an Australian who did not have his pay-book on him – another offence. We moved off and the Australian indicated to me that he was going to make a bolt for it. He rolled off the Jeep in the darkness and disappeared into the night. The Redcaps realised their error almost immediately and I got a couple of slaps around the head, presumably for failing to say anything. Then, to my surprise (and relief), they returned my pay-book, telling me to get back to my camp and keep my mouth shut. No questions asked, I quickly returned to camp. I assume the Redcaps would have been in some trouble had word of the escapee come out at their headquarters. Close shave that one!

On another foray, shots were fired at a pal and me as we crept through a Korean village on our way back to camp. We had to run for our lives as bullets whistled around us. The shooter was an irate South Korean army officer who, we learned later, had come home on leave unexpectedly and found a soldier in bed with his wife. The soldier escaped and the wife apparently concocted the cover story that she was being raped. According to the soldier it had been a straightforward 'business transaction'. The Korean officer went on the rampage with his army revolver, intent on taking revenge on any British soldier he came across. Unable to find the culprit, he reported the 'rape' next day, and the entire camp was lined up for an identification parade. The Korean woman had a close look at each of us, including the guilty party, but was unable or didn't want to identify anyone. Whether it was rape or the woman simply augmenting her income, as many of the young Korean women did in the absence of husbands serving in the Korean Army, who knows? They were hard and desperate times for many Korean women, with husbands in the army earning a mere pittance or, worse still, already a casualty of the awful war which had raged in South Korea for several years.

Korean houses were mainly of clay construction with thatched roofs. All were on one level but were raised slightly off the ground. During the winter, in the tunnel below the house floor, people burned whatever material they could lay their hands on. Material for burning was in short supply and trees could not be cut down by law, so straw and brush were used, gathered from under trees on the hillsides. This created a kind of crude central heating system and, while there was often a smoky haze in the houses, they were very cosy. I was once given a bowl of stew in a Korean house. It consisted mainly of vegetables with only a small amount of chicken, but was very tasty. I believe that small fish, consumed whole, were another regular element of their diet. One of the soldiers' songs had the line:

I've been to Korea and it's not very nice,
For all that they eat there is fish heads and rice.

This was sung to 'So Long, It's Been Good to Know You'.

Most of the Koreans slept on the floor on fairly thin mattresses. But one Korean woman, who definitely did not sleep on the floor, was one who became a 'partner' of an RASC driver. He went over the wire almost every night of the week to visit his Korean girlfriend, bearing gifts of whatever he could scrounge in the way of food etc. One night, he stole an unoccupied, metal-framed army bed from one of the tents. With it balanced on top of his head, he climbed the barbed-wire entanglement and headed into the night. He presented his gift to the very surprised Korean girl. I gather his sex-life improved greatly after that. The missing bed remained an unsolved mystery to the CO.

We made friends with some Koreans, including those who worked in the camp doing mainly cleaning work, but also some local people who passed by our camp. I became quite friendly with one 'Mama-san' (a motherly type of person) who agreed to take on board some of the camp's washing. She was as honest as can be and always returned with the correct number of items, clean and neatly pressed. They had no electricity in the country areas, so presumably she used an old-fashioned 'iron'. We paid her in 1st Commonwealth Division currency (issued by the army to the soldiers in their weekly pay) which was considered worthless by the Koreans. Somehow they managed to exchange it for US dollars or their own currency which was the won.

Many of our rations were supplied by the Americans, and included a lot of poor-quality, badly-cooked turkey (which we grew to hate), chicken, mince and stew (out of tins), 'bully' (corned) beef, tinned bacon (absolutely revolting) and dried vegetables (including dry potato mixture which the cooks never seemed able to mix properly). The food was sufficient but lacked variety and, because so much of it was processed, flavourless. If we were out on convoy and anywhere close to an American camp, we'd drop in there for lunch. The Yanks had far better food than us. Some of the rations were the same but they had greater variety. They also had luxuries that we never saw, such as steak, roast beef, a wide variety of fresh fruit, trifle and even ice cream. They took it all for granted and, if they stopped off at our camp, they would turn up their noses at what was on offer. On one occasion, we stopped off at an American camp and went into the mess hall (they had the luxury of prefabricated huts) where the usual piped music was playing – but the atmosphere was palpable. Apparently, there was no ice cream on the menu that day and the US soldiers were close to mutiny. Ice cream – bloody hell!

There was no piped music in British Army camps, but our tent did have a wind-up gramophone and two 78rpm records. We had many visitors and the same two records were played over and over again until we'd go almost mad. One day, the spring broke and some thought that would be the end of it, but one soldier needed his music and was able, after some practice, to spin the record on the turntable with both hands

– he was almost able to maintain the appropriate speed – almost. It should have put me off music for life.

I mentioned earlier that our winter clothing was far superior to what the Yanks had and that they would give anything for a pair of our boots or one of our parkas. I should emphasise that the Americans had huge stocks of every conceivable kind of supplies, and appeared not to have the strict quartermaster sergeants of the British Army, who would barely issue a pair of socks without a lot of argument and an accompanying countersigned memo. The day came when it was decided that our platoon was in need of electric lighting, instead of lanterns and candles, for the long winter nights. The LAD electrician had 'come across' a small generator and was in need of an engine to operate it. He headed off to an American supply dump, armed with a pair of 'commando' boots, and returned later in the day with a Jeep engine. A bloody good day's bartering I would say. The engine was connected to the generator, electric cable strung from tent to tent, and bulbs and fittings, acquired by another skilled barterer, completed the lighting system. As long as someone remembered to keep the Jeep engine supplied with petrol and it was given a service from time to time, this setup gave us light. It was still operating when I left Korea.

Midway through my tour of duty, as was common, I was given a week's leave in Tokyo – actually it was officially referred to as 'Rest and Recuperation' but, if ever the army got a description wrong, this was it. We were flown from Seoul to Tokyo in a massive American Globemaster transport aircraft, not unlike the Hercules used today by many armies, including our own. On arrival at our 'rest camp' in Tokyo, which had previously been a Japanese midget submarine base, all our clothes were taken from us. We had a shower and were issued with new army kit but, of course, before dressing there were the inevitable bum and privates inspections. We were finally given a brief but very specific lecture; enjoy

Korea 1954 – about to depart for Japan on 'Rest and Recuperation'.

yourself, don't be on the streets during curfew (midnight to 7am), you've been allocated a bunk in a dormitory but you don't have to use it unless you wish. but – don't get VD or you will be returned to Korea instantly. So endeth the lesson.

With a pocketful of back-pay we were in town before you could blink. I ordered a very ornate tea set for Mam, which the shopkeeper shipped to Scotland for me (June and I still have it.) I went to an ice-rink for a couple of hours' skating, but the Japanese girls would have nothing to do with soldiers – quite right too. It was then off to one of the hundreds of beer bars and a chat with one of the many pretty hostesses. If you found the 'right one', a deal was struck and you had yourself a partner for the full week. They summed it up by saying, 'You will be my husband and I will be your wife.' It was a remarkable arrangement which worked well. In Tokyo, all the 'business girls' were licensed and examined every few days by a doctor. My 'wife' (Micki) spoke very good English, appeared to be well-educated, had a great sense of humour and was good company, as well as being a wonderful lover. On my last day in Tokyo, she accompanied me in a taxi to the rest camp and we were both in tears as we parted. We were genuinely sad. Like everyone else who boarded the Globemaster on our return to Korea, I was absolutely exhausted and in great need of proper rest and recuperation. I was brought back to my senses when the American pilot announced that one of the four engines was unserviceable and we would be flying on three only: 'But, hey buddies, we can fly on only one if need be.' I was not reassured and was glad to land safely in Seoul.

My time in Tokyo was not entirely frivolous though. I did a considerable amount of sightseeing during daytime. Tokyo was a bustling, modern city with an amazing transport system. I was travelling on a very modern train one day when the carriage filled up at a station. I rose to give a Japanese lady my seat. She bowed to me and I bowed back, she bowed again and I once more returned the compliment. This went on for a few moments until I realised that if I did not stop bowing to her, she would never sit down. I stopped bowing and she promptly sat down. Giving a seat to a female was not the local custom, I learned, and it was not uncommon to see men roughly push women aside to grab a vacant seat on a train or at the cinema. A visit to the Ginza Market was an amazing experience, where haggling was the order of the day – there was no such thing as paying the price quoted. I always promised myself a return visit to Tokyo but, sadly, I have not yet made it back.

A few months after my Tokyo visit, I was promoted to corporal. My 'friend' the captain had moved on and we had a new CO who was a totally first-class officer and a decent human being. This ended my days on attachment to 'B' Platoon, and I moved back to the LAD. My new duties there were to carry out the army's '406 Inspections'. This was a monthly inspection when each vehicle was examined from top to bottom for cleanliness and road-worthiness, with recommendations made for level of servicing and repairs required. It also included a short road test. The cleanliness of the vehicle, plus other aspects of daily maintenance, including keeping nuts and bolts tight, was the driver's responsibility. More than a couple of faults necessitated the driver being reported for negligence although, in practice, he was usually given a chance to correct the faults if they were only minor. Other faults, wear and tear etc. were reported on the '406 Inspection Sheet', and the vehicle was then passed to a craftsman mechanic for the necessary repairs. I have to say this was a highly efficient method of vehicle maintenance – 'one up' for the British Army. I enjoyed the new work and responsibility, which meant cleaner hands as a rule, although sometimes the corporals did have to 'muck in' and do repair work.

It also meant that, occasionally, I would have to take on the duty of guard commander, with responsibility to the duty officer. The first time I was guard commander I got the execution of one of the parade drills wrong and had to go through the guard inspection twice. Only then did the duty officer allow the guard to march off to the guardroom – to my embarrassment, but to the amusement and glee of the duty guard. I didn't get it wrong next time though so lessons were learned again.

On one occasion when I was guard commander there were some real hard nuts in the guardroom cells. Some years later, I was to see the face of one of these guys in a newspaper – wanted by the police for a serious crime! Unknown to me, this bad lot had had some booze smuggled into the cells during the day and I only learned about it when they got drunk, became obstreperous and came to the notice of the duty officer. I was in front of the CO next day, but got off with a warning when it was established that the beer was smuggled in before I went on guard and, since I was out on my 'rounds' when the commotion began, it was felt I was blameless. Phew.

I was, and to this day still am, hopeless at getting out of bed first thing in the morning. Once free of training establishments I rarely made it to breakfast, and would only emerge when it was time to go off to start the duties of the day. When promoted to corporal, I was given another duty and that was to take turns with the other corporals to call a parade after breakfast, issue an anti-malaria tablet (Paludrine, I think they were named) to each of the REME soldiers and ensure that it was swallowed. I must be honest and say that the parade had often already assembled when I finally got out of bed. I would then rush out and issue the tablets. A poor example but hey, we all have weaknesses, and that is one of mine.

When I was attached to 'B' Platoon and working late at night under electric lighting, I would be surrounded by hundreds of mosquitoes and was bitten many times. I was supposed to work with my arms and neck covered, but on hot summer nights this did not seem feasible. The inevitable happened and I contracted malaria. I woke up one morning with a raging fever and reported sick. I was taken by ambulance to the army hospital where I was put to bed immediately. I had a high fever and was delirious for a few days, suffering incredible hallucinations. I lost a lot of weight and only after a couple of weeks was I finally released, extremely weak. The doctors threatened me with a charge of failing to take my daily Paludrine tablet, but I denied this, although I kept quiet about working with uncovered arms and neck at nights. I had some recurring symptoms when I returned to the UK. While these eventually disappeared, I regret that I am barred forever from being a blood donor.

I enjoyed my time in Korea. Although there were occasions when I felt very homesick, this was compensated for by a continuous flow of letters to and from home. Mam was a great writer and I made a point of writing to her every week. At first there was also a stream of letters from June, but inevitably I got the 'Dear John' letter. A Dear John was the final letter from a girlfriend, or in the case of some poor buggers, a wife, to say that the relationship was over. When such a letter was received, the soldier concerned made it known to everyone by pinning it to the dartboard in the tent. Everyone was invited to read it and throw darts at it every evening until the next one arrived. June and I had talked about the long time I would be in Korea, and I'd said to her, 'Well, if you get fed up waiting for me, I'll understand.' When the letter arrived I was, nevertheless, devastated and in the doldrums for a while. The lads all did their bit though and helped each other get through such a loss. Soon I was throwing darts at June's letter like the rest of them.

Towards the end of my service in Korea, another letter arrived from June. This time, she asked me to forgive her. She said the relationship she had with a young man in Scotland had broken up and she wanted to resume contact with me, at least until I got back home. The relationship was resumed, blossomed and, in due course, we became husband and wife.

Each soldier was supposed to serve only one full winter in Korea because of the extreme cold but, by late 1954, I was into my second winter. In due course though, word of our transfer to Japan and onward passage to the UK came through. A huge 'piss-up' was arranged for our last night – several of us were moving out at the same time. What a night it was! A lot of tears were shed. Addresses were exchanged and promises made to keep in contact. I have to say, it was a very subdued bunch of guys that boarded the Bedford QLs next day. The inevitable insults flew as we left the camp for the last time – 'Get some fucking foreign service in!' or 'You poor bastards. We're going home!' from us. The responses were equally crude, if predictable: 'Fuck off!' Next day we were in Pusan, and the following day we were back in Kure, Japan. We were going home – or so we thought.

homeward Bound – a new life beckoning

n arrival in Japan in November 1954 it was back to the Kure Battle Training Camp where we expected to be for only a few days before embarkation. A couple of days later, we boarded trucks and were transported to the docks where a troopship waited. We handed over our kitbags for the hold, went on board and were allocated bunks, but we had barely reached the troop deck when an announcement came over the Tannoy instructing our group to return to deck. The appalling news was broken to us that there had been a planning error (or more accurately, a cock-up – not all that uncommon in the British Army). We should not have embarked and were to wait for another troopship, probably in January. We retrieved our kitbags and an hour later we were back in the Kure Battle Training Camp. Promises of being home for Christmas or the New Year were out the window and there were some very upset soldiers, including myself! This was not life threatening however, just another of the many army blunders for which they are renowned. Once again the question was posed: how do we win wars with this kind of administration? Needless to say, the friends we had bid farewell to a few hours earlier were 'near wetting themselves'!

Next day we were allocated duties for the waiting period – mine was to oversee the packing of reconditioned Bedford engines into crates for dispatch in a nearby Japanese workshop. I found out immediately how bad the workmanship was in these workshops. The Japanese, I assume, were still pretty mad at losing WWII, so the workers did not give a damn about their British Army employers. My responsibility was to ensure the reconditioned engines were securely packed into wooden crates which were then shipped to Korea. The Japanese workers were mostly lazy buggers and had to be pushed all day to get the work completed. At the drop of a hat, one in particular would join me beside the workshop heater and ask me pointless questions. To prolong the inevitable – being sent back to work – he first offered me the services of his daughters (showing me photos, and they were pretty but extremely young girls) and later, the services of his wife! These offers were of course refused and he and the others were sent back to work with a threat of a whack around the ear – the only language they appeared to understand fully. Some of the workers were despicable human beings in my view.

While in Kure, I was astonished to learn of the huge waste that was taking place. Almost daily, barges were being towed out to deep water, and massive amounts of unused spare parts dumped into the sea by the British Army. Excess to requirements apparently, it seemed that dumping these valuable spare parts was the cheaper option to transporting them back to the UK. I heard of one case where a hugely expensive Rolls Royce engine, still on the secret trials list, was also dumped into the sea because it was too difficult to account for its presence in a particular warehouse. British Army trucks were also being sold off at giveaway prices to Japanese buyers, along with free spare parts.

Most nights while in Kure, a crowd of REME lads (including myself) would go into town and drink in one of the many beer bars. Each had several hostesses who not only took your order, but poured your beer into a glass, lit your fag and sat with you at the table, sipping very expensive soft drinks which the soldiers had to pay for. It was from the high profit margin on these soft drinks that the girls earned most of their wages, plus tips. Unlike the Tokyo beer bar hostesses, these girls were 'not for sale', and requests for extra services were invariably turned down, especially by those in the bar we frequented – Club Chotti. The one I made a beeline for each night was Judy – a slim, pretty girl with the most gorgeous eyes. I became very attracted to her and had many long, interesting conversations with her, as well as the odd kiss and a cuddle – but no more. Her parents had died in the Hiroshima atomic bomb attack. Luckily, she was away from home at the time. She expressed no bitterness towards the Allies for this horrendous attack, mainly on civilians and, in fact, agreed with the Allies' stance that it shortened the war, saving many lives. She was forced to work as a bar hostess because there was little other alternative post-war employment in Kure, apart from trading her body. I foolishly promised I would keep in touch with Judy on my return to the UK and she expressed a desire to continue the relationship there if she could get the necessary papers. However, the 'out of sight, out of mind' syndrome came into its own yet again, and I had no further communication with her after I left Kure. Maybe she was only bolstering my ego anyway? For most of us, sex with the Kure girls was not on the

Corporal Ian Green in Kure, Japan.

agenda this time because we were so close to returning home and it seemed wise not to 'push our luck'. This decision had the same controlling influence during the return sea voyage.

My duties in the workshop continued over Christmas and into the New Year of 1955, when we finally received news of embarking on the ss *Captain Hobson* in January. We were overjoyed at this news and the thought of returning home.

When we boarded the ss *Captain Hobson*, we were not a little surprised and delighted to find that there were no huge troop decks but, instead, two and four-bunk cabins. It appeared that the ship, usually working on the emigrant routes to Australia and New Zealand, had been requisitioned by the army to clear the backlog of troops being pulled out of Korea. The easing of tension on the Korean front-line meant a huge reduction in troop strength there. Real home comforts – and the food was also excellent. A bonus for me was that the *Captain Hobson* was much smaller than the HT *Lancashire* and had a totally different motion on the water, so I never suffered from seasickness on the entire homeward voyage.

The voyage was most enjoyable, with shore leave at all the usual places. But we were all a bit more mature and restrained. There were few duties, so it was a lazy, relaxed journey, and we all worked hard at building up the tan already started in Korea. As we were leaving Singapore there was a bit of excitement when the ship ran onto a sandbank. It was pulled off by a tug but then divers had to go down to examine the hull for damage. There was none and, after a couple of days, we resumed our journey. The incident was reported in the UK press, and my family knew of it before I had time to write home.

The friendships established in Korea had continued in Kure and, on the journey home, I spent most of my time with Korean pals, Pete Childs and 'Yorky' (for the life of me, I cannot recall his surname, but obviously he was a Yorkshireman). The three of us, and a couple of others, were very close.

Army pals Pete Childs, 'Yorkie' and Ian on the *Captain Hobson* homeward bound.

Early in the voyage, I reached my 21st birthday on the 29 January. I had a record request made by my buddies played on the ship's broadcasting service and then they bought me some beers in the evening. I was to have another celebration in Edinburgh on my arrival home, which was a less sober affair.

Some of our spare time was spent attending lectures by officers on the subject of employment choices and prospects after demob. One such talk was by an officer who had spent some time as a police inspector in Hong Kong. He suggested the police as a career opportunity for some of us and that sowed a seed which germinated some months later.

As we entered the Bay of Biscay, always a wild area, we hit a huge storm and, for a day or so, during which time the ship was simply weathering the storm and making little progress, no one was allowed on deck. During one night, a huge section of the ship's railing was washed away and lifeboats damaged and still I wasn't seasick, while others were having a terrible time of it – amazing.

On arrival at the docks in Liverpool on the evening of 22 March 1955 there was great excitement as we were each called on the Tannoy to report to an officer to be given our de-embarkation instructions. Several of us, who were by then near our demob date, were issued with rail tickets and leave passes for two weeks, with instructions to report in due course to Aldershot for demob. This was just what I wanted and, next day, in full marching order, kitbag retrieved from the hold and complete with my faithful Lee-Enfield .303 rifle, I was walking down the gangway. Can you imagine the expressions of members of the public today if they saw soldiers in the streets with rifles? Not uncommon then, of course.

There was little time to say cheerio to friends, but all the usual promises of keeping in touch were made – in absolute sincerity. It was a sad end to so many friendships, some of which had begun at the embarkation camp in England 'so long ago', and a few tears were shed – but most of us were heading for home, so there was also great joy.

I somehow got messages to Mam, Dad and June of my impending arrival at the old Caledonian Railway Station in Edinburgh, and then made my way through the customs hall. Every soldier was stopped and questioned about what gifts and goods they were bringing into the UK. I thought it was best to be absolutely honest and listed the more valuable items, including my fairly new Voigtlander Vito II camera. I found I was dealing with a really decent customs officer who refused to accept my valuation of the camera and kept suggesting a lower value. After a couple of times, I cottoned on to what he was doing and, when I agreed to his valuation, he advised me there was 'nothing to pay' – and winked at me. A lad at the table next to me was having different treatment. I knew he was always broke and never had a penny to buy any gifts. The officer dealing with him was not convinced that he had absolutely nothing to declare and, by the time I moved on, every possession had been emptied onto the table – and the customs officer was scratching his head in disbelief! Another soldier I knew, who had brought home a Chinese sub-machine-gun in his kitbag, got through unsearched, and was very relieved as we all headed for our respective trains.

A few hours later, I got off the train in Edinburgh to be met by Mam, Dad and June – tears of joy were the order of the day. June had to return to work so I went home to Convent Cottages with Mam and Dad where I was reunited with our wee dog, Toodles. Mam had been writing to me for some time, saying that Toodles was getting old and had difficulty walking. According to her, he was waiting for me coming home. He struggled out of his bed, wagging his tail, and gave me a great welcome home. He died a few days later.

Mam was looking so much better than when I left, and Dad looked less harassed. I didn't dare tell him I probably had not kept my nose as clean as he might have wished, but there were still lots of tales to be told. Neighbours welcomed me back and gifts were handed out. It was so good to be home.

I broke the news that I had started smoking in Korea where every soldier received a free weekly ration of 50 cigarettes and a box of matches. I got loads of 'stick' from Mam and Dad about this because, prior to Korea, I had been dead against smoking – and had given them both a hard time for doing so. I then got the shock of my life to find that Mam had kept every letter I had sent her from Korea, all neatly tied together in date order. I came across them again when clearing the house at Stenhouse after her death – and I could not throw them out.

On the evening of my arrival home, I went out to meet June and we held hands all evening. When I took her home late that night, we kissed and cuddled at the bottom of the stair in Balgreen Park, and I always remember June saying to me, 'Well, you've lost your shyness, eh?' Many more romantic times to follow.

I handed my rifle in to Redford Barracks for safekeeping until my de-embarkation leave ended. When I collected it from the REME armourer, he told me the sights and firing-pin were badly damaged, but that he had repaired them. Just as bloody well I never had to fire it in anger at the Chinese.

My 21st birthday was celebrated a second time in great style. Brother Jimmy, Johnny Swierc and I went out on the town one night during my leave. Dad could not go because he was in bed with lumbago. The three of us got very drunk and were thrown out of two pubs in Lothian Road – for drinking whisky out of a carryout bottle in one, and for being too noisy in another. When we got back to Convent Cottages, I succeeded in getting Dad pissed, and finally fell down drunk with my head under the sideboard. I think, later on, good old Mam somehow got me to bed.

A rather bonny young June.

While on leave I was to have my third and final run-in with the Redcaps. I was wearing army uniform daily because I had no civvy clothes that fitted, and I suppose there was a bit of the 'peacock' in me – a wish to show off because I still had the 1st Commonwealth Division flashes on my uniform, plus the corporal stripes of which I was very proud. Anyway, I was heading for a bus on Colinton Road one morning, with my beret folded neatly under my epaulette on one shoulder, when the Redcaps rolled up in a Jeep (seemed the only transport they ever had). They were both lance corporals, so they had to address me as corporal, but I got a dressing-down for not wearing my beret on my head and still wearing the Commonwealth Division flashes. A warning was administered, and I was told, 'You are not in Korea now, corporal,' – which was tinged with jealousy, I think! There was a great deal of pride amongst the soldiers who had served abroad, and envy amongst those who had not.

The leave was soon over, and it was a tearful but temporary goodbye to June at Waverley Station. Aldershot was a bloody awful place, consisting mainly of army barracks and pubs full of soldiers either coming or going. Each morning, while we waited for all the procedures to be completed, we were paraded and given litter duties. So many soldiers had been there before us that a cigarette end, or even a matchstick, was about as hard to find as 'gnat's piss' or local virgins. The entire parade disappeared in seconds like 'sna aff a dyke'. Remarkable, but that's old soldiers for you!

Our army service record books were made up to show all our achievements, and with a short reference for any future employer. The entry in my service record reads:

> He is cheerful, sober, honest and hardworking and is well-liked by his comrades. He has carried out his duties as a vehicle mechanic well. He is keen, takes a pride in his workmanship and is willing to work long hours. He is thoroughly recommended to any prospective employer.

Not so sure about the sober bit.

The great moment arrived when we attended a huge warehouse containing civilian clothes and, with only marginally more care than when issuing our first army kit, we were each provided with a suit, a raincoat (civilian coat, dirty-old-man type), shoes, shirt, socks and a tie – the complete demob suit. Some smart bugger advised us that if you gave the 'tailor' a couple of pounds you would get far better gear. What a load of rubbish that proved to be. We left barracks later that day, all wearing identical brown pinstripe, double-breasted suits, trilby hats and dirty-old-men raincoats – all looking the bloody same. This was really embarrassing stuff to be seen wearing in public and I recall, when I got back

Serial No. D/566.

Army Form B.108

Certificate of Service

Army No. 22798573

Surname GREEN.

Christian or Fore Name(s) IAN. DAVID

Enlisted at EDINBURGH

Enlisted on 31.3.52

Corps for which enlisted R.E.M.E.

Warning

If this Certificate is lost or mislaid no duplicate can be obtained. If, however, loss is due to exceptional circumstances a certificate on Army Form B108A may be obtained on application to the officer-in-charge, Records, concerned.

The person to whom this Certificate is issued should on no account part with it, or forward it by post when applying for a situation but should use a copy certified by a responsible person.

Any alteration of the particulars given in this Certificate may render the holder liable to prosecution under the Seamen's and Soldiers' False Characters Act, 1906.

Soldiers on leaving Her Majesty's Service are hereby reminded that the unauthorised communication by them to another person AT ANY TIME of any information they may have acquired which might be useful to any enemy in War renders them liable to prosecution under the Official Secrets Acts.

(This page must be entirely ...)

Description of Soldier on leaving the Colours.

Year of Birth 1934   Height 5 ft. 10½ ins.

Complexion FAIR   Eyes Blue/Grey   Hair DARK

Marks and Scars (Visible)   NIL

Final Assessments of Conduct and Character
(To be completed personally by the Commanding Officer)

Military Conduct Very Good.

Testimonial (To be completed with a view to civil employment)

He is cheerful, sober, honest and hardworking and is well liked by his comrades. He has carried out his duties as a vehicle mechanic well. He is keen, takes a pride in his workmanship and is willing to work long hours.

He is strongly recommended to any prospective employer.

The above assessments have been read to me. Signature of Soldier

(Signature of C.O.)

Place

23 MAR 1955

Date   Unit

2

Certificate of Transfer to Army Reserve

Date of Transfer 20 APRIL 1955

Rank and/or Appointment on Transfer CORPORAL

Cause of Transfer On expiration of his period of Colour service
Para 389 (1) Q.R.s (1940)

Corps from which Transferred R.E.M.E.

Service with Colours on Date of Transfer 3 years 21 days

Place LEICESTER   (Signature)

Date 29 MAR 55   Officer in charge R.E.M.E. & R.A.V.C.   Records

Certificate of Discharge

Date of Discharge 30th March 1959

Rank and/or Appointment on Discharge Corporal

Cause of Discharge Para 634 (VII) Q.R. 55.
Termination of first period of engagement'

Corps from which Discharged R.E.M.E.

Service on Date of Discharge (a) with Colours 3 years 21 days
(b) in the Reserve 3 years 344 days

TOTAL SERVICE 7 years NIL days

Place Smith Negation Lees   (Signature)

Date 7 May 59   Officer in charge R.E.M.E.& R.A.V.C.   Records

---

Service with the Colours showing Transfers, if any, to other Corps			
3			
Length of Service Days	149	208	29
Length of Service Years	1	1	—
			3	21
To	26.8.53	22.3.55	20.4.55
From	31.3.52	27.8.53	23.3.55
Country	HOME	JAPAN – KOREA	HOME
Corps	R.E.M.E.	R.E.M.E.	R.E.M.E.

Army Certificate of Service.

home, I never wore any of it again. I remember a couple of us going into London to the theatre to pass the time before catching overnight trains home. Everywhere we went in London, someone seemed to say, 'Hi lads, just demobbed?' It was that obvious.

On 20 April 1955, I ceased to be Corporal 22798573 Ian Green, REME and became plain Ian Green again after three years and 21 days exactly. In a way, it was strange because, for three years, I had been more or less controlled and cared for by a system, and now suddenly I was on my own. That was it though – I was no longer in the Colours but had become a paid army reservist.

How do I sum up three years of army service? Probably quite inadequately.

Some unbearable treatment at the hands of a few little Hitlers comes to mind, but I think I was undamaged by the experiences. I believe I ended up a better person, with an even greater and valuable sense of discipline and responsibility – and certainly with the ability to look at things more humorously. It also resulted in a more confident and mature person who had seen a lot of the world and experienced what many people might only read about. But the one strong abiding memory is of the wonderful and unique spirit and camaraderie that we all shared in the army, which I was never to experience again so strongly. The friends I made then will never be forgotten. My only regret is that I failed, as I think most of us did, to keep in touch with such good friends. But hey, life is always moving on and takes new turns. Often, there seemed no time to look back – until, sadly, late in life, I feel a need to revisit my past as I am doing in this book. I now seriously regret not finding the time to keep in touch.

Back home, the task of starting a new career became paramount. I did not fancy returning to gardening because wages were then only above the poverty line, and thoughts of marriage and bringing up a family on a minimal wage did not seem attractive, even though the work was. One morning, I left home to attend the Army Resettlement Centre for help and advice. I was informed that my army mechanical qualifications were not accepted in the vehicle repair industry as 'time-served', so a period as a motor mechanic 'journeyman', with a greatly reduced wage, made that option also a nonstarter.

The interviewer suggested the police – apparently desperately seeking recruits at the time. The lecture on the Captain Hobson flashed before me and I said, 'Why not.' With a recommendation from the interviewer, I went straight to the Edinburgh City Police Recruiting Department in

Chambers Street. My height, weight, sight and general health were all regarded as above standard, and my interview appeared to go well. I was advised to return at a later date to sit the necessary entry exams. I went home and Mam asked me, 'Did you get a job, son?' I replied, 'I think I might be joining the police.' She almost fell off her chair.

I duly attended, sat the police entry examinations and failed. I was pretty devastated because I had, by then, set my heart on following this profession. Apparently, my weakness in mathematics had once again let me down. I had scraped through on a couple of subjects and sailed through on others. The exams were very extensive and searching. It seemed that I was a borderline case and because my army service and references all stood me in good stead I was asked to return in three months to resit the exams. In the interim period, I did a bit of home study. At my second attempt, I am grateful to say I passed.

In the intervening period I simply found a job, any job, and worked in the rubber mill in Fountainbridge. Quite frankly, I would have gone mad working in a factory and I again found the workmanship absolutely appalling. I was employed in the tyre-building department where tyres for buses were built by hand on machines. The process, which needs no explanation here, culminated with the tyre going into a hot mould and set into the required shape. The experienced men were all on bonus – the more tyres built by each man on a shift, then the bigger the bonus for him. To achieve targets the workers took various short cuts, leaving out essential materials in the process of building each tyre. They were pretty closely supervised, but the inspector could not be everywhere at once, so the experienced tyre-builders got away with murder, which probably resulted in tyres that were not as safe as they might have been. I would never have achieved either the speed of these men, nor would my conscience have allowed me to take short cuts. I was happy to get out of the place.

I also considered starting my own business at this time. Having wide experience of truck maintenance, I felt there was an opportunity to start a small haulier business, initially with one truck. Ex-army trucks were being sold off fairly cheaply at the time, so it seemed worth a try. Mam was dead against it and, while I had some money set by from the Korean 'bounty' paid to all army servicemen for every month served in Korea, her advice prevailed and I dropped the idea. Instead, the bounty went towards my eventual marriage.

At this time I also took the precaution of visiting my doctor who was not a very humorous man. Somewhat embarrassed, I blurted out that I had recently returned from Korea and, while there, I had 'been with women'. I felt a check-up was necessary in case I had picked up anything. I could not bring myself to say what I should have said – 'I had sexual intercourse with prostitutes and I may have contracted VD.' He showed some surprise and annoyance, but provided me with a letter for the VD Ward at Edinburgh Royal Infirmary. Arrival there proved to be seriously embarrassing, but then no more than I deserved, I suppose. The waiting room was full of what were clearly prostitutes and grotty-looking guys. I wanted the ground to open up and swallow me. Eventually, I was seen by a specialist who examined me and took blood samples without being accusing in any way. In fact, he said I had been very wise, and he only wished that others like me would do the same. I asked him if I could wait for the results, but he laughed and advised me it would take a couple of weeks when the results would be sent to my home. Panic! 'Will the letter be in a plain envelope?' says I. 'If you wish,' says he. Slightly relieved, I left with his last words, 'You are likely to be okay because most venereal diseases would have shown up by now.' A couple of weeks later, a letter arrived giving me the all clear.

Just prior to my police training I was on a date with June one night, had stayed in the stair at Balgreen Park just too long and had to run to Corstorphine Road to catch the last bus to Haymarket. I saw my bus coming and went into overdrive. I dashed onto Corstorphine Road, across the front of a stationary westbound bus, right into the path of an oncoming car. The car was travelling fast, but somehow I managed to stop in mid-stride. Instead of being struck head-on, I received a solid but glancing blow to my right side, and was thrown several yards along the road where I landed in a heap. I came to my full senses with people crowding around me asking if I was okay. Apparently, the car had accelerated away from the scene without stopping, and suggestions were made that the police should be called. I thought to myself, 'This might stop my entry into the police. Maybe I've also committed some offence.' So, as there were no apparent serious wounds or breakages, I refused all further assistance and boarded my bus which had remained at the scene after the accident. I limped home and woke up next morning feeling as if I had been through a mangle. I went for a haircut and fainted in the hairdresser's chair, but again refused medical assistance and went home. A few days later, I was as right as rain but, from that date to this, I never cross a road in front of a stationary vehicle.

On 16 August 1955 I attended the Edinburgh Police Clothing

Department, also in Chambers Street, and, along with several others, was sworn in. I was issued with full police kit – two uniforms, two police caps, several shirts, a heavy overcoat, a raincoat, waterproof leggings, white and black gloves, black ties (later to prove quite useful for funerals as well), a notebook, a police baton and, the most useless bloody pieces of equipment issued, a whistle and chain (more on that later). Boots, socks and underwear were each officer's own responsibility, although socks had to be dark in colour and boots black, of course. We were also issued with two very important law books – *The Road Traffic Law Book* and *The Aberdeen Manual on Common and Statutory Law*. If anyone else on the training course I was about to go on was to learn everything contained within those two manuals, then they were a better man than I. However, most of it became 'required reading' (or study) and even bed-time reading. It was then onto a bus, and the Edinburgh City Police contingent for the August 1955 Scottish Police Initial Training Course to be held at Whitburn Police College was on its way. A new and exciting chapter in my life beckoned yet again.

PART II

life in the 'copshop' – on the beat

n 1955, the Police College at Whitburn was an ex-army camp and only a temporary home for the Initial Training Course of the Scottish Police. An estate house at Polkemmet (Polkemmet House) accommodated the Second Year Training College. Moves were already afoot to acquire Tulliallan Castle and its extensive grounds, near Kincardine, where not only the Initial and Second Year courses would eventually be accommodated, and training courses for CID officers, Traffic Department, sergeants, inspectors and superintendents, including many officers from abroad, could all be catered for under one roof. Later in my service I attended courses at Tulliallan Castle, as a sergeant, a training sergeant and later as an inspector. I could never say I enjoyed the stays there, although it was certainly a great place of learning, which provided a wonderful opportunity to 'compare notes' with officers from other forces.

On arrival at Whitburn College, half the people on the course, including myself, were allocated beds in army-style billets, while the other half was farmed out for bed and breakfast in the homes of the local population. After the issue of training materials, we were welcomed by the director of the college and instructors who talked to us on the history of the Scottish Police Force, the place of the 'bobby' in society and discipline within the police force. The need for extensive study was impressed upon us. The next day we were straight into the routine of classroom lectures, practical exercises, physical training and parade-ground drilling. The latter two were a piece of cake to 'old soldiers' and, to be honest, this side of our training was simply taking up where I had left off in the army. The theory consisted of the study of Common Law (the law of the land handed down from generation to generation from time immemorial), Statute Law (as drawn up by parliament) and Police Procedures.

The classroom work was very intensive and failure to pay full attention to the instructors soon resulted in individuals falling behind. There was a great need to further study the subjects delivered each day, so most evenings found me with my nose stuck in one or other of the manuals and instruction books. If I am honest, I have to admit I struggled with the theory throughout the three-month course and I had to work harder than some just to keep my head above water. We were allowed to go home at weekends and even then I would take work home and spend some hours on additional study. I was determined that a failed education was not going to be a serious obstacle to making the grade as a 'bobby'.

Exams were a regular feature of the course, allowing instructors to assess our progress. I regularly found myself having only 'scraped through', although not through lack of effort. As the final examinations approached, I committed myself totally to extra study, rarely visiting the Whitburn pubs during the week. I simply had to work hard and my determination to succeed again came to my rescue. The effort paid off and, while I was never likely to be top of the course, I did manage fairly respectable marks, placing me just slightly above the middle of the class.

Discipline was military in style, although I don't recall any tyrants amongst the instructors, such as my corporal friend at Blandford. They were from the many different police forces in Scotland, all volunteers, seconded to the college for a couple of years. Smartness and bearing were considered very important, and regular inspections were held on the small parade ground within the college, where we were drilled almost daily.

Some instructors were absolutely 'made' for the job and able to get the message across clearly, even with some humour. Some were a bit 'dry', and it could be hard to stay focused. There was a sergeant from Glasgow City Police who covered the subject of being a 'beat bobby', which included the powers of observation, how to deal with the public and so on. The first time I ever heard the expression 'ned' (a ne'er do well) was from this sergeant – sorting out neds appeared to be his crusade in life. Quite right too. I became a bit disillusioned in my latter years of service when neds had to be handled with kid gloves. The tough 'cops' of the '50s and earlier, many from the West Highlands and Islands, had a wonderful no-nonsense attitude, so sadly missed today. The do-gooders of this world destroyed that and so much more.

During the course, a very tough cross-country run – to be completed in a specific time – had to be undertaken by all recruits. I achieved this and came home in the first half of the pack. Swimming and life-saving were also compulsory and we were bussed weekly to a nearby swimming pool. I could not swim a stroke and, worse still, had an intense fear of water. The swimming instructor was a gem of a sergeant who told me just to get into the water at the shallow end and, at my own pace, gradually move into deeper water. 'When you are able to duck your head below the water and hold your breath for a few seconds, I'll teach you to swim.' He added, 'Take your time and tell me when you are ready.' I followed this advice, gradually overcoming my fear of water over a week or two. I then started swimming instruction. The sergeant proved just right for me, patiently but firmly pushing me first to swim (the breast and back-strokes), then to dive, submerge in the deep end in full uniform, recover items from the bottom of the pool, and even 'save' a colleague – things I had never expected to accomplish. One day he said, 'Okay, you're ready for your swimming and life-saving tests.' He would brook no argument, and I qualified for the life-saving certificate at my first attempt. I would never be a great swimmer, and to this day cannot do the crawl, but swimming was a new experience and a great social asset, especially on beach holidays when I simply loved snorkelling.

Halfway through the course the guys in the bed and breakfast accommodation moved into the billets, and the billet guys moved out to the bed and breakfast. I found myself in the home of the most wonderful couple you could imagine, who reminded me so much of Mam and Dad. They were friendly, hard-working people from the local mining community. He had been a coal miner since a boy. When I studied in my bedroom in the evenings, there would be a constant supply of cups of tea and home-made scones or whatever, and every morning I was wakened with a cup of tea and toast. They seemed to know when I had studied

The First Year intake at the Police College, Whitburn, 1955.
Ian is third from the right, second row.

long enough and would invite me into their living room for a blether. When it came time for the passing-out parade and end-of-course dance, they generously invited June to stay in their other spare room. I am ashamed to say I cannot now recall the names of these lovely folk.

At the end of the course, there were the now inevitable farewells to be made, but most of us knew we would meet again on the Second Year Course at Polkemmet, assuming we made it through the first year on the beat! The Edinburgh City Police contingent, including new friend Ronnie MacKintosh and others, was instructed to report to the Recruiting and Training Department in Chambers Street, where we underwent training on Force Procedures and received instruction on local byelaws. More study in the evenings, of course.

On my first journey from Convent Cottages to Chambers Street, in uniform, I boarded a double-decker bus in Colinton Road at rush-hour. I felt two distinct emotions on my first day out in uniform. I felt very proud, but also extremely anxious that I might immediately be confronted with a difficult situation which I could not handle. There were no personal radios or mobile phones to call for instant assistance or advice in those days. Well, I suppose it was bound to happen to me. When the bus stopped at the next stop, the conductor was upstairs and a horde simply piled onto the bus, packing even the platform. The conductor descended, saying that some passengers must get off. Not a movement. The conductor spotted me 'hiding' inside the lower deck and said, 'Okay constable, get them off – this bus is going nowhere.' He then folded his arms across his chest and glowered at me. With a rising feeling of panic, I mustered my most compelling voice and uttered my first official words, 'The bus is overcrowded – some of you have to get off.' Low and behold, about ten passengers immediately got off, and the conductor rang the driver to proceed. I could not believe it, but it did give me an early indication that most people are very law-abiding and will react promptly to a request or instruction from a figure of authority, especially a policeman.

The following day, the entire course was required for emergency street duties at a huge fire which had broken out in Jeffrey Street, making it necessary for streets to be closed off and diversions put in place. A feeling of really being of some use and doing the job penetrated my anxious brain and very quickly it seemed normal to be controlling access to traffic and pedestrians. Not a taxing duty, but an opportunity to become accustomed to being in the public eye.

We finished at Chambers Street two weeks later and the course members reported to their respective divisions on the following Monday. At that time, there were four divisions in Edinburgh City Police: 'A' Division operated out of Braid Place Police Station and covered roughly the south side of Edinburgh; 'B' covered the central area and part of the north and west suburbs out of Gayfield Square Police Station; 'C' Headquarters were at the West End Police Station and responsible for mainly the west, northwest and southwest; while 'D' covered 'Sunny Leith', Portobello and the northeast. Policemen always called it 'sunny' Leith.

I was assigned to 'C' Division, and reported to the chief superintendent at the West End Police Station in Torphichen Place along with Ronnie MacKintosh. Ronnie was an ex-regular infantry soldier with an incredible appetite for drink – and he was never too fussy whether it was beer or spirits. He was a most likeable bugger though, with a great sense of humour and hundreds of stories. He became even more hilarious when he got drunk at functions. Ronnie could drink until he rendered himself incapable of any kind of speech or movement, but continued to smile and laugh while remaining rigid against the nearest wall. Ronnie's likeable nature made him popular with everyone – from the rich to the poor. For many years he worked the Ravelston Dykes area, both as a beat policeman and later as a community policeman (the 'friendly bobby' as they were nicknamed) when the Panda car system was introduced. He was an absolute hit with the toffs of Ravelston Dykes, who spoiled him rotten. I was responsible for introducing Ronnie to his wife-to-be, Harriet.

I was PC 137-C and Ronnie was PC 147-C. My number had become vacant when the previous PC 137-C, Pax MacDonald, who came from the county of Moray and Nairn like me, was promoted to sergeant. Pax was from Nair, while I was from Forres, just along the road. A fairly spooky coincidence and there were more of those to follow me through my life.

Pax was a sergeant in 'C' Division and I came to know him very well because of our Moray and Nairn connection. He had at one time desired to be a priest but something had prevented this and instead he'd joined the police. I knew of at least two other policemen who had followed this strange path. Pax was one of the most generous and understanding policemen I ever met, with infinite patience to match. It was not uncommon for him, as station sergeant, to put his hand in his pocket and send a constable out to buy fish-and-chip suppers for all the inmates of the police cells on a Friday or Saturday.

Pax later became my mobile patrol sergeant – when I was the regular patrol van driver – and we became even closer. I will forever feel ashamed that I went on duty one New Year's Day (early shift – 6am to 2pm) after celebrating most of the night. At the end of the shift, Pax invited me into the police box at Pinkhill in Corstorphine where the shifts changed over and asked to speak to me alone. I thought, 'Now I'm for it.' But not at all. When I tried to apologise, he generously said, 'You were fine – just a bit tired.' He then pulled out an unopened half-bottle of whisky, poured me a dram and expressed his thanks for being loyal and always helpful to him, adding to my feeling of shame for having let down this fine man. He never showed ill will to any man, and always saw some good even in the most evil people.

We came on night shift on one occasion to learn that there had been a murder in Melville Street and that the suspect was the deceased woman's son who, by coincidence, was known to Pax. Within the hour, we came across the suspect wheeling his bicycle along a street off Queensferry Road. Pulling up alongside him, Pax handled him in his inimitable style. Within seconds, the suspect was in the van and on his way to the CID at Police Headquarters in the High Street. He was eventually charged with beating his mother to death, and duly convicted. My first encounter with a murderer – a poor, pathetic soul.

On one occasion when Pax was station sergeant I brought in an accused man who had, amongst other things, assaulted me by kicking me several times 'with his booted foot' (police jargon). Pax seemed unwilling to believe that the, by then subdued and very polite, man feigning innocence had kicked me and twice asked me to confirm this. I was becoming slightly peeved, so I rolled up my trouser leg – Pax was as shocked as I was to find a lump on my shin the size of a hen's egg. He apologised profusely, immediately slapping a charge of police assault on the accused, and I was packed off to the Royal Infirmary for treatment.

Pax sadly died at a very young age, leaving his wife with a large family to bring up. He left many colleagues, including myself, shocked and greatly saddened by his untimely death.

To get back to my first day at the West End Police Station, this was spent being shown the workings of the station, plus introductions to the various station personnel. Ronnie and I were allocated to the same 'shift' (team) and given our duties for the following day when I was to report for early shift to the police box at Magdala Crescent. I duly turned up at 5.45am, as was the requirement in those days (15 minutes to exchange beat information before the changeover). The night-shift officer departed quickly, needing his bed, and I was left alone in the police box awaiting the arrival of the senior beat constable for that day. I sat, uncertain what to do, as the minutes ticked on towards 6.15am, frightened to touch anything in case I 'broke' it. The phone suddenly rang, scaring the living daylights out of me. I gingerly picked it up to be informed that the senior beatman had slept in but was on his way, and I should 'Do nothing, touch nothing – just hide in the box with the light off" until he arrived. Great to feel you have the confidence of your fellow colleagues.

The standard police box was constructed of cast iron and in Edinburgh they were painted blue. Each box was equipped with a desk, a stool, a low corner-seat, a rack for files, coat pegs, a small, inefficient single-bar electric heater and a wash-hand basin which on occasions doubled up as a urinal. This was against orders, of course, but nevertheless everyone knew it happened, and coincidentally a bottle of disinfectant was supplied regularly to each box. There was an internal phone connected directly to the parent station and an outside phone for use by the public in emergencies; by simply opening a small, hinged panel-door, the caller was linked to the station. Many boxes also had air-raid sirens on the roof – a hangover from World War Two, but checked regularly in case of use during a nuclear attack. I always thought the plan if there was a nuclear attack was to stick your head up your arse and pray. If police boxes could speak, however, they would have some fascinating tales to tell – and there are many hilarious stories involving police boxes.

One box was situated on the south side of Princes Street, directly opposite South Charlotte Street. In the latter days of points (traffic control) duty, at a time when the number of woman constables was increasing, a pointsman, seriously in need of a 'pee', dashed off the junction and into the box. He slammed the door behind him, whipped 'it' out and was doing what comes naturally in the sink when, to his horror, he turned to see a young and somewhat amazed woman constable sitting on the corner-seat. The constable stopped in mid-stream.

The same box was the scene of another great tale. When the number of policewoman had increased quite dramatically, it was decided that they would be fully incorporated into shift patterns. This of course meant they would have to work night shift for the first time. I suppose the equality rule had some good points. Some weeks later, the duty sergeant was making his rounds visiting the beat constables. On arrival at the police box, there was no light on inside. He opened the door to be confronted with an unforgettable scene. Two almost naked officers (one a male and the other a female, I hasten to add) were 'having it off' over the desk. I'd like to think the constable's explanation was, 'I am showing her my beat, sergeant!'

In my early days, the police box at Tollcross was situated on an island in the centre of the Tollcross junction, and became a haven for a number of beatmen, patrols and pointsmen. On occasions several constables would gather in the box, exchanging important police intelligence of course, but also having a smoke. One day, a pedestrian standing on the island was astonished when the door of the box burst open and out poured somewhere in the region of six to eight constables, accompanied by a billowing cloud of smoke. As the final officer emerged from the box, the astonished pedestrian asked, 'Is there a downstairs in this police box?'

One final police-box story is of a young constable, apparently attempting to emulate the older tough cops, who took an unruly ned to his box in Polwarth to administer some corporal punishment. But as soon as the door closed, the ned whacked the policeman and ran off, leaving him almost unconscious on the floor. The constable was honest enough to admit what had befallen him. He complained sourly that it was bad enough being assaulted, but having his 'piece' (sandwiches) stolen was too much to bear!

Days turned into weeks, weeks into months and, with the passing of time, my confidence grew. Then, one week, I found I was detailed for traffic control duty (points duty). I was allocated the No. 2 Point at the West End – No. 1 Point was controlled by an older officer, nearing retirement, who had volunteered for permanent points duty. On arrival at No. 2 Point, which controlled the pedestrian crossing at Binns on Princes Street and had to be worked in complete unison with No. 1 Point, the older officer indicated a desire to speak to me – 'Get your fucking arse over here, now.' I was then told, in no uncertain terms, that if I 'fucked up' or failed to follow his lead, he would stick his boot up my 'arse'. With those few encouraging words, I stepped into the middle of the road with my knees knocking. It didn't take long to get into the swing of it though, and after a while it became quite robot-like. On the couple of occasions that I did 'fuck up', the No. 1 pointsman would think nothing of bawling me out – to the great enjoyment of the pedestrians on my crossing, and to my total embarrassment. This same pointsman was the regular recipient of 'gifts' (some might say bribes?) from passing drivers, and on occasions would have to waddle off to the nearby police box to unload 'goodies' from his bulging pockets.

I continued on points duty for a month or two, and at times I would take over No. 1 Point. It was imperative to have your wits about you as you dodged tramcars whistling around you, as well as motor traffic coming from all directions. Some of the more impatient drivers clearly wondered why this young idiot was slowing down progress. It was a great way to get to know a lot of people in a very short time though. Every tram driver, conductor, delivery driver and pedestrian had a (mostly) cheery word or some humorous banter as they passed by – and of course some of the 'spoils' came to the rookie. Some of the tram and bus crews were real characters. I often speculate where that breed of transport worker has gone.

In bad weather, points duty was the worst bloody job in the world, with water running down inside your collar, up your arms, out your arse and through your cheap boots – until you were like a 'drookit rat'. Many a time I was close to tears. Not many years later, pointsmen were removed from the principal junctions in Edinburgh to be replaced by automatic traffic signals. It was in the name of progress, of course, but the drivers could not banter with a traffic light, so it was the beginning of the end of day-to-day contact between the police and the public. More, and worse, was to follow though. Some of the points volunteers found it hard to fit back into shift patterns on the beat after years on a nice eight-to-four or nine-to-five.

After my spell on points duty, the task of learning to find my way around every beat in the division resumed. This entailed being shown 'the beat' by all the regular beat officers in the division, both day and night beats, so that the time came when I could take over, temporarily at least, any vacant beat resulting through illness, holidays or whatever.

The beat system that operated in those days was as follows: 'c' Division was divided into four sections, which were then subdivided into beats (six beats to a section). Each beat was then divided into a number of patrol areas, or 'turns' as they were referred to. Each hourly turn had a precise path to be followed, which entailed walking every street on that turn. This meant every street was visited once, or probably twice, during an eight-hour shift, unless the officer had been temporarily assigned to some other public duties requiring a heavy concentration of police, e.g. football matches, royal visits etc. The hourly turn brought the beat officer back to his beat box or to another police box/telephone point, from where he had to call the divisional telephone operator and report his position and wellbeing. An accurate log was maintained by the telephone operator at Divisional Headquarters. 'Ringing-in' was performed throughout the eight-hour shift. It acted as a safeguard against an injured officer lying for a long period on his beat, and enabled supervisory officers to pinpoint the beat officer's position during his tour of duty. Before departing on his turn, the officer was required to make an entry in the Box Journal as to which turn he was on, or where he was making a call to, so a fairly accurate picture of his whereabouts was always available. This was before personal radios or mobile phones had been introduced. The system depended on the beat officer following his turn accurately (and therein lay a weakness in the system, leading to all kinds of confusion, and officers being reported for not being on their turn). Three shifts operated at that time – early shift, late shift and night shift. Each shift of men went on night shift after two months of working a week on early and a week on late shift alternately. Night shift lasted one month (resulting in a lack of social life, apart from one useless day off each week). Uncivilised? You better believe it.

Later, the shift system changed to a four-shift system: each team worked a week of night shift, a week relieving the days off of the other teams, a week on early shift, and a week on late shift. Days off were included on each shift except night shift, when each team worked a full week and then had two days off. This was much more civilised and greatly enjoyed by all.

On night shift, after seeing the drunks home and clearing up any cases of breach of the peace and disorderly conduct, such as 'peeing' up closes and in shop doorways, the principal duty was checking property, i.e. the security of business and other premises, such as churches and clubs. If you were following the approved beat turns as per orders, this resulted in each of these premises being visited by a constable twice in the eight-hour shift, probably more if the premises were particularly vulnerable. Most of the time it was tedious because all was secure, but it was necessary to remain alert. You never really knew when you would walk out into a back green and find a housebreaker at work on a rear shop window, or perhaps already in the premises. You were then confronted with the problem of getting assistance for the arrest of the criminal(s). The police whistle was the only, somewhat useless, means of communication you had, so often you relied on assistance from a member of the public – and in those days it was invariably forthcoming, there being good relations between most of the public and the police.

I made several arrests when working night shift, which earned me Chief Constable's Commendations. These were entered on your record sheet, but it also gave most officers a wee boost to be recognised in this way. Commendations were published on daily information sheets delivered to all stations and police boxes. One such commendation came as a result of arresting a well know criminal, Eddie Laing, which was to have a strange turn in later years.

It could be very lonely in the middle of the night examining property in remote places and often, on some beats at least, seeing no one but the sergeant for hours on end. It could also be quite eerie in some locations – which meant keeping tight control of your imagination. I knew some officers who found night shift to be really stressful. It was the fear of the unknown, I suppose. A couple of policemen I knew whistled loudly or made a lot of din as they entered potentially dangerous areas, presumably to warn any possible housebreaker of their approach. Personally, I adopted the stealth approach in the hope that I would nick one in the act.

I recall a situation where an officer came across a broken second-storey rear window of an off-licence shop and a whole stash of bottles on the ground below it. There had presumably been two housebreakers, one inside lowering down bottles (the 'loot') on lengths of string while the other collected it below the window. The latter brave lad had made off on the approach of the constable and left his mate to face the music. He became aware of the presence of the officer and, subsequently, the reinforcements (the 'cavalry') when they arrived, but he refused to budge. A cordon was placed around the shop (laughingly referred to by policemen as 'throwing an accordion around the premises') and we all sat tight to await the arrival of the off-licence key-holder. The criminal knew the game was up and gave us a running commentary of how much he was drinking. By the time the key-holder arrived, the housebreaker was totally 'pissed' and had to be carried out.

Each shift (the fire brigade refer to them as watches) had an inspector in overall operational control, with one sergeant in charge of each section. The sergeants, as a rule, would visit each beatman on his section twice during an eight-hour shift, and the inspector invariably visited each beatman, plus each section sergeant, once during that period. In the absence of the shift inspector, an acting inspector (a sergeant in the running for future promotion) would take over – the same system applied with acting sergeants replacing regular sergeants. This part of the system worked really well and, until changes were implemented later, resulted in well-experienced constables and sergeants being promoted to the next rank for which they were well-prepared.

In later years, an Accelerated Promotion System was adopted, and a recruit with a university degree was promised (and given) the opportunity to apply for accelerated promotion at a very early stage in their service. And if successful on the Accelerated Promotion Course at Tulliallan, they could be sergeants at, in my opinion, too early an age, and certainly before they had enough police experience. This also meant that the normal promotion list was severely slowed down, resulting in resentment amongst older officers on the brink of promotion through the normal system. I believe that some very good promotions came through the Accelerated Promotion System, but I have to say there were as many total failures, which we were then stuck with – boys leading men. All in the name of progress.

Each division had a chief superintendent at the 'top', his deputy was a superintendent and, below him, were a chief inspector plus various administrative positions for inspectors and sergeants. On any shift, each divisional station had a station sergeant, station clerk, including civilian employees, and a divisional driver (they always seemed to be lazy buggers who did not want to get out of their van for any purpose). The station sergeant was responsible for the dissemination of incoming public calls and divisional radio traffic, with the added responsibility for accepting arrests and processing these for court and their onward transport to Police Headquarters. The station sergeant's job was most taxing – he had very quickly to learn how to type and complete the myriad forms that were swamping all police forces. If he had a really busy night (Fridays and Saturdays usually), he would have to work on to complete the court reports after his shift colleagues had gone home. Funny, you never see any bugger preparing such reports on 'The Bill'.

There were specialist departments in all divisional headquarters, including traffic enquiry departments. These departments dealt with the investigation of all road accidents from which prosecutions for careless, reckless and dangerous driving were likely, plus all road accident deaths, and all other sudden deaths (where the doctor would not grant a death certificate even though the death was not deemed suspicious). There were also divisional plain clothes departments with responsibility for all licensed premises (pubs, hotels etc.), the issue and renewal of firearm certificates, and many other licensing matters. These departments were also responsible for all vice (prostitution etc.) within their divisions. By the way, I was once explaining this to a group of people where one bright spark actually thought I meant 'we were responsible for the vice' in the first place. Not quite, although I knew some officers who I would not have trusted with my granny.

As a probationary constable on day shift, there was a process of being shown the hourly turns and getting to know the A to Z of the beat. It was necessary to know all the personalities to be found in that area, including local criminals, gang leaders, prostitutes, extroverts and alcoholics – 'hooks, crooks and comic singers'. The local gossips (very useful in gaining information on local 'goings-on') had also to be cultivated. In those days, the information accumulated by many regular beatmen, stored in their heads, was astonishing and a never-ending source of intelligence to the CID and other departments. A regular beatman was worth his weight in gold – the 'front line' of the service, and at the very heart of police/public relations. Many residents befriended their beatman and, if he was worth his salt, he could resolve many family and other disputes, plus other day-to-day problems, with a 'quiet word' or a 'cuff around the ear' (now seriously outlawed). Sadly, this tried-and-tested, although I must be honest and say occasionally abused system of policing was destroyed by new and supposedly more efficient systems which replaced the beat system. In the opinion of many of us, not for the better – from that day on, contact with the public was seriously eroded and eventually became almost nonexistent. Very sad.

There are many stories about how some of these experienced officers dealt with beat problems. There was one officer – 'Basher' – who worked the Grassmarket area (then considered to be the 'wild west'). He had an awesome reputation, but apparently never used his notebook. His method of sorting out the roughnecks was to take them up a side street, remove his tunic jacket and proceed to have 'a square go' with the culprit – which invariably ended with the latter coming off worse. Basher was loved by the local population and, when he reached retirement, the community on his beat took a collection for him. The chief constable got wind of it apparently and 'nipped it in the bud'. I believe the money went to charity. These legendary beatmen were all big, brawny officers, many from the West Highlands, whose very size proved a point.

I knew one particular officer in the West End Division, an ex-soldier with a considerable army boxing record, who came out of that same mould. One night, Jimmy went to a house-row (a domestic dispute) and when he and his colleague walked into the house, the wife was bruised and bloody, having apparently been beaten up yet again by her drunken husband. No witnesses of course. Jimmy was trying to get the wife's version of events, but all the time the drunk was interrupting and nipping Jimmy's ear. Without looking at the husband, Jimmy reached out with his right hand (he had massive hands by the way) and grabbed him around the throat, lifted him off his feet and pinned him against the living-room wall. Jimmy continued listening to the wife's version, while chummy struggled to get free. Jimmy held on until the man started to go blue and only then did he finally let this somewhat deflated clown slide to the floor. When he had partially recovered, the brave boy was 'invited' into a bedroom, while the other officer remained with the injured wife in the living room. The sound of a few thumps ensued, followed by moans and groans. A moment later, Jimmy re-emerged rubbing his knuckles, commenting to the wife, 'He won't touch you again but, if he does, you come and see me at the police box.' Problem solved to everyone's satisfaction, with the possible exception of the husband – although he would otherwise have spent all weekend in the cells and been fined by the court, which would inevitably have come out of the wife's purse. Summary justice I think we call it – or maybe it was just common sense in an era when abused wives simply would not act as witnesses against husbands and, despite regular assaults, continued to run the home with not a thought of leaving. Where would most of them have gone in those days anyway?

I remember another family in Whitson Road, where June and I were eventually to get a rented house from the council. Almost every Friday or Saturday (sometimes both) the husband and teenage sons would arrive home 'out of their skulls' and, as the 'cairry-oot' was consumed, inevitably a fight would develop between the father and the sons, or between the brothers, or any other combination. The result was always the same – blood would flow freely, splattering the walls and furniture. The living room would be a shambles, with upturned furniture, broken glass and smashed ornaments. The poor, frightened wife and mother would call for the police, but would never press charges against her husband or the sons. She just lived with this weekly nightmare. The husband and sons were warned over and over again but, when the drink got a hold of them, reason went out the window. The wife was a tiny, gentle wee woman who struggled valiantly to keep a clean and tidy home and despite the carnage each weekend, a call back midweek would reveal no traces of the spilled blood. The living room would be back in the best possible order under the circumstances. I felt for that poor wee soul.

Unfortunately, these sort of domestic disputes were all too common.

Only occasionally was a wife prepared to take a stand against the abuse and act as a witness to the assault. Even then, by the time the accused and witnesses arrived at the station, the wife was likely to have reconsidered her position, and would as often as not withdraw her allegation of assault. Not surprising really since, on the occasions that a husband reached the court on Monday, he would usually be released after being fined, and would head back home seeking revenge. Frustrating stuff to deal with as a police officer, but these poor women had an awful life.

During the spring of 1955, I asked June to marry me (very romantically, under a holly bush in Corstorphine Road, as I waited for a bus). June said yes, so the next step was to ask her dad. (Yes, we did that in those days.) He agreed, although he was somewhat taken aback when I told him we were planning to get wed early in 1956. We were engaged in April. It was necessary then to receive the permission of the chief constable. A detailed enquiry into June's background was made to ensure that she was a suitable person to be a police officer's wife. Can you imagine the chief constable getting away with that nowadays? From stories I am told these days, it appears that officers with convictions are now being admitted into the police, never mind their spouses. Anyway, the chief constable gave his blessing to the union.

We were married in Craiglockhart Church of Scotland on Saturday 28 January 1956 followed by a reception at The Gothenburg pub in Slateford with many relatives and friends. It was a day to be remembered – a very happy occasion. June chose the date which was as close to her 21st birthday as possible. I was 22 on 29 January, and June was 21 the following day. The bridesmaids were Betty McLennan (June's sister) and Gertrude Tevendale (my cousin), and my brother Jimmy was my best man. Dad made a beautiful bouquet for June, as well as all the buttonholes. He also gave Jimmy and me two very large drams before we left to go to the church, so we breathed whisky all over the poor minister.

We spent our first night in East Claremont Street, in a small flat we had rented from two elderly sisters – who gave us a hot water bottle as a wedding present. A kind gesture, but we didn't need a hot water bottle that first night.

We had a week's honeymoon at June's Aunty Kate and Uncle Jack at Thorpe Lea Road, Egham in Surrey. June's sister Betty and husband John would settle there after their marriage a couple of years later. On the coach journey back to Edinburgh we did not have enough money to buy breakfast at the early-morning stop. We had to walk from St Andrew's Square

Family group at June and Ian's wedding, 1956

to the West End Police Station to collect my wages as we did not have another penny in the world.

In retrospect, my conclusion is that we married too young, before either of us had contemplated such things as house purchase or the arrival of babies. Still, we loved each other and they say if you are in love you don't need anything else. Some of the hard times we suffered in our early years of marriage might have been avoided, however, if we had 'bided our time'. Young and foolish, eh? One of my party pieces for years was to sing, 'They tried to tell us we're too young,' but honestly we were.

It was not totally satisfactory living in East Claremont Street while working in the West End Division, and transport became a problem at times. One night shift, for example, while working a beat at Morningside, the only bus going back into town early on Sunday morning was at 5.45am I asked my section sergeant if I could leave my beat a little early to catch this bus and was told bluntly, 'No.' I was forced to embark on a walk from Morningside to East Claremont Street – a fair stride. The driver of an electric milk float came upon me about Tollcross, took sympathy and offered me a lift. The damned thing only travelled about ten miles an hour, only marginally faster than walking, but I was very thankful to rest my weary legs after a night of walking the beat.

A few months after our marriage, we learned of a basement flat which was available at Western Terrace at Murrayfield. The house was occupied by Mrs Duncan, widow of the owner of the family firm of Duncan's Chocolates. The rent of the basement was free in return for maintenance of the small front and moderate-sized rear gardens. We also had to liaise with Mrs Duncan's housekeeper and June or myself had to be on call should Mrs Duncan be left alone on any occasion. This was an excellent arrangement and I feel we got the occupancy of the flat because of my gardening skills, as well as being a police officer. I had only recently rented two allotments at Balgreen Road, which were nearby, and I now lived in the centre of the West End Division, so everything was clicking into place.

On occasions when Mrs Duncan went on holiday, we would be invited to make use of her television and her wonderfully furnished sitting room. This was real luxury since we could not afford a TV. June was provided with a continuous supply of the superb Duncan's chocolates, and occasionally, when I was working in the front garden, Mrs Duncan would give me a 'fiver' for my efforts, despite my protestations. We had three happy years there, and Mrs Duncan turned out to be a lovely and generous landlady.

We had only just got settled in at Western Terrace when June came home one day with confirmation that she was pregnant. She had been absolutely desperate to have a baby as soon as we got married, but I was a bit apprehensive because of our difficult financial situation. Nevertheless, we prepared for our first baby, and from the outset I was convinced it would be a girl. On 18 February 1957 our daughter Linda was born and I was over the moon that my wish had been granted. I was on night shift when Linda was born – no excused duty for such an event then. I wandered round my night beat in a state of nerves, but eventually, in the early hours of the morning, news came through that both were doing well. What a relief. Clutching a bunch of flowers, I went to Simpson's Memorial

Four generations of the Green Family.

Maternity Hospital later in the day to confirm that we had a beautiful daughter and a very happy June.

As the task of learning all the divisional beats was completed, the time arrived to attend the Second Year Police Training Course at Polkemmet House. This was a beautiful old estate house, and we were living in comparative luxury, with about four beds per room. Most of the lads I had met on the First Year Course were there, and we all exchanged notes on progress in our individual forces. It transpired that one or two had fallen by the wayside and were no longer in the police. Ronnie MacKintosh and I had become good friends by this time and his insatiable appetite for a drink saw us out on the nearby town more than I would have wished. However, I was determined to do better on the Second Year Course, so I devoted a lot of spare time to study, and by that time I was finding I was assimilating the information more quickly – and importantly, retaining it in my brain. I enjoyed the course and when the final results were published, I was well up with the leaders and was cock-a-hoop. I also came in second on the long-distance run and was 'capped' as goalkeeper for the Second Year Course against the First Year Course. We won, and I had a good game. My confidence was now steadily building!

After Polkemmet, it was back to 'C' Division in Edinburgh City Police and, in due course, I was confirmed as a fully-fledged police officer. I settled down to a spell as a regular beatman on the Broomhouse/Broomhall and Sighthill Industrial Estate beat on the Third Section. Broomhouse was a wild place then, with some notorious families and numerous convicted criminals living on my 'patch' as they say in TV police programmes (not a term that we used though). Domestic disputes and complaints of noisy neighbours were common, young gangs roamed the streets at night and the minority of decent people who lived in Broomhouse had a bloody awful time of it, despite 'polis' efforts. One of the residents in those days was one of the Bay City Rollers and his family. It was not uncommon for the early version of the band to rehearse in the back green of the house, to the annoyance of neighbours!

It was in Broomhouse that I made my first arrest of a housebreaker who I caught in the act of attempting to jemmy his way into the local grocery store – an old converted double-decker bus. He heard my footsteps as I was about to arrest him and took off with me after him. He hurled the jemmy away into deep grass, so I threw my police cap near it because I knew we'd need it for evidence. I finally made my arrest near a telephone box. I slung him into the box while a helpful resident made a telephone call from his house, offering to bring out his Alsatian dog to 'sort out' the criminal. I declined the offer. The CID arrived shortly afterwards and I was on my way to my first Chief Constable's Commendation.

Quite near this same telephone box was a three-storey tenement to which I had a call one morning on early shift. A toddler had somehow clambered up on a couch which was close to the window in the living room and, in the absence of the mother, had climbed onto the window ledge. The window was open and the child had taken a nose dive from the top floor onto a concrete path below. According to witnesses, it had landed on its head. I was expecting to find a dead child when I reached the locus (more police jargon) but it was only bawling loudly. Mother and child were rushed to hospital, but allowed out after examination and x-rays revealed no substantial injury – quite extraordinary!

There was no such thing as a quiet day on the Broomhouse beat and every conceivable incident occurred there. One day on bicycle patrol, I saw a motor scooter pass by and realised the rider was a known criminal. I would have gone in pursuit but the old police bicycle was not built for speed (or comfort for that matter). I was left standing (or more accurately cycling) but knew where the young bugger lived. I made for this house, hid my bicycle in the back stair and then waited just inside the tenement door. A few moments later, I heard running feet, and a panting young criminal entered his common stair and was nabbed on the spot.

A year or so earlier when being shown the Broomhouse beat by a seriously grumpy old beatman, who hated recruits and refused to walk the extensive beat, I had to sit on the crossbar of that same bicycle while he rode around in the early hours of the morning. We got some really funny looks from milkmen and other early workers. Quite frankly, I felt a bloody fool but was frightened to say a word.

Sunday morning was bicycle-maintenance morning, when the police bike had to be cleaned, oiled etc. An entry had to be made in the box journal to the effect that the maintenance had been done. One young idiot officer took the maintenance thing a bit too far and removed all the axles, ball-bearings etc. and then, like Humpty Dumpty, it couldn't be 'put together again'. He wrote in the journal – 'Maintenance of the beat bicycle could not be completed', and the various components were left on the box desk. The late-shift officer was not pleased.

Calling on relatives to inform them of the death of a loved one was never an easy task, but one Sunday morning I had to call on three families and deliver the unwelcome news of three entirely unrelated deaths.

One recipient of the bad news fainted and fell into my arms on the doorstep.

Getting your photo in newspapers was not an uncommon event and one day I was sent to Saughton Road North where a large subsidence (or hole in the road) had occurred. It turned out that the hole occupied an entire carriageway and traffic diversions had to be put in place. I was standing at the scene, just happened to be looking into the hole, when an *Evening News* photographer arrived and snapped me. The photo was in the evening paper with the caption – 'A large hole opened up in Saughton Road North today – the police are looking into it.' Unfortunately I have lost that paper cutting.

Night shift invariably brought some excitement. On one occasion, I had finished my rounds in the Sighthill Industrial Estate and was cycling down Cultin's Road (which was on the city boundary) when I came across a safe in a harvested cornfield. It had been stolen from a factory and very recently been blown open (the heat of the explosion could still be felt). Needless to say, the notes had all gone, but 'half-crowns' and 'two-bob' pieces had been scattered widely when the charge blew. I got a message to the CID via a passing motorist, and gathered up as many of the coins as I could find to pass on to the CID. For the rest of the night shift, I stopped off at the scene of the safe-blowing a few times and, on each occasion, found a coin or two which went to a charity close to my heart.

On another night shift, I was cycling down Broomhouse Road and, as I approached the entrance to Broomhouse Secondary School, heard what I can only describe as 'excited sexual noises'. I stopped, switched on my torch and, lo and behold, my light revealed a sight never to be forgotten. A couple, who I estimate were in their late 60s or early 70s, both semi-naked and with various items of clothing around their ankles, were against the wall having a 'knee-trembler' (police speak for sexual intercourse while standing). A wee 'cairry-oot' of beer and spirits lay on the ground beside them. There was a frantic struggle to rearrange clothing, and the old fellow, by way of explanation said, 'Sorry constable, I was just necking'" I replied with the timeworn police response in such situations – 'Well, put your neck back in your trousers and get off home!'

A few years later, at the same location, I was on motor patrol with my sergeant when we came across a parked car which was rocking quite violently as we approached with headlights blazing. The windows of the car were totally steamed-up, and the inmates were so involved in their passion that, only when we opened the car door, did we find two completely naked bodies locked in each other's arms. They were in the back seat and all their clothes were in the front. Our sergeant, always full of mischief, asked the young lad for his driving licence, which entailed him having to get up and reach over – when all was revealed. It then transpired that the girl, who was still at school, was the sergeant's neighbour. She was told to get dressed and get off home. As she left she implored the sergeant not to tell her mum and dad. He did not. Ah, young love.

The sights a police officer sees and the things he experiences are quite remarkable, and a couple of humorous examples are worth mentioning. I had to call on a nurse at her home address well after midnight one night and advise her that she was to report at the hospital next morning for an early operation. She offered me a coffee which I accepted but, when she sat down on the couch, she moved right up beside me and allowed her dressing gown to open up, revealing almost everything. I finished my coffee and left. Being the innocent lad I was, I never worked out what she had in mind.

In Gorgie Road one night, an American serviceman reported that he had gone with a woman to her house to have sex but, when he got there, a male threatened him and stole his wallet – then kicked the lad out the door. We accompanied him back to the flat and a knock brought the woman to the door completely nude. As she danced about in anger, with the dangly bits dangling, she screamed at us, 'Well, are you all wanting a screw or what?' We declined the offer. When we got into the house, we quickly recovered the American's wallet, although the cash was gone. He was happy to get his identity papers back and would press no charges. I suppose he must have walked back to the Kirknewton US Air Base and had enough time to contemplate his foolishness.

On a more serious note, I attended a house fire in Broomhouse. The fire brigade was already in attendance, and amongst the firemen (now firefighters) was June's brother, John, who had recently joined the brigade. When the kitchen fire was extinguished, I entered the house and was astonished by what I found. It was occupied by a husband, wife and three children, all of whom had escaped without injury. It was the state of the house that appalled me and the fire crew. It was filthy and stank throughout, but it was the kids' bedroom that really shocked us. The beds and cot were urine-soaked and covered with excrement, and under the bed there were actually piles of faeces. The kids had drawn on the bedroom walls – unbelievably with their own excrement. The Social Work Department was called but, instead of removing the kids to a place of safety as I had expected, the husband and wife were given the day to scrub the house from top to bottom. Fresh bedding was obtained from some voluntary source, and the house was given the okay later in the day by the Social Work Department. For a while afterwards, I popped in on my way past and, while the house was never immaculate, the woman had been given a real fright and was at least trying to maintain a decent level of cleanliness. You may well ask yourself, how people can live like that.

The Sighthill Industrial Estate expanded quite dramatically during my time on the beat, and there was an interesting mix of businesses. There were several factory watchmen anxious for a blether, and I occasionally popped in to see them, if for no other reason than to give them some support and confidence. It was a heavy night-shift patrol getting round all these premises, especially on windy, cold and wet nights – not a pleasant patrol.

There was a potato crisp factory on the estate. On one occasion, when I dropped in to see the watchman on late shift, a general commotion was taking place in the packing room, with screams and howls of laughter. We slipped quietly into the factory to find the packing-room girls with one of their workmates, stripped from the waist down and spread-eagled on the conveyor belt. They were attempting to push crisps where crisps were never intended to go, and the recipient was screaming holy murder. Apparently she was getting married the next day and was being 'prepared' by her mates. I knew of husbands-to-be getting their 'tackle' blackened with boot polish but that was a bit extreme. I never ate that make of crisps again!

There were gangs in almost every housing estate, and on occasions there would be confrontations between opposing groups, which often ended up with injuries requiring hospital treatment. The arrival of the police always sent the gangs running in all directions, so detection was impossible. Batons, axes, knives etc. were often recovered after they had gone.

The Broomhouse gang had to be continually moved on from shop fronts and other locations where they congregated to the annoyance of local residents. I got to know most of them by name but could never pin anything on them in the way of an offence. On one occasion, however, as I was passing the gang, they started whistling the theme music from Z-Cars (one of the early TV police 'soaps'). This was blatantly 'taking the piss' (although admittedly quite humorously) and I felt the situation required attention or I might become the subject of scorn. I grabbed hold of the one I regarded as the gang leader, warning the others not to interfere and to clear off. With some mutterings, they reluctantly did so. I walked the lad quite a distance to the police box, during which time he subjected me to abuse. Inside the box, I have to admit that I assaulted him. Not seriously, but enough to take the wind completely out of his sails – needless to say, the big, brave gang leader, without his gang around him, proved to be a pathetic little boy and out of his depth. As he left the police box, I instructed him that every time I passed in future, whether he was with his gang or not, he would address me as Constable Green. The amazing thing is that he did, and from that moment on, if I appeared on the scene, the gang would disperse without a word of warning from me. This reinforces my earlier thoughts that the world has turned upside down, common sense having been abandoned nowadays.

Years later, I was confronted with another gang from Stenhouse and Whitson, who were terrorising the residents. Again, there never appeared to be any evidence or witnesses prepared to take a stance against any of the gang. They became very cocky and would shout taunts at the police. One day, the leader gave me abuse from a distance and then took off. I had an idea where he was bound for and drove a short distance to the Water of Leith near Murrayfield Ice Rink, hiding the police car and then myself in the bushes by the riverside. A few moments later, he came running along the path. All I had to do was to reach out and grab him by the scruff of the neck. I pulled him to the nearby bridge, hung him over the parapet upside down and threatened to drop him in. He screamed holy murder and pleaded for mercy, at which point I hauled him back onto his feet and posed the question, 'Will this stupid gang of yours stop now?' This one was no better than the previous clown and, after apologising and pleading for leniency, he promised me that 'his' gang would behave in future. I certainly had no further problem with them, and the malicious damage and endless complaints from local residents reduced dramatically. Summary justice again, perhaps?

After a couple of years on the beat, the powers that be decided that a new system of policing in the outer areas of Edinburgh (the 'c' Division Third and Fourth Sections) was to be adopted. The system still relied on six beatmen on each shift of each section, but with a police patrol van, manned by a driver and the section sergeant, augmenting the beat system. In practice, the sergeant had the discretion to uplift one or more of the beatmen and transport them quickly to incidents. The patrol van also attended to all '999' and other urgent calls and was in radio communication with both Divisional and Police Headquarters. This meant a rather faster response to calls than the previous situation where the beatman received the message on his return to his police box and then made his way to the incident on foot or bicycle.

Selected constables who had driving licences were immediately attached temporarily to the Traffic Department ('E' Division) for driving instruction. After successfully completing the course, I became the relief driver of the patrol van. The regular driver had been in the RAF during the war and had some of the most unbelievable stories to tell. One story he told was that he was flying with a Polish pilot and each time they approached a landing, the pilot pushed back the cockpit hood and stuck his head out as if he was listening for something. Our colleague, without blushing, then explained that when he asked him for an explanation he said, 'Don't tell anyone, but I am blind and I am listening for the ground coming up.' One night, when he was regaling us with yet another ridiculous tale, I unkindly told him that he was a 'fucking liar', and he threw a cup of hot tea all over me. I deserved it I suppose, but had to be pulled away from him.

One of the advantages with the mobile patrol system was that at least some of the beatmen on the section would go to the West End Police Station for refreshments (or 'piece-time' as we called it). This was a luxury after sitting in the police box in Broomhouse Road on winter nights, with snow blowing in and drifting underneath the ill-fitting door, when I would quickly eat my sandwiches accompanied by a cup of tea, and then rush outside to get warmed up. Interestingly, there was never such a thing as an official refreshment period entitlement for police officers, just some government committee recommendation which some senior officers were quick to remind you of. Actually, the term 'superior officers' was used a lot, but I never accepted that term because in my early days in the police, I found some so-called 'superior officers' I worked with were far from superior, and some seriously lacked any kind of humanity towards their colleagues.

I recall an occasion as a recruit when I was being shown the beat on Gorgie Road on early shift. Two of us were on a turn, both wearing raincoats, when visited by the shift inspector. This bloody idiot bawled me out for wearing my raincoat on what was a dry day (the instruction was that raincoats would be worn in wet weather and overcoats in dry, cold weather) but said not one word to the senior constable. The inspector made a big issue of the incident, threatening to have me 'out of the job', despite my explanations that I had to make a decision about which coat to wear before leaving the house at 5am and did not have my equipment stored in the box. It would not have been so bad if he had bawled out both of us.

The mobile patrol van on the Third Section had the call sign 'ZH Whisky 50'. The early patrol vans were very basic Morris vans which were both unstable and susceptible to regular breakdowns. They had no heating and in the winter we had to be wrapped up in overcoats and gloves. They were later replaced by Vauxhall, and improved models of Morris vans. These vans built up huge mileage readings which went 'round the clock' and more. About the time we got the more modern vans, our regular driver moved on to another department, and I became the fully-fledged 'Whisky 50' driver on our shift.

These were happy days, and the Third Section bonded into a really close-knit team. The rivalry between the Third and Fourth Sections was fierce, and improved efficiency dramatically. Each officer of the Third Section was a character. There was John Tully, who was almost obsessive about his personal tidiness to the exclusion of almost everything else; Tommy Hogg, one of the most dedicated police officers but with no concept of time; Jock Wait, a Borderer whose father owned a pub to which Jock fell heir when he retired; Frank Bell, a very meticulous and dedicated officer with a very serious personality; Kenny Reid, a close friend of Tommy Hogg, who went on to join the Mounted Section; Ronnie MacKintosh and others who came and went.

To give you an idea of John Tully's need to be always immaculate – one evening he was acting sergeant and we had stopped at my old police box in Broomhouse Road. As we watched, a passenger aircraft passed overhead on its approach to Turnhouse (now Edinburgh) Airport. Someone remarked, 'One of these days a plane is bound to crash at Turnhouse Airport.' A moment or two later, a wireless message was received – 'ZH Whisky 50 attend at Turnhouse Airport where a passenger aeroplane has overshot the runway and crashed in a field.' We looked at each other in total disbelief (another spooky occurrence). John Tully's immediate classic response was, 'I need to go home first and pick up my Wellington boots.' John was persuaded by the rest of the crew that this was an emergency, and I set a course for Turnhouse at high speed.

On arrival there, John and a couple of other officers went to the plane which was on a marshy bit of land, with its nose stuck in the soft ground and the tail up in the air. The air company employees were on the scene within minutes and painted out the name of the company, even as people were being helped from the scene. I remained in the van and relayed information by wireless to Police Headquarters. This was before 'Air Crash Contingency Plans' had been published, so we were all on a learning curve that night. I continued to relay information on the situation to headquarters as new details became available and quite soon it became clear that there were no serious injuries amongst the passengers and crew. A number of ambulances arrived to take some passengers to hospital with minor injuries and suffering from shock. Very quickly, the 'cavalry' arrived, and soon all was well under control. The next day, word was relayed to our team from the chief constable's office that our action at the scene of the crash had been exemplary and the flow of information by wireless communication clear, concise and informative – a well-deserved pat on the back for our superb team.

We had a series of section sergeants over the next few years, including Pax MacDonald, mentioned earlier. One was an ex-CID officer who, on promotion to uniformed sergeant, came to us. Jimmy Campbell was a hugely-experienced officer who was a great source of assistance to us all. He never 'used his rank' excessively on anyone and always had the welfare of his 'troops' close to his heart. He also loved a joke and was great at social functions. Jimmy took me under his wing and I have a lot to thank him for. He also befriended my Dad who he met at various flower shows and would go home with Dad's prize-winning onions and other goodies. Jimmy would continually tell him how well I was doing and what a 'good cop' his laddie was – very embarrassing.

I found myself in a couple of funny situations with Jimmy. We were sitting stationary in Corstorphine village one evening when a semi-drunk, 'upper-crust' male approached us and started abusing us about everything under the sun. I was waiting for Jimmy to jump out and arrest him, because he had a quick temper, but instead he said, 'Fuck off you ignorant, toffee-nosed bastard' He gave the man a hefty push on the chest, turned to me and said, 'Drive on.' Definitely not in any of the police manuals.

One morning, we were parked at Western Corner while the owner of the gardening shop was setting out his goods on the pavement at the shop front. This man always wore the kilt, by the way. He came out the door carrying quite a large sack of grass seed and slipped on the pavement. The whole sack of grass seed went up in the air, emptying onto the poor shopkeeper who was now on the ground with his kilt around his ears. (No, he wasn't!) Jimmy, who was writing in the van journal, had missed the fun and was astonished to find me in hysterics. The shopkeeper got to his feet, brushing grass seed off his kilt while attempting to regain his composure, and tried to make some explanation. I couldn't resist it and, through bursts of uncontrollable laughter, I said, 'Could you do that again? My sergeant didn't see it.' 'Drive on,' said Jimmy again.

I suspect that Jimmy saved my job when June was hospitalised as a result of a national tuberculosis-screening campaign. Our daughter Linda went to Mam and Dad at Glenlockhart and the plan was that I would stay at home at Western Terrace in compliance with our arrangement with Mrs Duncan. Things went fine until I moved onto early shift. Now I have to admit that I sleep soundly, could do so on a bed of nails as a rule, and I am really difficult to awaken early in the morning. When I was at home and working as a gardener, Dad used to have the unenviable task of rousing me. He would physically lift me off the bed and drop me back down before he would get any kind of response – so, being on my own, trouble was around the corner. I sought advice and set two alarms to go off simultaneously on a tin tray with spoons on it, likely to rouse the dead. I went to bed very early, set the alarm for 5am and woke up about 7am, with Jimmy Campbell knocking loudly on my bedroom window. Apologies, and more apologies. That night, I went to bed about seven o'clock, with the same alarm clock arrangements in place, only to be again awakened by Jimmy knocking on my bedroom window around 7am. Seriously embarrassed, I had to make arrangements with the housekeeper that I would be living for a while with my father-in-law at Balgreen Park. He got me up each morning, with great difficulty, but I made my shift for 5.45am Jimmy did not give me a hard time. He covered up for me and I was not reported.

I regret to say that all too soon Jimmy was returned to the CID where he finished his service but sadly died early in his retirement – another great loss.

Another mobile patrol sergeant was Willie (name withheld) who had been in the Traffic Department when he was involved in a very serious police car crash. This had resulted in a long spell in hospital and a back which gave him continuous pain. It could make him really crabbit, but we developed a good relationship and I found he was a very fair sergeant you could speak openly to without having rank flung in your face. Willie, I fear, sought refuge in the bottle and drank too much for his own good both off and on duty, which could have caused serious consequences for both of us. I shudder to think of some of the escapades Willie got us into. On a couple of occasions I had to take him home in the early hours of the morning before the shift was ended. I think our inspector at that time was at his wits' end with him but had, I presume, sympathy for the pain Willie suffered.

While I worked with Willie, I became eligible to sit my sergeant's exams. My by now built-in determination to succeed had me studying like mad and I felt fairly confident I could pass the police duties exams. I was less confident about the educational exams, which had to be sat in conjunction with the police exams in those days (no longer required). As I recall, we had to sit exams on history, geography, English and mathematics. I was able to cover the first three subjects with home study, but mathematics was yet again almost beyond me. By chance, Willie's hobby was working out mathematical problems and he was a huge help to me with this subject. He tutored me to an advanced stage, both on duty during quiet spells and through homework. As a result, I sailed through the sergeant's exams with flying colours – to my own personal delight. Willie was ecstatic. I was then prepared to rest on my laurels but he said, 'No way.' I was entered for the inspector's exams the following year and again passed all subjects. I will forever be thankful to Willie.

There was one occasion when we came across the drunkest motorist I had ever seen. We saw a Bentley travelling erratically eastwards along Corstorphine Road. The vehicle was as often on the wrong side of the road as the right and had one or two very close calls with oncoming vehicles. We finally stopped the car near Donaldson's Hospital and, when I opened the driver's door, the drunk driver fell out into my arms. He was speechless, incapable of movement, and how he had managed to drive the car at all was beyond me. He was arrested and placed in the police van. To my delight, I was instructed to drive the Bentley to the West End Police Station, and the woman passenger, the driver's sister, insisted on travelling with me. As soon as I got into the car, she hauled her dress up to her waist and assured me that, if I let her brother off, I could do whatever I wished to her, then or later. I said it was a most attractive offer but 'no deal'. I drove her to the West End Police Station where she became a real nuisance until we got her a taxi home. I have to say she was not the most attractive women I have met but she had a nice pair of legs 'right up to her bum and back down again', as some officers said.

While Willie was my sergeant, we experienced one really busy Saturday night shift. As soon as we came on, we had a call to a road accident (or VA in police jargon – vehicle accident). We dropped off an officer at this fairly minor 'bump', and immediately got another VA call to near the zoo. As we pulled up there, a third call came in regarding yet another VA at Western Corner. Willie chose to deal with the zoo accident, and I drove on alone to Western Corner. There I found a two-car accident, with the driver of one vehicle alleging that the other driver, who was accompanied by another male, was drunk. I advised the first driver that, since I was alone, he would have to witness the police procedures I had to follow, and he agreed. As I approached the alleged drunk, it immediately became clear he was under the influence of alcohol and not capable of driving. I advised him of my suspicion, told him I was arresting him and administered the usual caution (before the days of breath-test kits).

I put him in the police van and went back to speak to the other driver, only to see the accused leave the van. With his colleague, he came at me menacingly. I felt I was in serious danger and, despite warning the men repeatedly, when I attempted to place the accused back in the patrol van, they set upon me. I drew my baton but, before I could even attempt to use it, one of the men grabbed it and wrenched it out of my hand. I was left with the leather strap wound round my hand in the approved manner. (If held in the 'approved manner', it was considered that the baton could not be taken from your possession – so much for the official version.) I was then dragged to the ground by the men, and I believed in that moment I was fighting, if not for survival, certainly to avoid serious injury. I recall the three of us rolling around the pavement at the bus stop, and people in the queue 'politely' stepping aside without lifting a hand to assist me, while I was taking a beating. The other driver was dancing around us, ineffectually telling the two men to stop. Somehow, I recovered my baton, so at least I was not about to be beaten up with it. The melee moved onto the carriageway while I shouted for help. At last, someone chose to help. This Good Samaritan proved to be an American airman in a passing car. He asked me the pretty obvious question, 'Are you in trouble buddy?' I screamed, 'Yes – there's another policeman dealing with an accident at the zoo. Get his help to me immediately'. With a 'Sure buddy', he drove to the zoo and got hold of Willie.

I continued to take a hammering but I recall, at one point, there was a leg in front of me. I thought I would take my anger out on this leg if

Policeman Attacked After Car Accident

An Edinburgh policeman was punched in the face and kicked on the legs by two young men last night at the scene of a car accident in Corstorphine Road. He was forced to use his baton to defend himself.

This was stated at Edinburgh Sheriff Court today when the two men, John Slater Watson, motor salesman, of 3 Tinto Place, and James Healy, 48a Coburg Street, Leith, pleaded guilty to the assault and to committing a breach of the peace.

Sheriff Substitute K. W. B. Middleton fined each of the accused a total of £15.

Describing the incident, Mr D. B. MacFarlane, Depute Fiscal, said Watson had been driving a car which crashed in Corstorphine Road. Healy was a passenger in the car. The policeman suspected Watson was under the influence of drink and said he was going to apprehend him.

Watson started punching the officer and Healy jumped on the policeman's back. He was kicked on the legs and had to defend himself with his baton.

TWO BLACK EYES

The policeman received two black eyes in the fight and one of his legs was badly bruised. He was treated at the Royal Infirmary for his injuries.

Watson told the Court that he had been shaken by the crash. He was pushed towards a police-van by the officer and was given no time to explain the circumstances. Healy said he thought he had only pushed the policeman away. He might have struck him "in the heat of the moment."

Ian attacked on duty.

nothing else, and ladled into it with my baton. I suppose this is when the whole thing turned into farce because it later transpired that the leg I had been 'beating to pulp' was, of all things, a bloody artificial leg. The 'cavalry' then arrived and I was saved from an unpleasant end. However, I finished up in the Royal Infirmary yet again – after I had presented my evidence to the station sergeant, of course.

A very spooky thing happened to me (again) when I got home. Hoping not to alarm June, and trying to hide my black-and-blue face and body, I sneaked quietly into bed, whereupon she said, 'You're injured.' I said I had a few bruises but June retorted, 'No, it's worse than that.' After she tearfully examined my bruises, she recounted how she had 'wakened up' in the middle of the night with her (deceased) mother standing at the bottom of the bed. Her 'mother' said, 'Ian has been hurt, but he is okay.' And the 'vision' disappeared. Now I am afraid I take a bit of convincing about this sort of 'ghostly' appearance, but June swears to this day that she had this experience. Maybe there was a telepathic connection between our two minds and somehow June then dreamt the appearance of her mother. I don't know. The mind is a strange and greatly unknown place. Of that, there is no doubt.

The two men were all locked up and appeared in court on Monday. They were fined for police assault and the driver subsequently lost his driving licence on a drink-driving charge. I never carried my police baton again throughout my service, despite police regulations. Police assault was not uncommon, and exciting moments lay ahead, but nothing as bad as that, for a while at any rate.

I really enjoyed driving the mobile patrol van and even became so confident about my driving ability that, at one point, I applied to go on the Traffic Department course for possible selection as a Traffic Department Officer on patrol car duties. I was accepted for the three-month course.

I enjoyed the challenges and became a much better driver, but there were aspects of the course which gave me second thoughts about being a traffic patrol officer.

There were two of us on the course, and another coincidence came to light when I learned that we had both attended Rothes Primary School at about the same time, although neither of us remembered the other. Our driving instructor was a superb driver. I will long remember the day he told us we were next to undergo training in high-speed driving. He drove the car to Glasgow as a demonstration, giving us a running commentary throughout the journey. He covered the distance in what seemed like only minutes and at speeds in excess of a hundred miles per hour – without the two 'learners' ever feeling apprehension. When we stopped on the outskirts of Glasgow, the engine was so hot that it was smoking. This was a police driver at the peak of his chosen profession. I was impressed.

On the course it was not uncommon for us to drive to Aberdeen or Inverness in a morning or afternoon and, as we took turns to drive, we had to maintain a continuous commentary. One day, we were in the Grampians. Dennis, the other trainee, had run out of things to say, there being no other cars about, no pedestrians, no changes in road surfaces etc. So, understandably, he dried up. 'Your commentary,' reminded the instructor. Dennis thought for a second or two and said, 'There's a sheep on top of that hill.' It was a moment of light relief in what was mostly serious business. When we started high-speed driving, I was not totally comfortable. At the speed of 100mph, you are simply eating up the road at an alarming rate. When the instructor urged me to go faster, and I saw the speedometer passing 100mph, with him still shouting, 'Faster', I stopped looking at the speedo and simply concentrated on a 'safe landing'. I am afraid I have always been a realist (some say a pessimist), but I had visions of some important bolt shearing or a tyre bursting at a 120mph (plus), and decided there and then that this was not for me.

I did finish the course, passed the very challenging advanced driving test and then went on to work with one of the garage mechanics to learn something of the basics of motor engineering. This part was no problem after three years as an army motor mechanic. The next stage was to go out with car crews, either as a passenger or as a replacement co-driver on occasions of sickness or other reasons. Most of the crews were fine, but some had been together so long that comradeship had taken a severe knock. There was one crew in particular who did not utter a word to each other, or me, for the entire shift and only communicated when some official task called for speech. Very sad.

Incidentally, the theory examinations were bloody tough and, if you were to be confident of passing the Highway Code test, you really had to know every word from cover to cover, including who printed the bloody thing. The day of the driving test, I was accompanied by the instructor and the E Division Chief Superintendent, whose presence made me nervous. His uncomplimentary comments throughout were seriously off-putting and, while I had been warned to ignore them by the driving instructor, it was easier said than done. He was not a nice man.

At the end of the course I had an interview with this same man who, I learned, was regarded widely as a bit of a fool, not to put too fine a point on it. He informed me that I would probably be called back to serve in the department when a vacancy occurred. I told him that, after what I had seen within his department, I would actively resist any permanent transfer to E Division. He told me in his bullish manner that, if the Traffic Department wanted me, I would have no say in the matter and was told to 'get out'. Thankfully, I was never recalled to the department, and I resumed as mobile patrol driver on my previous shift on the Third Section. It was an unhappy secondment to a department which needed good leadership at the top and better team spirit, in my humble opinion.

Life continued for a while as before on the Third Section mobile patrol and then I was seconded to the CID for a couple of months for work experience. I had no desire to seek a permanent transfer to the CID. My reason for this was simply that I was seriously at odds with the behaviour and attitudes of some CID officers. While I hasten to emphasise that most police officers I worked with throughout my service were good, honest and dedicated officers, I have to say there were a few in the CID, especially in my early police years, who should have been weeded out. Frankly, I distrusted them. Such concerns were shared by a number of other uniformed officers and apparently by at least some ranking officers at divisional level.

My time with the CID was interesting, but I learned little due mainly to the fact that only unsolvable cases were passed to me. When I did somehow find a culprit for a stolen bicycle CRF (Crime Report Form), I was told bluntly that I did not have sufficient evidence when, in fact, there was certainly enough to submit a report to the procurator fiscal. Most of the CID officers lacked time for assisting attached officers anyway because their case loads were, in all fairness, enormous. The result was that most of the time I felt I was in the way. Going 'for pints' seemed high on the agenda of some officers. And when I was invited along, I was invariably expected to pay (supposedly a 'tradition').

CID officers I worked with later reckoned this was a bad time for the Criminal Investigation Department and that massive improvements later occurred. I would agree. Mainly, I think, when the CID based at Police Headquarters was broken up somewhat, with many CID officers then operating out of the various Divisional Headquarters, much more transparency and accountability were assured. Nevertheless, I continued to find CID officers who were prepared to ignore the views of uniformed officers and I took exception to an oft-used 'joke' that 'a uniformed officer wouldn't recognise a stolen car even if he tripped over one'. Once again, it was a relief to return to uniformed divisional duties and reality. Don't get me wrong, there were some outstanding CID officers who were let down severely by some others.

It now seems a bit unreal that drivers of mobile patrol vans would undertake the pursuit of stolen vehicles and drunk drivers, travelling at speed to 999 calls in vehicles which were poorly designed in the first place. There were, of course, specific instructions that these vans were 'not to be used as pursuit vehicles'. But can you contemplate a young, enthusiastic police officer turning down the challenge of arresting a 'tea-leaf'? Some great captures were made by mobile patrol van drivers, including myself, but there were also occasions when driving too fast was the cause of 'bumps' (police car accidents). In all cases of police vehicle accidents, the driver would be called before a Police Internal Accident Board, usually given a hard time and sometimes suspended from driving police vehicles. I attended only one such enquiry and, while I believed I was not responsible for the accident, my 'old friend' the Chief Superintendent of E Division would accept not a word of my explanation. He called me a liar and so on, but could only administer a caution at the end of the proceedings. I don't think he liked me.

On one occasion, I would seriously have been in trouble with the board had the event ended in an accident. I was attending a 999 call to a 'suspected housebreaking in progress'. The acting sergeant for that day switched on the blue flashing light, headlights were turned to full and I was thundering down Clermiston Road towards St John's Road. Cars were parked in a continuous line on my nearside, narrowing the road considerably and, when I was well down the hill, I saw a car turn from a side street into Clermiston Road, turning north towards us. With blue light flashing and full headlights, which I was flashing on and off rapidly, I assumed the oncoming motorist would see our approach, but he seemed to misread the situation totally, and certainly was making no effort to give me a clear road. By then, the car was opposite the line of parked cars and I was running out of road, both in width and distance. I thought of braking but I was doomed to enter a skid which would certainly have taken me 'through' the oncoming car.

I did the only thing possible and aimed directly for the centre of the gap between the oncoming car and the parked vehicles, muttering a prayer. The van shot into the gap, with little to spare on either side. While I held my breath for what seemed the inevitable 'crunch', we sailed through unscathed. I looked at the acting sergeant and saw that he had turned as white as a ghost. He was only able to blurt out, 'What driving! How did you get through that gap?' I stopped the van, asked the acting sergeant to get another vehicle to attend the 999 call and, with shaking legs, I walked back to the car which had also stopped. I was about to embark on a lengthy and grovelling apology, but the driver beat me to it. He said he had panicked when he saw the oncoming police van, with lights flashing, froze and could not react. I mumbled something about being on a 999 call and that I had to get to the scene quickly. Apologising for frightening the living daylights out of the petrified man and his wife, I left 'while I was still ahead'. We were both sobered by the experience, but the acting sergeant kept repeating, 'What a piece of driving, Ian!', while I kept thinking, 'What an amazing piece of luck.'

One busy night, we picked up a 'D & I' (drunk and incapable) with the intention of taking him home. En route, we got a 999 call to a housebreaking and had no option but to take the drunk along. After details of the housebreaking had been noted, we returned to the police van to find that the drunk had urinated on one of the officers' parcel of sandwiches. Needless to say, the D & I was locked up instead of being taken home.

The early models of the Morris vans were stubborn old bastards. One went through a period of stalling at junctions, almost any time we stopped. As was common then, the batteries in the vans seemed unequal to the task of powering a VHF radio, lights, heaters etc., and continual restarting drained the battery. Near to the locus of a 999 call, the bloody thing stalled yet again, so the usual procedure was adopted – all hands out of the van, give it a push and get it started. As the officers worked up a bit of speed, they pushed the van round a corner and into the next street – the locus. The originator of the 999 call emerged from his house and shouted, 'Bloody hell. Would you not have been quicker if you'd left the fucking van at the station and walked here?' Nice one.

On another occasion, a mobile patrol van roared up to an incident, the doors burst open and half a dozen policemen poured out before the vehicle had actually stopped. A passerby commented humorously to the press, 'It was like the Keystone Cops.'

Before they built sub-stations at Corstorphine and Oxgangs, the two mobile patrol crews took their refreshments at the West End Police Station. Our sergeant on ZH 50 would occasionally be one named Peter (name withheld). He had a reputation for being a bit dreamy, or not quite with it, and was referred to on occasions as being like Mr Magoo. The sergeants ate in the sergeants' room, while the rest of the crew ate in the constables' room. Halfway through the refreshment period, Peter phoned the constables' room and said, 'Burglar alarm at Sighthill Industrial Estate. Get the team into Five-Zero and I'll join you.' The team assembled in the van in seconds, but no sign of Peter, so it was 'tally-ho' and off we went on our own. Half an hour and a false alarm later, the team were back munching their sandwiches, when Peter burst into the room and demanded to know, 'Why have I been bloody well sitting waiting in Five-Zero for the past half-hour?' It transpired that Peter had been sitting in the old Five-Zero, sold off at auction months previously to a joiner who, by a strange coincidence, also operated out of Torphichen Place, and nightly parked the ex-police van (with broken door locks) opposite the West End Police Station. Peter took some convincing that he'd been sitting in a joiner's van while the real Five-Zero attended the call.

About this time, training for dealing with the outcome of a nuclear attack had to be undertaken at a training centre in Ardmillan Terrace. This entailed groups of police officers attending a course for a couple of days, where they received numerous lectures and were shown government films. It was all a bit of a joke to most of us because the whole thing had a 'Mickey Mouse' feel to it – the idea of running about with a ladder and a shovel looking for casualties after a nuclear attack seemed ludicrous to most of us. We were shown a film on how a control centre would operate, in which the reports coming into the communications centre were attached to a string with a clothes peg, and then hoisted to the upper control level where the CO sat. It became a pantomime when one cynical officer asked, 'And what happens if the piece of string breaks.' The class subsided into hysterics.

Later, officers were selected to go on 'Nuclear Attack Convoys' and travelled across the country from location to location in 'Green Goddess' fire engines (later to be brought out of mothballs when the fire brigade went on strike) and other ex-army vehicles. The lads on these exercises had a great time, but none felt it would be a saviour in the event of a real nuclear attack, so it was back to day-to-day events.

A young constable, Andrew Watson, was about to be married and go off on honeymoon. At the time, Andrew worked on the Fourth Section Mobile Patrol of C Division. Fearing that his colleagues would 'tar and feather' him, he contacted the administration department and asked for a change of beat for his final night shift before being married. On 'the night', Andrew was happily walking round his temporary Dalry beat, when he was descended upon by the 'Flying Fourth Mobile', who snatched him and drove him to Oxgangs. There, they removed his trousers, leaving the rest of his uniform otherwise intact, and left him to find his own way back to the police box in Orwell Terrace, where the Fourth Mobile deposited his trousers to await his arrival. Andrew's long walk from Oxgangs to Dalry and his encounters with members of the public in his Y-fronts were a source of amusement for months.

Road accidents were a common occurrence on the Third Section because of the several main arterial routes, and I attended some very serious crashes. One night, under the charge of Acting Sergeant Tommy Hogg, we attended a real bad 'pile-up' involving several vehicles on Corstorphine Road at Balgreen Road. On arrival, the junction was strewn with pieces of wreckage, badly-mangled cars and injured bodies. It was carnage – one person was dead and a number badly injured. We got what information we could from the injured before they were whisked off by ambulance to hospital. Then we got on with the job of taking statements from uninjured passengers and other witnesses, noting details of vehicles plus their damage, marking and measuring the positions of vehicles after photos had been taken and clearing the road. The rest of the night was taken up with writing the witnesses' statements, including those of the police officers, and a VA (Vehicular Accidernt) report was compiled. This information was then left for the Traffic Enquiry Department. Tommy Hogg was full of praise for the night's work, and I later got a call from the investigating officer – 'Well done to all.'

A short time later, my shift inspector advised me that I was being temporarily attached to the Divisional Traffic Enquiry Department, with a view to remaining in that department for the usual two years. I agreed and kind of assumed that my work on the above road accident was instrumental in my selection for the department. I was about to enter a new era in my police career, and would remain with divisional departments for the next five years. Another new set of challenges.

life in the 'copshop' – specialisation

I moved into the Traffic Enquiry Department of 'c' Division and joined a bunch of really nice guys. All were hugely-experienced uniformed officers, prepared to help the 'new boy'. They included Peter Morton, Arthur Kingscott, Harry Scott, Jimmy Sinclair, Bob Edwards, Donald Morrison, John Muir and Tom Fergusson, some of whom came and went. I settled into the ways of the department quickly and will be forever grateful for the help I received from these excellent officers. After a trial period, I was confirmed as a fully-fledged member of the department. I loved the very interesting work and busy days and, importantly, it was also a very happy department. There was always good banter amongst the enquiry officers, but a huge amount of work was accomplished.

Individual caseloads were high – each officer rarely had fewer than eight on the go at the one time and quite often as many as 12. The most important lesson I learned very quickly was not to take home worries and concerns about cases; walk out the office door at the end of your eight hours and leave it all behind. If you did not, then you'd worry yourself sick and that would quickly have an effect on home life. This was a useful lesson for the rest of my police career and in later retirement.

The work mainly involved enquiries into VAs (vehicle accidents) where there was an allegation of careless driving and, occasionally, reckless and dangerous driving. For some reason the court was always reluctant to go ahead with reckless and dangerous driving and, only occasionally, with causing death by dangerous driving. A VA Report Book was submitted by a beat officer to the department and allocated to an enquiry officer. It was then a question of interviewing all the witnesses, collating police officers' statements, visiting the accident scene and drawing a plan of the locus of the accident. In addition, productions (physical items of evidence) were documented and finally, a Summoning Report was submitted to the chief inspector who would examine it with a fine-toothed comb and send it back for amendment if there were any errors. The standard of police reports in 'c' Division was very high at that time.

The final approved Summoning Report was then sent on to the

Procurators Fiscal Service. The PF allocated to the case would decide if there was a case to answer and since there usually was, the accused would be summoned to appear in court to make a plea. If he/she pled guilty, the case was dealt with by the sheriff there and then, but if the accused pled not guilty a date was set for trial. Regrettably, enquiry and other officers spent a lot of hours at the sheriff court waiting to be called as witnesses, often being dismissed either because the police witnesses were not called or the accused changed his plea to guilty at the last moment. The problem still occurs to this day.

Fatal road accident enquiries had to be undertaken in far greater depth, and a Sudden Death Report was required for the PF at an early stage of the enquiry, followed by a final Summoning Report. This invariably included photos of the accident scene, productions and other additional evidence. A fatal accident enquiry included accompanying a relative to the mortuary for body identification, always a sad and stressful duty to perform. The enquiry officer would then, in turn, have to identify the body to the postmortem doctor (pathologist). The chain of identification had to be complete.

Sudden deaths (where there were no suspicious circumstances, but where the medical practitioner was unwilling to supply a death certificate because he had not seen the patient for a considerable time or for some other reason) were also the department's area of responsibility. These cases also involved identification of the body by a relative to the enquiry officer or the pathologist and, in most cases, necessitated the attendance of the enquiry officer at the postmortem. This was to identify the body to the pathologist, take notes as necessary and obtain a death certificate in due course for the relatives. These doctors were immune to opening up cadavers, but I always had to work hard to retain my composure. Some pathologists would get very excited about aspects of the examination and invite me to look closely at some interesting part of the brain or other organ. A bit too gory really but, my goodness, my knowledge of the human body increased dramatically.

During the investigation of an alleged careless driving case, if it became apparent that there was no case to answer, i.e. insufficient evidence or conflicting witness statements, the Vehicle Accident Report would be completed to that effect and passed for approval to the chief inspector who would sign it off. Insurance companies also had access to information contained in such reports. If there was a case which was on the borderline, it might be necessary to see a PF, give a verbal résumé of the circumstances, after which he would make the decision to proceed or 'write the accident off'. This meant getting to know each PF and developing a close working relationship with them. There was one who was a very nervous type. He would often light his pipe when I was talking to him to hide his obvious embarrassment. On one occasion, after getting the pipe going 'full steam', he accidentally struck it with his hand. The pipe flew into the air, emptied its burning contents over the flummoxed PF and all the papers on his desk. Almost a fire brigade job, poor man.

A common practice before taking a case to the PF for a decision was for the enquiry officer to get the attention of all the other enquiry officers and go over the circumstances in detail. A consensus of opinion would then be sought to assist the decision-making process. This worked well because it was sometimes possible to get too close to the case in hand and miss key factors.

One fatal road accident case I failed to complete to my entire satisfaction involved a woman who was knocked down in Lothian Road at the Caledonian Hotel pedestrian crossing. We had no witnesses to the accident, the driver had not stopped and the accident only came to our attention later through an ambulance/hospital death report. All we had was a body that clearly had been in a road accident during the very busy evening rush hour, but no witnesses. In such circumstances, it was common to enlist the aid of the *Evening News*, or even television on occasions, and make an appeal for the driver and witnesses to come forward. This was done. I also enlisted the help of fellow enquiry officers and we attended at the locus of the accident exactly one week later, when we stopped everyone passing over the crossing within half an hour before and after the estimated time of the accident.

As a result, we came up with two 'eye witnesses', both, I think, through the *Evening News* appeal. One witness said he was there on the evening in question, about the right time, and saw a woman dash onto the road without looking properly. She was struck a glancing blow by a car, he thought,

A newspaper plea by Ian for witness to a fatal road accident.

EDINBURGH POLICE SEEK VEHICLE

Police are still trying to trace a vehicle involved in an accident on November 12 in Lothian Road, Edinburgh, opposite the Caledonian Hotel, in which 78-year-old Mrs Agnes Gilroy, 152 Morningside Road, was knocked down and received injuries from which she later died.

The vehicle may have been a car or lorry. They are also trying to trace a man who helped Mrs Gilroy to her feet. The accident occurred between 5 and 5.30 p.m.

Bequest To University

in the heavy flow of traffic. He reckoned that the driver may have been entirely unaware of the accident. The other witness described a similar accident at the same locus but was adamant it was not on the date in question. He was interviewed very thoroughly, but stuck to his statement that it was the day previously, and confirmed, because of his work routine, that he was nowhere near Lothian Road on the date we were investigating. The ambulance service corroborated that our date was the correct one. Both witnesses confirmed that the injured woman was being cared for by other witnesses and that a crowd had gathered, but the two witnesses had left the scene immediately. They also provided conflicting descriptions of the deceased and her clothing. Posters were sited at the locus but not another witness came forward, the driver was never traced and a very inconclusive report went to the PF. I spent a lot of time and effort on this fatal accident enquiry but with a very frustrating negative result. There is nothing as strange as reality.

Another accident I investigated occurred on Glasgow Road just east of the railway bridge near The Maybury. The bridge caused a distinct hump on the road, and vision eastwards was restricted because of this. A car travelling eastwards came over the hump and was alleged to have been travelling far too fast. It ploughed into the rear of the last of a line of vehicles held up at the Maybury Roundabout, creating a concertina effect and resulting in substantial damage to a number of cars. A line of tyre-rub marks (we were never allowed to call them skid marks) had been astutely measured and positioned by the mobile patrol officers at the scene, as was the clearly indicated point of impact. Point of impact is invariably indicated by broken glass and other debris from the colliding vehicles. I completed the enquiry and there seemed no doubt it was a clear case of careless driving. The driver pled not guilty.

I don't know why I did this, but I returned to the locus again the day before the trial, drove eastwards until I had a view over the hump of the bridge and pinpointed my position exactly. I was called to the witness box when the tyre-rub marks and point of impact were discussed in detail. The sheriff then asked me the question I somehow had anticipated: 'Constable Green, exactly what would be the position of a vehicle when the driver finally had a clear view over the hump in the road?' I was able to locate it precisely on the plan I had submitted, but the sheriff said, 'Are you certain, Constable?' 'Yes,' I replied and I was committed. The sheriff indicated that he would postpone his decision until Monday to allow him to visit the scene personally. He returned to the bench on Monday and, in his summing-up, he said, 'Constable Green was absolutely correct in his measurement and I find the accused guilty.' Why did I do that the day before the trial – my subconscious perhaps? Had I not done so, I may well have been forced to make an estimate and made a bloody fool of myself. Well done the sheriff though.

A 'court' story, alleged to have happened at Police Headquarters, then in the High Street, is worth repeating. One of the local High Street worthies had been arrested yet again for being drunk and incapable and was being held until the Burgh Court sat in the morning. It was a quiet night at HQ and, to relieve the boredom some of the staff decided to play a prank on the 'drunk'. The Burgh Court, which was housed in Police Headquarters, was opened up and officers took on the mantle of the various court officials, including the magistrate. The 'drunk', or more correctly the accused, was wheeled in before the 'court' and given a long lecture by the 'magistrate', who declared the punishment would be 25 years imprisonment (or some such silly sentence). The accused was then removed from the 'court', protesting loudly at the excess punishment and returned to his cell. In the morning when he was being prepared for court, he was adamant he'd already been to court, but was assured he must have been 'dreaming'!

There were some very unusual cases in the Traffic Enquiry Department, so life was never dull, and the busy life in this department continued for two years.

In the meantime, June and myself had added to our family with, first, Andrew who was born three years after Linda and later Stephen, who was born within a year of Andrew's birth. That was a bit of bad family planning. When June called on our doctor to have him confirm the pregnancy, he humorously remarked, 'Oh well Mrs Green, you are one of those unfortunate women who only needs to see her husband's trousers hanging on the back of the door to become pregnant.' It was okay for him to be flippant but we were panicking.

We had by then moved to our first council house at 76 Whitson Road where we spent many happy years. The neighbours there were really fine people and included the Greig and Miller families. Apparently the arrival of a police officer (me) in the area had an immediate effect on the neighbourhood, resulting in less malicious damage, fewer housebreakings and a drop in crime in the area. I did, however, have to make it clear after a spell that our home was not a police station as well-meaning neighbours arrived at our door, day and night, with found property and minor complaints.

New Year was always an amazing occasion at Whitson Road where we and our neighbours had an 'open door' policy – all welcome after the 'bells'. Our house was at the centre of the celebrations and for many years as many as a hundred people would pass through in one night. It came to an end though, when one Hogmanay a group of strangers arrived. They were very drunk and showed no respect for our home at all, so we had to ask them to leave. We later found that a bottle of whisky had gone with them and, worse still, they had substituted it with a bottle of cold tea. This was the only occasion we had such a problem, but we decided to call it a day for a while after that.

Linda, Andrew and Stephen attended the local Balgreen School, and June started teaching Sunday school at Saughtonhall Congregational Church. I helped to maintain the garden around the church (doing my community bit), but I bloody near fell off my chair when the minister called on us and invited me to become a deacon of the church. I explained to him that I was a non-believer, an atheist in fact, but I was more astonished when he replied that it did not matter. I convinced him that that would be quite dishonest in my book, so he let it rest. Me, a deacon of the church, I ask you.

My two allotments at Balgreen Road were by then flourishing and producing a steady supply of fresh fruit and vegetables, which helped eke out our rather poor police weekly wage. My brother Jimmy, a joiner by trade, who made various conversions on our house at Whitson, also built me a small greenhouse in the back garden. My old Korean buddy, Alex Boyes, did all our decorating. From time to time, Alex and I would 'hit the town' on a Saturday and go to a club in Torphichen Street where there was always a good sing-around which I enjoyed taking part in. I was never a great singer but liked to have a go in those days.

I soon became involved in showing vegetables and flowers at local flower shows, and was fascinated in growing exhibition chrysanthemums. Again, my determination to be successful drove me on and, within a year or two I was competing at the highest level, exhibiting my prize chrysanthemums from the Borders to Perth. There were a few acknowledged top-class growers around at that time (two from the small town of Selkirk alone). While I simply could not compete in the top six-vase classes (i.e. six vases each of five blooms, and a different variety in each vase) because I did not have the facilities or cash needed to grow a huge number of plants, I was able to hold my own in the three-vase, single-vase and mixed-vase classes, winning many prizes and certificates. I think

: *AUTUMN BLOOMS*

The flowers that bloom in the autumn added a touch of colour to Carrick Knowe Church Hall, Edinburgh, where Carstorphine Horticultural Society staged their annual show. Judges and officials are pictured admiring the prize blooms of Mr I. D. Green, of Whitson Road, Edi

Judges admiring Ian's three-vase entry of winning chrysanthemums.

Dad was very proud of me and would help me stage the blooms (it took a lot of gentle care with a cotton bud to get the petals all sitting perfectly). We did fall out one day though when he came to my allotments and started criticising my feeding (fertilising) methods. I stupidly told him to mind his own bloody business and pointed out that he had never achieved the success I had with chrysanthemums. A conceited outburst which I regret to this day. We made it up over a drink though – Dad and I both liked one or two or three or four or more. The trouble with drinking with Dad was that he drank 'nips' while I drank pints. He would say 'Slainte' and tip the whisky down his throat while I took my first sip of beer. He'd then say, 'Right, we'll hae another wee drammy.' I never drank anything but pints in those days and Dad never drank anything but whisky, so I'd have to miss out on a few while Dad got merry.

I was severely 'wound up' over chrysanthemums by my pals in the Traffic Enquiry Office. From time to time I would give them plants and also blooms after exhibitions, and they all knew how consumed I was by the hobby. One of them saw an opportunity to set me up. He came into the office one morning to inform me that one of the plants I had given him had a stem with one colour and another stem with a totally different colour. This had me drooling at the mouth with thoughts of a cash register ringing. To explain: exhibition chrysanthemums are hybrids created by cross-pollinating by breeders. When a very good specimen is raised from the resulting seed, the breeder then propagates by taking cuttings from the parent plant and steadily increases stock until it's available for sale to enthusiasts. Now, occasionally, one of the propagated plants will 'sport' – i.e. it will throw up a stem on a plant with a totally new colour but with the same good characteristics as the original hybrid. When this happens propagation then occurs from the sport. Growers will pay a lot of money for such a sport. I was getting all excited, telling my colleague to let me visit and collect the plant, only to find first one and then another having a quiet laugh at my expense. It had all been invention which had produced the desired result.

Mam and Dad's Golden Wedding.

I had also taken up trout angling, visiting various rivers and lochs with the Police Angling Club. My first season was a bit of a disaster because I had been used to fishing in my early days with worms and maggots etc. – when not poaching. The Police Angling Club was 'fly only', so there was no opportunity to use my previous skills. My first 'go' on Loch Leven (then the 'Mecca' of trout fishing) was with the club. I was in a boat along with one of the West End divisional drivers – Bob – and my brother who was a guest. Bob was one of the most crabbit buggers in the police and was no better on a social occasion. We hit Loch Leven that day at its best, Bob was hauling in these lovely one-pound trout, and brother Jimmy had bagged a couple. My nylon cast with four artificial flies kept landing on the water like a pile of spaghetti, despite my efforts, but eventually a trout, which must have taken sympathy on me, managed to select a fly from the tangled mess and went off like a torpedo. I had absolutely no idea how to 'play' the trout. It went everywhere, round the boat, under the boat and bloody nearly jumped into the boat on one occasion. My antics were infuriating Bob who cursed me up hill and down dale using every curse in the 'soldier's vocabulary'. In exasperation, he grabbed the landing net and, as my trout raced past him yet again, he stuck the net into the water. The trout charged straight into it and Bob 'wheeched' it into the boat – a beautiful trout of one and a half pounds. I was so elated I hardly fished again that day, but also the fear of further curses kept me quietly seated while I ate my sandwiches.

I was 'hooked' from that moment. Go for it Ian, no stopping until you are at the top again. I practised, studied the art of fly angling in depth, and the following year I progressed so far that my efforts achieved a clean sweep of the Police Angling Club trophies. I was hopelessly consumed by fly angling and managed to join another club – The Edinburgh Walton Club. I became the Walton Club Champion which qualified me for the Scottish Angling Championships the following year. My tail was up and nothing could stop me. I was second in the Scottish Angling Championships, being beaten by only a couple of ounces. What a disappointment but, at the same time, what elation because the top 12 qualified for the Scottish Team to compete the following year against England, Ireland and Wales at Loch Leven. I knew Loch Leven like the back of my hand and had an uncanny knack of knowing where the trout would be and what imitation flies would be 'taking'. I had one bonanza day when fishing with the Edinburgh Walton Club, bagging 16 beautiful Loch Leven trout, all a pound or over.

Annual presentation of prizes at Police Angling Club dinner. Ian is fourth from the left.

The international match was an amazing day which I will never forget. I don't think I had ever been so proud in all my life up to that moment. June was slightly unhappy with me going fishing while she was in hospital about to give birth to Stephen. Looking back, it was one hell of a choice, but fishing for Scotland, my one and only chance as it proved, was too much to pass by. I had another incredible day and, out of the four countries, I had the second best catch, again beaten by a few ounces for the best catch of the day. Scotland was also beaten into second place by England, but what an experience for probably the youngest lad of the four teams. I treasure my team badge and internationalist tie which I wear with pride.

I continued fishing for years and have some wonderful memories, including the day I was fishing the River Tweed with the Police Club when I caught two salmon in quick succession while fishing for trout. It is no mean task to land a salmon of around ten pounds on trout-fishing tackle, and a salmon fisher watched me land both with some admiration. I had no permit to fish for or catch salmon, but the salmon fisher and her gillie kindly let me keep the larger of the two – ten and a half pounds – while they 'snaffled' the other. I have to say, I arrived home that night in a pretty inebriated state. There is a great fishing poem, which goes:

The Scottish International Angling team at Loch Leven before taking on England, Ireland and Wales. Ian is third from the left, back row.

The fisherman riseth early in the morning,
Goes forth with great hope in his heart,
And returns in the evening,
With the truth not in him.

Well, a big bloody salmon proved the truth was in me that day.

My brother Jimmy and I planned a fishing trip to the Highlands one year and fished the lochs from the Assynt Hotel every day for a week, with more or less nothing to show for it. Jimmy caught a nice sea trout the first day, but after that it was bloody little 'tiddlers' as the sun shone mercilessly from a blue sky (the exact opposite of good fishing weather). On the last day, maybe because of our frustration, Jimmy and myself had an argument and, while I was all for putting it behind us, Jimmy barely spoke all the way home the next day – a disaster in more ways than one.

The Police Angling Club also made fishing expeditions to the Western Highlands and good catches were usually the order of the day. Not only was the fishing good, but we ate well and there was some good craik. The total catch was usually divided equally amongst the group before we headed for home.

The Angling Club was instrumental in me being involved in the organisation of a 'folk club' in the Police Club at 28 York Place in Edinburgh, which was to be the beginnings of my 'musical interlude'. It started off as a one-off fund raiser by Davie Scougall, myself and others of the Angling Section, but proved to be so popular that the Police Folk Club (later to be named by some 'folky' humourist as 'Fuzzfolk') eventually settled into a fortnightly event. It went on to become one of the best folk clubs in Scotland, but more of that in a following chapter when I will expand on my musical involvement.

You may ask yourself: (a) how did I manage to fit in all these pastimes while bringing up a family and holding down my job as a policeman and (b) how could I afford such pursuits? Well, along the way, Dad introduced me to Jimmy McCalman (father of Ian McCalman of The McCalmans folk group). Jimmy had spent many years working with the nursery company, Dobbies of Edinburgh, but had left to start up his own business on The Mound – a shop selling all manner of garden supplies. Jimmy and his wife Isabel were lovely people and so very, very generous to June and me.

Jimmy quickly expanded his business and was in need of a part-time deliveryman, and I fitted the bill nicely. He paid me cash, but we also had an arrangement in which some of the rewards of my labours went towards the loan of Jimmy's car for our holidays. So started family camping holidays to Devon and Cornwall and around Scotland – holidays we could never have afforded since I had no car of my own. The money Jimmy paid me subsidised my fishing and gardening hobbies, but there was one unfortunate side effect. I was so busy fishing, gardening, delivering and being a policeman that I was guilty of neglecting family life to some extent. It did not seem so at the time but, in retrospect, I believe I was so anxious to achieve success on so many levels that, to my regret, this hectic life did get in the way of personal relationships. My association with the McCalman family, however, led to a friendship, with Ian in particular and he and I remain friends and business associates to this day.

I think in the hierarchy of 'c' Division it was considered that, if an officer successfully completed two years in the hectic environment of the Traffic Enquiry Office, he deserved some sort of reward, and in those days that meant the next move was to the Divisional Plain Clothes Department. I spent three years in this department – some of my happiest years in the police service. We were under the direct control of the divisional chief inspector to whom the department reported on a daily basis, but we had no other supervision and were left entirely on trust to do the job. I can never recall any officer in the department betraying that confidence. Okay, we 'played' occasionally, but we all worked extremely hard and the results were there for all to see.

In the department I was teamed up with Peter Morton (we worked in twos) with whom I had also worked in the Traffic Enquiry Office. I could not have asked for a better partner. He was a tall, imposing officer, a real decent man with a great understanding of police work, and a colleague who would back you up to the hilt in any situation. We knew instinctively how each would react – in the year or two we worked together there was never the hint of a wrong word between us. Peter showed me the ropes of plain-clothes work and my professionalism improved greatly under his guidance.

Invariably, when two police officers make an arrest, the accused person will quickly show his dislike for one officer while cultivating the goodwill of the other (the 'good guy'). On occasions when an accused took umbrage at Peter and befriended me, I loved to wind him up by saying, 'Yeah, my mate is a real bastard but you will be all right with me. I'm a real good guy.' Then I'd watch Peter's expression. Just devilment, but the sort of 'ragging' that could only work between good mates.

Peter and I got into some really 'hairy' situations but came out of these ever stronger as a team. I recall one Saturday evening when we were doing the rounds of the pubs to ensure they were being managed effectively. We walked into Bissett's Bar in Morrison Street, only a stone's throw from the West End Police Station. As soon as we opened the door it became apparent that a real 'stramash' was taking place – punches were being thrown and the bar was in uproar. The manager recognised us immediately and screamed, 'Do something.' We both shouted, 'Police officers' and Peter launched himself at one of the principals while I grabbed another, only then realising that he was a great hulking coalman from the local coal-yards, in for a 'quiet refreshment' (probably about 12 pints!). It was like grabbing hold of King Kong, and before I could say, 'Be gentle with me' we crashed right through the outer glass door, landing on the pavement outside. By some stroke of sheer good luck, I was on top of my coal heaver and managed to place one knee on his throat in an effort to subdue him. At this point a passing woman set about me with her folded umbrella, screaming, 'Leave that poor man alone.' An angry 'King Kong' was one thing but an elderly lady with an umbrella was too much for one night. Thankfully, the 'cavalry' arrived in the nick of time and I lived to tell the tale. By coincidence, a close friend of mine was standing on the other side of Morrison Street waiting for a bus and recognised me as we entered Bissett's. He later described the scene of seconds later: 'It was like a scene from a wild-west movie when you and the coalman crashed out through the glass door and rolled onto the pavement. I wished I had a camera.' At that same second in time, I wanted my Mam!

On one occasion Peter and I were doing a watch inside a pub at Oxgangs, looking for a man who was alleged to be illegally collecting bets in the public bar each Saturday. We dressed up in dirty old overalls, with muck on our faces and hands and went into the pub to quietly have a pint on expenses while we kept watch. Not bad having a pint on the chief constable. Anyway, we sat there making a couple of pints last a long time when we were approached by another drinker who said, 'Hi polis, just having a quiet pint?' Our cover was blown – a quick, red-faced exit.

We were watching a licensed club in Slateford one day, as a result of complaints of out-of-hours illegal drinking. We had the use of a laundry van from a helpful member of the public, who was also a special constable, and were sitting observing the club when a lady approached and handed me a bag of laundry. All we could do was note her name and address and later pass the laundry to the owner of the company. Our cover as laundrymen was apparently better than at the Oxgangs pub and remained intact.

From time to time, after newspaper and other complaints about a certain house in Danube Street that was being used as a brothel, we would stage a fairly extensive watch on the house concerned. This would entail two or more unmarked police cars parked in the surrounding area, while an observation post – the trusty laundry van – would be parked close to the alleged brothel. A driver transported Peter and me to the locus, locked the van and left us hidden in the back with only a peephole at the front and rear providing a view of the premises. A very necessary bucket (for our 'comfort breaks'), a thermos flask and some sandwiches sustained us for several hours.

It all sounds a bit silly now but, to avoid the press listening to our messages on the police radio, we used 'walkie-talkie' sets to communicate with others on the watch, and to further ensure the security of our messages, we invented names for the various participants – the female brothel-keeper was the 'Queen Bee', the 'drones' were the clients etc. – you get the picture? It was, of course, necessary to identify the 'drones' and interview them at a later date, so each was followed home by one of the waiting cars and the address quietly noted. I remember calling at the home of one of them some weeks after the watch and suggesting to the male that we should interview him privately. 'Not at all,' said his wife, adopting a high-handed attitude. 'We have no secrets.' The woman's face was a picture when we explained to her husband that we had seen him visit the brothel on the date in question.

When enough evidence of activity in the brothel was obtained, we'd apply to the sheriff court for a warrant to enter the premises, always on a busy Friday or Saturday. (Some, including the brothel-keeper, assured us that their busiest time was during the week of the General Assembly of the Church of Scotland, but I would not know about that) On one watch, prior to one of many raids that were made on the premises, we witnessed more than a dozen Chinese seamen enter the brothel together and leave only minutes later. On the night of the raid, I mentioned this to the girl I was interviewing and she said, 'Yes, I remember there were only three girls on that night and we each serviced four Chinese. Mass-produced sexual intercourse.

The raids were to some extent light relief and the looks of surprise on the faces of the men literally 'caught with their trousers down' as we burst into the bedrooms were a picture. We were welcomed politely by the charming brothel-keeper who would advise all the girls to, 'Be honest and tell the truth to the lovely gentlemen – I will be pleading guilty as always.' She was a remarkable woman, with numerous convictions in respect to the brothel. She swore that she waited until she knew that a certain sheriff was on the bench before pleading guilty, in the belief that he would be 'sympathetic' and lenient. Her husband was a timid wee man who appeared to be the tea-maker.

I recall on one raid of the brothel we were confronted by a young girl who went into hysterics when interviewed. Apparently, she was saving up for her forthcoming wedding and was petrified her husband-to-be would learn of her 'dark' secret. She was assured it was safe with us. Often, after a raid, the parting quip from our friendly brothel-keeper was, 'There's a free invitation for all you gentlemen to return for services from my girls when you're off duty.' She was some lady.

Raids on licensed clubs was another common occurrence, due mainly to the fact that pubs and hotel bars closed at 10 o'clock in those days, and licensed clubs were the only place where a 'late drink' could be obtained. Noise in the early hours of the morning as the late-night revellers left the club would often result in complaints from neighbours. Some clubs were seriously badly run and, to emphasize this point, I recall raiding one of them – let's call it the Bakers' Club to safeguard the guilty. When we rounded up the considerable number of drinkers, not one single person in the club that night was an actual member.

Peter and I were given the task of obtaining evidence on two shops in Edinburgh suspected of selling pornographic photos and films (before the days of sex shops). Peter expressed the view that he was not sure about his acting skills, so the task fell to me to visit one of the shops, while he remained nearby in case I got into difficulty. I am blessed (or otherwise) with the remnants of a Morayshire accent and, since I was brought up in a farming community, I felt I could get away with the guise of being an agricultural machinery salesman visiting Edinburgh for the day. I boldly entered the first shop. My 'story' was accepted and, after numerous questions, I was given a piece of paper with a code number and advised to call at another address (the other suspect shop). The shopkeeper said to me, 'I have to be very careful you understand because, for all I knew, you might have been a cop when you walked in here.' I managed to retain my composure without bursting into laughter and replied, 'Me, a policeman? You must be joking.' (Some might agree with that.) I headed off to shop number two where my coded note was accepted. I was asked what I was looking for and said, 'Some sexy photos to show some of my mates in Morayshire.' He took me into the privacy of the rear shop and produced hundreds of very explicit photos, informing me he could also supply reel-to-reel film but only on my next visit. I purchased a selection of the 'worst' photos, for evidential purposes, and left the shop with the promise to return again. I did too.

A warrant to search both shops was obtained and we raided them both simultaneously next day. The shopkeeper in the second shop got the surprise of his life when I appeared with other officers and recovered a huge haul of photos, magazines and films, all of a pornographic nature. He threatened me, 'I'll remember you.' Before we could submit our report to the PF, it was necessary to examine in detail every photo and watch every film, all of which were then labelled as productions for court. Watching one pornographic film after another became very boring and so, to relieve our boredom, the CID photographer played one reel in reverse. This proved to be hilarious – the film was far more entertaining when the sexual act was performed in reverse, ending with the male actor leaping out of bed, putting his trousers on and running backwards out the door. I leave some of the other reverse scenes to your individual imaginations. 'Little things amuse bairns,' as my mother used to say.

The shop owners were charged and fined, and all the material was confiscated by the court. I got a pat on the back from the inspector of the Headquarters' Licensing Department who had instigated the operation. He had thought it would take weeks to 'infiltrate the pornographic net' and I had accomplished it in one day. It was my personal charm of course.

The problem of underage drinking has been with us a long time, although some seem to think this is a recent phenomenon. Considerable effort was expended by divisional plain-clothes officers in trying to stamp this out, with regular visits to all the likely pubs, at weekends in particular. Peter and I became quite expert at identifying underage drinkers simply by surveying the bar or lounge for a moment or two. Likely suspects would then be removed, along with their drinks (evidence), and interrogated in the manager's office or other likely place. Denials from obviously underage boys and girls would be met with the well-rehearsed routine of a warning that, if they were later found to be lying, there would not only be a charge of underage drinking but also the more serious crime of wasting police time. That usually had the desired effect, whereupon the correct age would be blurted out. It was amazing, though, how often a false date of birth which did not tally would be blatantly reeled off.

Invariably we would convey the offenders to their homes (some as young as 13) and explain the circumstances to the parents. Most accepted the situation, but on occasions parents were quite hostile and refused to believe that their 'little angels' had been taking strong drink in a pub – 'How dare you suggest such a thing, Constable? I intend to report you to the chief constable.' There was no point arguing with them.

The renewal of, or application for, firearms certificates was another of our tasks and one which necessitated a visit to the home of the holder/applicant. Some firearm owners were extremely rich people who found it difficult to accept that a 'mere constable' should visit their lordly manors. I recall phoning one, informing him of my identity, whereupon he answered, 'Right, Inspector.' I replied, 'No, I repeat, it's Constable Green.' 'Okay, Inspector.' I eventually called at his home where he continued to address me as Inspector Green despite numerous reminders. Another I visited had recently retired and explained, on my arrival, that he had started doing his own decorating. He insisted on showing me his handiwork, of which he was very proud. To my astonishment, the strips of wallpaper either failed to reach the ceiling or the skirting board in places and, at the corners, he had simply not fitted it properly. There was a wallpaper curve at each corner of the room. It was funny and yet sad.

After close to two years, Peter moved on to become acting sergeant on his previous shift and for a time I worked with a number of temporary colleagues. One was an older officer who I will name only as Norman. This officer had an outrageous sense of humour. He was a 'professional' prankster who would greet every success with a great guffaw of laughter.

One of our less-welcome duties was visits to public conveniences, including the then Caledonian Railway Station, in response to complaints from the public. These complaints always related to blatant homosexual behaviour in public conveniences – men exposing their erect private members to other males, or two males handling each others private members in public. Dealing with the complaints entailed two officers entering a special cubicle with a one-way mirror where the urinal area and water closet doors could be viewed clearly. I hasten to add that this duty was not relished by any officer and could only be undertaken for short time-spans because the behaviour of these men caused mental stress to most officers.

On one occasion, I was on duty in the Caledonian Station cubicle with

Norman, and one man was in and out of the public convenience on numerous occasions during our observations. He was also taking a close interest in other men and exposing himself to them. Most merely ignored him and left the toilet quickly. He eventually entered a water closet. The lookout cubicle we used had access along the back and above most of the water closets. Norman, who always sought to lighten a dark situation, moved along to the rear of the appropriate closet where the suspect was found to be masturbating vigorously, not an offence in itself in private, of course. Norman waited for the 'appropriate second' and flushed the toilet from above. The suspect shot out of the closet like a scalded cat and was not seen again that day in the public convenience. Crime prevention?

I was astonished that the men we arrested for various indecent crimes came from almost every conceivable walk of life, and some were married men with families. But what was most surprising was that the Caledonian Railway Station toilets were known (for all the wrong reasons) throughout the UK, and men travelled considerable distances to make contact with men of a similar mind. It was not rewarding police work, it has to be said. One such arrest by two of my colleagues resulted in the male taking his own life by wading into the sea at Cramond and drowning himself – a very sad outcome.

One very humorous incident occurred one day when I was on late shift. One of the day officers had attended a pub in Morrison Street where a quantity of suspected stolen cigarettes was being sold on cheaply by a customer. The officer learned that all cigarette packets, at that time anyway, had a code on them which could be used to identify exactly where the cigarettes had been distributed to by the manufacturer. The day-shift officer had made 'diligent enquiry' and learned that the local cigarette sales representative was a 'Mr Bloggs' who lived in Currie. He was not at home, so the day-shift officer asked me to phone this gentleman in the evening and invite him to examine the cigarettes at the West End Police Station. I called in the evening and, assuming that the man was who my colleague thought he was, I launched into a spiel, inviting him to the station to examine the cigarettes and the code numbers and identify them for us. 'Fine,' said Mr. Bloggs. 'I will come in right away.' Then, as an afterthought, he added, 'I am delighted to do this officer but why are you asking me? I have nothing to do with the cigarette trade.' Clearly the wrong Mr. Bloggs! I never really understood why he was initially quite prepared to come and look at cigarettes he knew nothing about – nowt as strange as fowk!

I had a series of different partners after Peter moved on. One, in particular, I found difficult to work closely with. We did not see eye to eye on a lot of things but, when I suggested we go 'upstairs' and each ask for a change of partner, he was set against the idea, so I just soldiered on. Unfortunately, the very happy period in plain clothes was to some extent soured by my nephew David's criminal activities at that time. He frequently broke into Mam and Dad's home at Convent Cottages and several times stole items of value, plus cash being saved for holidays or paying bills. It was heartbreaking, and for him to do this to the two people who were so generous to him was unforgivable – although Mam forgave him every time. He was so brazen he would break in one day and call to see them a few days later. On one occasion, I was present when he called. I have to admit I saw red and plastered him.

David extended his housebreaking activities to other houses in the Craiglockhart area, while sleeping rough in the convent outhouses. Eventually there were warrants for his arrest and this seriously embarrassed me as police officer. I called on my chief superintendent and offered my resignation, but he would have none of it. So I took it upon myself to hunt David down in my own time. I called at numerous lodging houses and other likely places but, by sheer coincidence, I jumped onto a bus one evening to find the brave boy sitting upstairs. We were about to leave the bus close to the West End Police Station, when he broke free from me on the bus platform by jumping into the roadway while the bus was travelling quite fast. I failed in my efforts to recapture him that night.

A few weeks later, I went out Christmas shopping on my lunch break, and was in Tollcross when I literally bumped into David. I grabbed him and in doing so dropped my purchases. When I tried to retrieve them, he again broke free, and I pursued him onto a demolition site where some old tenements where being pulled down. He ran up the stairs of one, with me in hot pursuit and I came upon him as he climbed over a partly-demolished wall, three storeys high. I grabbed him by his jacket, and he turned and sank his teeth into my fingers (more permanent scars). He wriggled free of his jacket and dropped the three storeys to the rubble-strewn ground below, and I thought, 'That's the end of him.' Not so! He got to his feet and ran off.

A young schoolboy who had witnessed the chase called to me, intimating he would give chase – and with 'Be careful' ringing in his ears, he was off like a hare. The commotion caused someone to make a 999 call and a police car was on the scene as I emerged from the derelict building. Descriptions of both David and the pursuing schoolboy were transmitted by wireless, and David was arrested soon after near Princes Street. He was given a prison sentence and wrote from his cell threatening my life on his release. All bravado, of course. When he left prison David moved to England and I was finally free from the embarrassment he caused me.

I wrote a report on the actions of the schoolboy. He was called to the chief constable's office with his parents and given a CC's commendation – very well deserved. He was a brave young lad. For my part, I was also given a Chief Constable's Commendation, against my wishes I hasten to add. My chief superintendent called me into his office shortly after the event. He congratulated me and warmly praised my efforts to clear my name. Rumours were gleefully being circulated by some officers, who should have known better, that Ian Green's nephew was wanted on warrant. The super then did something which astonished me. He asked if I had lost some purchases during the incident. I apologised for shopping when on duty, but this was not his point. He wanted to know the value of the goods lost, took the sum from his own wallet and insisted I take it – a real gentleman. Incidentally, he was the spitting image of Harry Worth, the comedian, and that was his nickname.

Towards the end of my three-year stint I was preparing to go on duty one afternoon when I suddenly and unexpectedly collapsed in our lobby. I felt bloody awful and had no option but to go to bed. June reported me sick to the station. I thought I'd be okay after a day in bed but my condition deteriorated overnight and June called our doctor. He took one look at me and called for an ambulance. Apparently I had all the classic symptoms of pneumonia, and my condition worsened in hospital. I spent a couple of days with a very high temperature, hallucinating and drifting in and out of consciousness. A wee nurse on the ward was my saviour, I think. I learned later that she had given me endless bed-baths and watched over me for hours. I was partially conscious one day when a visitor came to my bedside. I overheard a conversation between him (Bob Edwards, I think) and a nurse. I heard the words, 'Yes, Mr Green has been very ill and we nearly lost him.' That shook me, I have to say.

When my time came to move out of the department, it was a big break. I had enjoyed the interesting and varied work with excellent officers who could 'play hard' occasionally but worked hard most of the time. Wonderful three years!

My next move was into the West End Police Station Operations Room as station clerk working under the station sergeant (sometimes referred to as desk or bar sergeant). Work in the ops room entailed controlling the divisional wireless traffic. By that time, we were using personal radios, so there were two transmitters and receivers to control and concentrate on while performing my typing skills honed in Traffic Enquiries and Plain Clothes. The first task at the beginning of each shift was to type out all the crime report forms which had been submitted in writing by beat officers in the preceding eight hours. These were then rushed to headquarters with other divisional mail, where it was sorted and distributed. There were also incoming phone calls from the general public and beat officers, plus a public counter to deal with. Not much time to let moss grow under your feet and, at times, quite stressful because of the various pressures. There was also the divisional driver to help out, but he had various runs to do, so often he was out of the office more than he was in it.

Our driver was George, a larger than life character who had, a few years earlier, volunteered for police duties in Cyprus where he had disarmed a terrorist and earned himself a commendation. In Cyprus all British police volunteers were automatically given the temporary rank of inspector during their attachment, and I think George found it difficult to settle back into uniformed duties in Edinburgh City Police. I often went fishing with him, occasionally to Loch Leven but, if the fish were not 'taking the fly', George would resort to bait (maggots mainly), which was banned on Loch Leven and most other lochs. That did not deter him, of course, and he was an absolute master at hooking trout in this manner, while I sat and fretted in case we got caught. Sadly, George died at an early age.

If the station sergeant had a lot of lockup cases in one night, it would sometimes fall to me to act as bar sergeant, accepting and processing arrests – great experience for the future.

After a period as clerk, I was moved back onto street duties as acting sergeant on my shift. This meant being the No. 1 relief officer on the shift and, when not acting sergeant, I would stand in as divisional driver, clerk and beatman – never the same beat for more than a day. I quite enjoyed the varied work, but the lack of continuity became wearing. About this time, I also had the misfortune to work with one of the most objectionable sergeants I had the misfortune to meet in the police. He was a rude and aggressive man who tried to bully everyone under his control, apart from his 'favourites' which, in my book, made him an even worse sergeant. How on earth this man was promoted (from 'B' to 'C' Division) I simply have no comprehension. We crossed swords immediately because, quite frankly, he was jealous of my divisional departmental experience and my abilities and I despised his bully-boy tactics. He tried at every opportunity to put me down. I learned later that, of all my supervisory officers, he was the only one to submit negative assessments on my work. I have absolutely no doubt this man single-handedly held up my then imminent promotion. I recall an argument I had one day with him but, before it developed too far, I asked, 'Is this a sergeant talking to a constable or are we on a level playing field?' He replied, 'On a level playing field.' But as soon as I began to win the argument, he snarled, 'Listen fella, you are talking to a sergeant and don't you forget it.' So much for the level playing field.

The problem became so bad that I went 'upstairs' and asked to be transferred to another shift to get away from this total idiot. The 'boss' persuaded me that it was not in my best interests to force the issue. He advised me that I was high on the list of promotion candidates and that it would be best not to rock the boat. When I insisted that I could not work with this sergeant, I was advised to talk to my shift inspector. I did so and we reached a compromise. I would move to the Panda cars based at Corstorphine Police Station, which had become operational during my time in plain clothes. I would take over ZHWhisky11 and would continue my acting-sergeant role both at Corstorphine (Third Section) and Oxgangs Police Station (Fourth Section) as required. This meant I was well away from the idiot sergeant who worked out of Torphichen Place. That probably suited us both.

I really enjoyed working on the Pandas and there was a particularly good team spirit at Corstorphine. We had many social nights out and the most amazing Christmas dinners at the station when some of the wives prepared the meal. Oxgangs would cover for us and later we would reciprocate.

There were a couple of officers who thought they were Stirling Moss – Richard and Joe. They drove everywhere fast and furious and, at the drop of a hat, would go flat out in the fairly basic Ford and Morris cars. On one occasion, when I was acting sergeant, I accompanied Joe on a busy Friday night. I told him twice to slow down but to no effect, so when he went through a red traffic signal for no justifiable reason, I told him to stop. I got out of the car and wirelessed for another Panda to pick me up. I never accompanied Joe again.

Richard, who also drove far too fast, could 'talk the hind leg off a donkey', and frequently did so first thing on early shift when we met at the station for cup of tea while receiving instructions and information. I was invariably like a bear with a sore head at 6am, and hated Richard's endless babbling. My requests to 'give it a break' went unheeded until one morning in a worse mood than usual I strode over to him, grabbed him by the uniform lapels and threw him against the wall, where he fell to the floor. Needless to say, I was immediately full of remorse and apologised profusely. He could only mutter, 'You are a bad-tempered bastard, Ian Green.' He was right. We laughed about the incident many times later, and the story travelled around the division on the 'bush telegraph'. Give him his due, Richard was one of the best car-thief spotters I ever met and this gave him a reason to go hell-for-leather in pursuit.

A request then came from Headquarters Licensing Department for me to be detached for a period to help with a watch on an illegal gaming club being operated by the occupier of a house on the south side of Edinburgh. I spent many nights (often freezing or wet) at the top of a ladder in a yard peering, with the aid of binoculars, into the offending house. We could clearly see 'punters' coming and going all night and could identify the occupier taking a share of each kitty (his 'puggy', as it was referred to in gambling circles). All this evidence was recorded carefully and, in due course, a warrant was issued for a raid. The raid was less successful than anticipated. The 'gamblers' insisted that no 'puggy' was taken, and that it was simply a game of cards between friends. Bollocks, of course! The case went to trial and the accused was found not guilty, despite good police evidence, which disappointed everyone because so much effort had been expended on the case. By coincidence, I knew one of the jurors who told me later that the not guilty verdict was far from unanimous, but she said some of the jurors suspected one police officer of lying. Thankfully, she said it was not me.

After the raid and court case, the licensing inspector held on to me at headquarters. He had a high regard for my police work and wanted me in his department permanently, which I would have enjoyed. My chief superintendent at the West End would not hear of it, saying he wanted me back in the division. Nice to be wanted.

I returned to my previous duties in the West End but, after a while, and believing I had been 'passed over', I applied for a vacancy in the Court Department at headquarters. I submitted my application, and next day when I reported for duty at Corstorphine, my new chief superintendent, a decent man and a bloody good copper, was waiting for me.

I was taken to a witness room where the chief super threw down my application and said, 'What is the meaning of this? Why are you applying for a dead-end job?' I impudently shouted back, 'A dead-end job for a dead-end officer.' Well, he blew his top and was heard throughout the station giving me HELL! When he calmed down, he persuaded me to tear up my application and, before he left, he said, 'I know your police record Ian and you are too good an officer to rot away in some department for the rest of your service. I can give no guarantees, but you have my assurance you are at the top of the promotion list. Take my word for that.' I was completely gobsmacked and a bit ashamed.

Some weeks later, I was called into hospital for a minor operation and was off work for a few weeks. Near the end of my sick leave, I was called to the West End Station to see the superintendent who said, 'You are being promoted to sergeant, and the chief superintendent, who is away at the moment, wishes to remind you of the conversation he had with you at Corstorphine. I don't know what he means but you might.' I did though. The super suggested I shave off my beard, which I had grown a couple of years earlier, before I went to see the chief constable. I belligerently said, 'If my promotion is dependent on me taking off my beard, then I don't want the promotion.' I think it could be said that I had become a bit 'bolshie' by that time.

I attended at Chief Constable John R Inch's office in due course and, when my turn came, he asked me if I was confident to take on the rank of sergeant. I replied, 'Yes sir,' whereupon he said, 'Congratulations, Sergeant Green'" As he shook my hand, he added, 'Do you feel comfortable with the beard?' I said, 'I do, sir,' and he commented, 'Yes, it suits you.' He then moved on to the next promotion candidate. On returning to my division, the super quizzed me and was somewhat 'put out' when I repeated the chief constable's conversation. He nevertheless wished me good luck and advised me that I was going to 'B' Division. I was sad to leave 'C' Division because I had felt, on the whole, very comfortable there and had made many good friends. The close contact was about to be broken.

CHAPTER SEVEN

the 'copshop' – promotion

I became Police Sergeant 24-B on 6 May 1975 and reported to Gayfield Square Police Station a few days later to be greeted by Chief Superintendent Alastair Hood. I had huge admiration for him and, by the end of my service, regarded him as one of the best chief superintendents I had worked with. I had known him as a constable in 'C' Division and bumped into him in our police travels over the years. He congratulated me and advised me that he had specially requested my transfer to 'B' Division on my promotion. That was a good start.

I commenced night shift the next day and was shown around the division over the following week. It is quite a step to move from a territory you know like the back of your hand to one less familiar. There is also the problem of getting to know the divisional personnel – their names and numbers, plus some knowledge of each one.

After a period as relief sergeant, during which time I worked on the three sections of the division and also performed the duty of station sergeant from time to time, I began to settle in, and was informed by my shift inspector that I was to take over the Drylaw Mains Section. The shift inspector was not a very inspiring character who was nearing the end of his service. He was not at all keen on making difficult decisions, as I was to discover, and I found him to be a strange man.

On taking over the shift at Drylaw, I quickly realised that there were some excellent officers, but three of them did not impress me at all. The first night on night shift I went on patrol with one of the latter, he immediately 'tested' me. He suggested that we attend a pub at closing time because, according to him, the manager had a problem clearing the customers at the end of permitted hours. I went along with this but, as soon as the last customer had left, the manager asked the constable if he would have his 'usual'. 'And what would the sergeant like?' I said, 'Thank you, but we don't drink on duty.' This was more to make the point to the constable than to the manager. I could see that he was not happy with this start under the new sergeant.

Within a few night shifts, I began to see a pattern emerging relative to certain officers who often seemed to 'disappear' during week nights. When I made a rendezvous these officers would appear from an identifiable location. I came to the conclusion that there was a 'drinking-on-duty culture' on my shift at Drylaw. During a briefing one night, I made it clear that drinking and driving police cars did not mix. I also made my position clear – I would not tolerate this. I could feel the hostility from some officers, but emphasised that the next instance of drinking on duty would be reported to the shift inspector. A couple of the good officers came to me quietly, saying that it was about time someone dealt with the drinking problem at Drylaw.

Some weeks later, one of the suspect officers arrived at the station for his refreshments. I could clearly see that he had been drinking and, at one point, he almost fell over a chair. I quietly left, drove to Gayfield Square Police Station, and reported my concerns and suspicions to the shift inspector. Back at Drylaw, the shift inspector interviewed the constable privately and then, to my astonishment, he said that he did not think the constable was bad enough for a doctor's examination and that he was taking no action against him, apart from giving him a verbal warning. He also instructed me to ensure that the officer did not drive again that night, which was a bit of a contradiction. I appealed to the inspector that an example had to be made if I was to deal with the drinking culture at Drylaw. Close to his retirement date, he clearly did not have the stomach for such action. While he was pleased with my efforts to stamp out the drinking, he said that he would back me no further. I was dismayed. However, the officer concerned was moved out of Drylaw shortly after and returned to normal beat duties.

I was even more dismayed when, a few months later, the same inspector called me in for assessment and again praised me for the way I was handling the drink problem at Drylaw. He then explained that he was planning to move me back 'up town' to sort out the same problem on the First Section. I complained that this was quite unfair on me, but the man clearly considered it okay for me to do what he could not, i.e. his dirty work. I felt quite disgusted and went away to consider my next step.

West Pilton and Drylaw housing estates really were the 'wild west' in those days, and every day produced some unusual incidents. Like the pub that was raided one day when two men entered the bar, jumped over the counter and stole the till and contents. The till was replaced, but the next day at almost the same time the same two guys (it was reported) returned and did exactly the same thing again.

The pub in Pennywell Road was visited one Saturday by a gang of hoodlums bearing a grudge. With pick shafts, they systematically smashed every bottle and glass in the bar. The manager and staff wisely locked themselves in the office until the culprits had left. When they emerged, they found the bar swimming in alcohol and littered with broken glass. In the meantime, some locals seated around a table in the corner continued to have 'a quiet drink' in the middle of the mayhem. When interviewed by the police, the group, who presumably wanted no involvement, declared innocently, 'What disturbance officer? We never heard a thing.' Astonishing.

The area was so full of criminals and people who had no love for the police that many calls had to have two cars in attendance. The occupants of one would deal with the call, while the other car remained on guard to avoid vandalism of the police car. Panda cars were on occasions scratched, mirrors broken and, on one occasion, the car was overturned. Witnesses to such vandalism were of course nonexistent.

One bizarre incident, which immediately became a banned subject, occurred one night in a crematorium. A bunch of 'animals' (which is an insult to all creatures) broke into the crematorium and forced open a number of coffins awaiting cremation, removed the bodies and placed them in the pulpit, at the organ and in a pew. What kind of human beings could do this as a prank? It was certainly a sick joke. A decision was taken to cover up the incident for the sake of the relatives of the deceased. It was also a common occurrence for one very old graveyard to be visited by criminals who dug up graves or broke into tombs and stole the jewellery often worn by the deceased when interred. Some people in this world simply have no conscience.

Some officers relished the challenge of working in such a violent environment as West Pilton and Pennywell and doing what can only be described as patch-up work to the many problems. I personally found it a totally depressing area with very little job satisfaction. My dilemma of being 'used' by my shift inspector was resolved when the chief super called me in to Gayfield Square and invited me to take over the duties of divisional training sergeant. This was a new challenge for me and provided the opportunity to be free from a very weak shift inspector for whom I had lost all respect. I accepted.

I commenced the following day and worked with the retiring training sergeant for a couple of days. Then I was on my own. There were few lecture aids and no lecture notes left by the previous training sergeant, so I virtually started from scratch, preparing overhead slides and lecture notes for myself. I also undertook a refresher course at home, studying criminal and statutory law, to get myself up to speed on these subjects. I had a working knowledge, of course, but inadequate for answering questions from bright young probationary cops. One especially good aspect about my new position was that it entailed a five-day week, with every weekend and public holiday off – a bit more normal than shifts which I always found difficult.

One weekend, June and I attended a party with very good friends Liz and Maggie Cruickshank. On the way home, with Liz in the back seat, we came across an incident in Slateford Road, near Ashley Terrace. A young lad was walking along the pavement quietly eating a bag of chips when he was set upon by a passing gang of youths who gave him a real going over with fists and boots. I stopped the car, and the assailants ran off. I shouted to the lad that I was an off-duty police officer and asked him to wait for my return. I drove quickly into the Wardlaw area to see the assailants walking along, bawling and shouting. I pulled in, instructed Liz to find a phone quickly and dial 999 while June and myself quietly approached the youths from behind. I then spread my arms and pushed the gang into a shop doorway. One with long hair immediately escaped from under my arms but June's 'dander' was up and she bravely grabbed his long hair and, as he struggled, she wrapped it around a street railing and hung on for dear life. While I wrestled with the other three in the doorway, their parents appeared from nearby and made threatening gestures towards June and me. I think another youth had run off and alerted them. I roared out several times that I was a police officer and if anyone interfered they would also be arrested – who was I kidding? It was beginning to look dangerous when a police van roared round the corner with reinforcements – the 'cavalry' saved the day again and probably our hides.

When we went back for the assaulted lad, he had gone, but the four youths were locked up for assaulting an unknown man, breach of the peace and resisting arrest. They all pled guilty at the court in the morning and were fined. I did what a police officer is expected to do, but June, especially, and Liz acted superbly under pressure. Sadly, Liz died prematurely a few years later. June sustained injury to one hand and subsequently was awarded criminal injuries compensation. She has trouble with one of her fingers to this day.

As training sergeant I worked closely with the chief superintendent, reporting to him regularly, and had also to liaise closely with shift inspectors regarding the progress, or otherwise, of their probationers. It was very rewarding work. I pushed the young officers hard with their weekly study and examinations, not for any personal pleasure, but because it was in their best interests when they sat their final examinations. It gave me great satisfaction, therefore, when a young struggling constable benefited from my 'encouragement' and finally made the grade. Some officers came back to me after they were confirmed and thanked me personally, but some did not approve of my insistence on 100 per cent effort. I was passing the officers' locker room one day after training classes when I heard one who always needed extra persuasion say, 'He's like Attila the Hun, that bastard.' He was referring to me. I popped my head round the door and said, 'See you next week Constable' His face was a picture. The same lad later wrote a very funny song about me which was performed in the Police Folk Club.

Training consisted of the young officers being allocated weekly study and, the following week, sitting an exam on the subject. The papers were marked by me, and at the next class the subject was dealt with in depth and misunderstandings cleared up. Much of the other training included practical exercises on dealing with road accidents, shoplifting cases, drunk driving and other day-to-day police work. An end-of-term exam was held which included questions on most of the subjects covered during the past term. Thereafter, each officer was seen by me, made aware of his exam results and assessed. My overall assessment of each young officer was passed to the chief superintendent and the shift inspectors. Officers who achieved poor end-of-term results quite often also received poor assessments. They would be seen by the shift inspector concerned and possibly the chief superintendent. I regret that, on occasions, I would be requested to give a final overall assessment on an individual officer's ability to make the grade as a police officer, and sometimes the answer simply was in the negative. I felt sorry to see such lads leave the service, but invariably they had been given numerous warnings from all concerned and failed to buck up their ideas, so were unlikely to be a great asset to the force.

There were no training classes during the summer because of annual leave, giving me an opportunity to improve my selection of training aids and plan for the next term. One summer I was seconded to Headquarters Recruiting and Training Department to help out at a time when recruitment was at a high level. I enjoyed the work there and learned additional training techniques but, by then, HQ had moved to a new custom-built building at Fettes Avenue where there was just too much 'top brass' around for my liking. I was quite happy to return to divisional training after a few months. By this time, Edinburgh City Police was no more, having been swallowed up by Lothian and Borders Police on 16 May 1975 in the name of reorganisation.

The following summer I attended a course for divisional training sergeants from the various Scottish forces at Tulliallan Police College. This was my first visit to the college as a student. The training was absolutely first class and did a power of good for my techniques. The use of various pieces of training equipment was dealt with in detail, and the art of speaking to a class was a particular focus. All training sergeants had to first undertake a short talk on a subject of their choice, with no time to prepare, and to speak non-stop for three minutes. Next, each student had to undertake the preparation and delivery of a 20 minute talk, also on a subject of their own choice. Finally, a subject decided by the training team had to be researched over a number of evenings and presented as a 40 minute lecture in front of not only the other students, as was the case with all the talks, but also in the presence of the training team. One female police sergeant got up to deliver her first talk and froze – unable to utter a word. After some guidance and help from the training team, she was later able to complete the talks and the course.

One funny incident occurred when I was doing my 40 minute lecture. I was working at the blackboard and, as a smart-ass aside, I said, 'Using all the police college training techniques, I will illustrate this by use of the blackboard'. The voice of the chief training instructor quietly came from the back of the room, 'Well don't face the blackboard when you're talking.' Spot on, of course, and it stopped me from making any further 'clever' remarks.

I considered that I had done well on the course and I'd enjoyed the good company of fellow course members and staff. When I got back to 'B' Division, my report eventually arrived from Tulliallan. The chief super said it was 'excellent', although it commenced with the words, 'Sergeant Green is a bearded officer.' Oh, the powers of observation of high-ranking officers. It was then back into the heavy weekly training schedule, taking full advantage of my Tulliallan techniques, a more confident and able training sergeant.

In the meantime my brother Jimmy had married Anne McLennan at one of the best weddings I have ever attended. It was held in Bridge of Orchy where Anne's parents lived and, after a meal in a hotel, we all moved to the community hall where the most amazing ceilidh developed (but not before the locals went home, changed into working togs and did the milking). The ceilidh went on until the small hours and then the Edinburgh party had to be 'poured' into the bus for the journey home. I was best man and did my 'master of ceremonies' at the ceilidh, but I was a pretty sorry sight by the time we reached Edinburgh. Yes, a few 'drammies' were taken that day.

Jimmy and Anne, after some few years in Edinburgh, decided to make a new start in South Africa where joiners were welcomed with open arms on the gold mines near Johannesburg. Mam, Dad and Elizabeth were invited out for a holiday the first year after they settled in, and then June and I were invited to visit. This meant saving up some annual leave to make a total of 28 days, but first we had to find some money to fund this expensive holiday – we were still living a hand-to-mouth existence. June suggested that we get a stall at Ingliston Sunday Market and, because I was off at weekends, this was doable. I was by then buying albums of folk music and selling them on at the Police Folk Club and festivals, so it made sense to extend the range to cover jazz, blues, country and western, rock and pop music.

The first week, we obtained a stall by queuing at Ingliston from 6am. We covered our costs and made a couple of pounds profit but, as week followed week, we increased stock, made some good buys of pop stuff and started to make better money. Close to Christmas, we turned over a thousand pounds one Sunday. The soundtrack of 'Grease' was all the rage at the time and I took a big chance by ordering a hundred 'Grease' LPs at a good price. June had a quick look round the market. We pitched our price just below other record traders and sold out. It was a long stand on cold days but there were many laughs to be had. I kept my identity secret because there were some 'dodgy' traders, such as the one who offered June a beautiful pair of leather shoes at a giveaway price, saying, 'They fell off the back of a lorry.' Wink, wink. I had also to keep an eye out for off-duty police officers because a second job or running a business was not permitted in the police. Every time I saw a police colleague shopping in the market, I had to 'duck out'. I really thought I had got away with it until much later when I was having my final interview at the end of my service. The chief super winked and said, 'I suppose you will be continuing with your stall at Ingliston?'

While June and I were planning our holiday to South Africa, Dad went into hospital where he had a cancerous kidney removed. I spoke to the hospital consultant who gave me the shock news that the cancer was aggressive and would return. He gave Dad about a year. I asked him if Dad knew. He confirmed that it had been fully explained to him, but that the family should leave it to Dad to decide whether he wished to discuss the matter with us. He never did and was to die almost a year later. The family agreed that Mam should not be told of Dad's true illness because we felt it was too much for her to cope with. I believe that not discussing it with Dad and failing to be honest with Mam are two of the most stupid decisions I made in my entire life. When she learned of his illness some months later from the family doctor, who unwittingly blurted it out, I rightly got hell from Mam, but you could immediately see her preparing herself for what was to come. She proved to be an absolute pillar of strength, nursing him day and night as his condition deteriorated. She was super. The lesson I learned is never to underestimate the inner strength of anyone.

For my part, I hadn't a bloody clue how to deal with Dad's illness (which I wasn't supposed to know about). I think I stuck my head in the sand. We carried on a charade, pretending all was fine, when both he and I knew it was not. I visited him almost every evening, but found myself standing at the door of the house attempting to compose myself before I could go in and 'play out the game'. At first, I always made sure there was a bottle of whisky in the house and we'd have a dram together, but latterly whisky made him sick (the cancer had spread to his bowels and elsewhere by then). So all I could do was pick up this skeleton in my arms and carry him to the living room for an hour or so, and then carry him back to his bed before I went home. He was, of course, a tough old bugger and did not go quickly, which would probably have been a blessing. So we had to watch him die slowly. I cried a lot. He died on a Saturday morning when there were several visitors in the house. Dad was unconscious and, to relieve the mounting tension, I took the males to a nearby pub for drink. We were gone only a wee while but, in that period, he died.

It was just so sad that he died without a chance to say the many things that remained unsaid. Given a second chance, I would have taken my courage in both hands, disregarded the consultant and discussed Dad's illness with him – and hopefully removed the barriers that the silence created. Saying nothing really wasn't an option. Life has to go on, though. Dad got a big sendoff from a huge turnout at the crematorium and we then each had to come to terms with our loss in our own ways. Dad's death seemed to sap the strength from Mam and she suffered greatly, never really getting over the loss. As she saw it, her whole purpose in life was gone and, although she outlived him by seven years, she was an unhappy soul.

Eddie McLennan, June's Dad, died next. June and I had had all the responsibility of his failing health and worsening dementia. June's sister Betty lived near London, and her brother John lived in Australia, so we bore the brunt of it. It was the same with my own parents, of course, because Elizabeth lived in Lancashire and Jimmy was in South Africa. Funny how often the responsibility falls to one couple. It meant a hell of a lot of running about for June and me and, while we did it willingly, the stress was considerable.

Some of the responsibility was removed when Eddie was finally admitted to an old folk's home. He was a pathetic soul by then and, on a visit, it was not uncommon for him to ask me many times, 'What shift are you on today, Ian?' Eddie had driven buses for the SMT for many years and, latterly, was a tour driver with the company and hugely popular with the tourists. He was a strange man. I never achieved a close relationship with him, although when I could not afford to go to the pub, he often dragged me along for company. I was also able to borrow his car on frequent occasions and, in repayment, I did most of the car maintenance. He was an overgenerous man. Some took advantage of this in his latter years and as a result he died almost penniless. I wound up Eddie's estate on behalf of the family. The two deaths coming so close together brought much sadness.

For years after Dad's death, I had a recurring dream in which I would meet him and say, 'But Dad, you died.' He would reply, 'No, son. I recovered from the cancer.' It was frighteningly realistic and, after a while, I chatted about it to my doctor who said this was not uncommon when suffering a great loss and advised that it would gradually recede. It did but occasionally the dream recurs to this day.

By this time, we had outgrown our house at Whitson Road but were no better placed financially to buy our own home, so we arranged an exchange and moved to 3 Morven Street in Clermiston. It was a big break to leave Whitson because we'd had many happy years there and the best of neighbours. But the new house had three bedrooms – ideal for our family needs – and it was built in post-war years so it was quite modern and on two levels.

Around this time June and I enjoyed many family camping holidays, especially in Devon and Cornwall, where we often met up with June's sister and her husband and their three bairns. We had some great times together and the weather was usually excellent. One quite strange incident occurred on one trip south. I'd bought an old Hillman Minx from a colleague and we set off for Devon one Friday in this old banger. When we were near Lancaster, the engine started overheating. We pulled into a garage where the mechanic looked at the thermostat, said it was faulty and promptly threw it away. On the road, and again the engine boiled up. We drove into Lancaster where the Hillman agent refused to look at the car – bastard. We then stopped at a Ford garage where the foreman mechanic was a really nice man. He offered to look at the car on Saturday morning, his day off, suspecting we had a burst cylinder-head gasket.

We took some spare clothes from the car and headed out into Lancaster. June then had a brilliant idea. She knew friends of her Dad – Mr and Mrs Powley – who lived in Lancaster, so we visited the local police station to see if they could trace the family. You have to understand, as always in those days, our holiday was on a shoestring budget and we had no money to pay for bed and breakfast for five. That would have ended the holiday there and then. The police came up blank, and by now the three young 'Greenies' were crying and June was getting in a state. We left the police station and were aimlessly walking along, devoid of ideas when, believe it or not, who should June spot coming towards us but Mrs Powley. For some reason, she had not taken her usual route home that Friday. We explained our predicament and were invited home to have a cup of tea and talk things over. Later we were invited to stay the night and, in the morning, Mr Powley accompanied me to the Ford garage where the foreman told me that he'd removed the cylinder head but the gasket was intact. A test then showed that the radiator was blocked solid and he had fitted a new one. He generously said there would be no charge for the cylinder-head gasket because it had been a wrong diagnosis, but there would be a fairly hefty charge for the new radiator and labour. That effectively meant the holiday was over, when in stepped the wonderful Mr Powley who said that he'd pay the garage and we should have our holiday – we could pay him back later. All was saved and we had a great holiday with the Stewart family.

What kind, generous people Mr and Mrs Powley were, the salt of the earth really, who I did not know at all and June knew only slightly. In due course we repaid our debt to them and, when they later visited Edinburgh, we invited them out for a 'thank-you' dinner. I also wrote a letter to the Ford garage, thanking the foreman for his generous assistance.

Accidents involving Andrew and Stephen were commonplace on holiday – one year Stephen was treated twice at Raigmore Hospital in Inverness and, on another occasion, Andrew was hurt on rocks in Devon. Returning to the car for the first-aid kit, Stephen slammed the boot lid down on June's finger, whereupon he fainted. Fun and games.

As they were growing up, I was seeing signs of both Andrew and Stephen getting out of hand, and I don't think this was helped by June who was covering up for some of their escapades when I was at work. She felt that I was too hard on them but, in retrospect we probably let them off with too much, in the name of being enlightened parents. Both of them were later to have skirmishes with the police, and again I was shamed by family members. This sort of gossip travels like wildfire in the police. In complete contrast to the boys, Linda was a joy to bring up and we never had any bother with her at all.

This was a very difficult period for June and me, and our marriage hit a rocky patch. We had got into debt when we were at Whitson Road some years earlier, but found our way through that problem. This time it was not just due to the stress surrounding the boys, which was considerable, but we seemed to be drifting apart for other less identifiable reasons. We must have had a strong bond though, and we survived the bad patch and came out the other side much stronger I believe. By all accounts, most marriages have their ups and downs, so I suppose we were no different in many respects. I tried to keep it from Linda and the boys but, later in life, I learned that they were more aware of the squabbles than I realised at the time – and the scars remain.

Andrew was no scholar, leaving school at the earliest opportunity. He went into the food-retail trade and seemed to be continually on the move. Stephen, on the other hand, had great prospects of going on to university, according to his house master, but refused to take advice from the school or us. He left school and joined the civil service which he very quickly grew to hate, mainly I think because he was unwilling to comply with their standards in dress etc. He had proved himself at school to have a real talent for rugby but threw that away also.

We subsequently earned enough from our sideline at Ingliston to pay for our visit to South Africa, which we arranged to coincide with the summer training break. We had never before been on a foreign holiday. By this time, our family were all working. We threw away the chip pan to avoid fire risk, and the two boys were given a stern lecture about behaviour – there were to be no house parties and Linda was left in charge. It made no difference in the end because the boys did have parties and led Linda a merry dance, which appalled me when I eventually got to the truth a long time after.

Our holiday in South Africa was amazing and I must say that Jimmy and Anne went out of their way to make it good for us. They lived in Springs near Johannesburg. We had a week in Durban and a few days in the Kruger Game Park. We saw many animals and it was a super experience, but the trip to Kruger had to be cut short due to Mam taking ill while on an extended holiday with Jimmy and Anne. At that point in her life, she was suffering badly from chronic bronchitis and was being prescribed all sorts of medication and breathing aids.

South Africa is a beautiful country, spoiled at that time by apartheid. I was continually saddened by what I saw and heard. Jimmy and his circle of friends, in all other respects lovely people, were just so racist. I also made a visit to a local police station to obtain a police cap for a colleague collector back home. There was no invite to come in and see round the station, as we would certainly have done in Scotland, and I found the police to be quite unfriendly. When I tried to compare notes with them on police work, they clammed up, and I was more or less asked to leave.

There was disgusting segregation on the Durban beaches, on the trains and buses, and even in shops. I tried to buck the system at the liquor store by going in the 'coloureds only' door, only to be refused service by the coloured assistant. He insisted that I go in the 'whites only' door and, when I agreed, the same assistant served me. I cannot think of anything so bloody ridiculous as 'white man' laws.

On my second day in Durban, I had my beard shaved off (by a barber originally from Balerno) and when I returned to duty, Chief Superintendent Hood actually congratulated me and informed me he did not approve of beards in the police service. I had never been aware of that and it made me think. Here was a man who had requested that I should be promoted to 'B' Division, and had then given me the position of training sergeant while all the time hating my beard.

Not long after my return to duty I was advised my term as training sergeant was coming to an end and was asked to train up my replacement over a period of weeks. When he felt ready to go it alone, I moved onto a shift where I was to take up the role of relief sergeant and acting inspector under one of the early female police inspectors. There was some resistance towards her from the older officers on the shift, but it seemed inevitable that that was how things were developing, and I settled down to working closely with her. I found her to be a good inspector – a lovely person, who developed a close relationship with her sergeants, in particular, and soon gained the respect of all. I enjoyed my period under her command and quickly settled into the new role.

It was while I was acting inspector that I received my first and only official caution. A photocopier had been installed for a trial period at Gayfield Square Police Station. On night shift, the inspector or acting inspector was given the key for that room, and photocopies could only be made under his supervision. One night, I made use of the photocopier for my own purposes and, bugger me, if I did not jam paper inside. I could not clear it and had to leave a note for the administration clerk the following morning, in which I said I had jammed the machine while doing some copies for my own use. I also said I would be happy to pay any costs for an engineer to clear the jam.

I went home thinking all would be well but, in the afternoon, I received a phone call to report to Gayfield Square Police Station to meet with Chief Superintendent Hood. It became clear the administration clerk, in an attempt to cover for me, had not reported my note of explanation, and it was only when the engineer handed the boss the offending (jammed) document that he realised immediately who the 'culprit' was. I was asked if I had used the photocopier for my own purposes and, in doing so, had jammed it. I confessed, explaining I had left a note for the admin clerk, taking full responsibility and offering to pay the engineer's costs. Both the chief super and super looked at each other, somewhat surprised, and Alasdair Hood said, 'You should not have been using the photocopier for your own purposes, but your honest admission of guilt is exactly what I expected from an officer of your calibre, Sergeant Green. You are being given a verbal warning on this occasion.' It was a caution, but with a wee word of praise. The story went around the division and then the other divisions like wildfire, and I was continually met with: 'Who broke the nice new photocopier then?' Very embarrassing and, to this day, I am still reminded about this incident when I meet other retired officers.

The photocopier incident did not have any serious effect on my career because, a few months after my caution, I was promoted to inspector – on 16 March 1983. I was very proud of this promotion because, on joining the police, I'd really had no such expectations or ambitions. Time moves on though and it was a quite different and more assured Ian Green who walked out for the first time, with the braided cap and two pips on each shoulder, from the somewhat unsure recruit of years gone by. I made one promise to myself. I would deal with my subordinate colleagues in a fair and decent manner at all times.

What was the first obvious difference as an inspector? Well, I was no longer 'one of the boys', certainly not with the constables, but neither with the sergeants and it was strange to have your refreshments in splendid isolation, being addressed as 'Sir' and saluted at. It was a solitary life, especially on night shift, when there were no other senior officers on duty and I was in sole charge of the division. 'The buck stops here' took on a new significance.

I consider I achieved a good balance as an inspector, but at times my patience was tested – there is always an officer who wants to push you to the limit. One such officer worked on a beat in Stockbridge and had been there for far too many years. He had developed some really bad habits, but also thought he was untouchable. I changed that when I moved him from Stockbridge to another beat where there was less chance of him 'living off' the misplaced generosity of local business people. He was not pleased, but the point was made. One sergeant remarked that the move was long overdue.

On 19 June 1982, Linda (Green) married David Brown (providing excellent joke material for the reception). David was a smart young soldier serving in the Royal Highland Fusiliers and was a member of the military band, playing coronet. He was highly regarded as a musician and was sent on advanced music courses from time to time. David was married in full military dress uniform. They made a colourful couple on the wedding day, at which a police colleague, Duncan Smith, a piper in the Lothian and Borders Police Pipe Band, played the guests in and out of church. It was a lovely, happy day. I booked a ceilidh band for the reception which went down a storm once everyone got into the swing of it. It was just so much better than the more usual excessively loud, crass wedding disco which I absolutely loath.

The only thing to cloud the wedding day was a CID enquiry into money removed by some unknown person from the safe of the shop Andrew was managing. No charges were made against any person, but this incident, coming almost on the eve of the wedding, did cause upset and embarrassment.

The marriages of both Andrew and Stephen were less memorable for a number of reasons which are best left unsaid, but suffice to say that neither lasted and each ended in divorce. Fortunately, Stephen had no children, but Andrew had two (Lyndsey and Craig) which, as always, created difficulties for the children and caused much stress for June and myself.

I next found myself in the embarrassing situation of having one of Andrew's close pals of that time, Gavin, attached to my shift. I got the impression that he was going to continue to treat me as a family friend and had to call him in and explain we were now on a different footing. He would be treated fairly, but the same as all other officers on the shift. Unfortunately, I had to speak to him again when he let me down when working with another shift inspector on the Saturday Princess Street 'shoplifting' patrol. I bawled him out and, while he stood there and took it, I suspect he'd expected more lenient treatment from his 'best friend's father'.

I did score a few 'brownie points' one very stormy, wet night when I gave the sergeants instructions to bring all the men into the station in relays and let them dry out at intervals throughout the night. This would have been frowned upon a few years earlier. I also insisted we have a Christmas dinner on night shift – good for bonding I thought. I was very fortunate to have good sergeants, and a happy shift was developing.

However, I had a serious disagreement with both the CID and the Procurator's Fiscal on one occasion. We all attended the scene of a death where a woman had fallen three storeys into the tenement back green. There was a history of violence against the woman by her son who lived with her and neighbours described regular disturbances, usually when the son returned home drunk at night. The woman had complained to some of her neighbours about his violence and bruises were common. On the night of the woman's death, there had been yet another disturbance in the house, with shouts, screams and thuds, followed by total silence. The body was found later in the garden. Naturally, there were no eyewitnesses, but sufficient circumstantial evidence existed, in my opinion, to charge the son and let the court decide. The woman was elderly, and to have climbed onto the window ledge and jumped out of her own accord, as was suggested by the CID, was quite ridiculous. I tried to persuade both the CID officer in charge and the PF that this was not an accidental death, but to no avail. I was not happy with the situation and submitted a full report of the circumstances and my own suspicions to the chief superintendent, which was in turn passed to the chief constable. I received a reply to the effect that my report was on file, but the decision of the PF was final in this case. It left a bad taste in my mouth.

The miners' strike of 1984 was a very sad event. Bilston Glen was the focus of their resistance in the Lothians, and I spent many days there on the picket lines where hundreds (sometimes it seemed thousands) of miners demonstrated. It was a strange situation, with the miners almost face to face with the police. Friendly conversations developed between individual miners and police officers and frequently there was quite humorous banter from both sides. Every so often, one of the strike leaders, usually from a position at the rear, would raise the ante and all hell would break loose on the lines. Aggression would erupt into violence as the miners tried to break our lines and enter the colliery, but the lines invariably held. One day, some miners stoned their own canteen, which was close to the road, and every window was smashed. We were advised by the senior police officer to ignore this vandalism and allow them to vent their anger on the building. Not sure I agreed with that. On another occasion, some miners managed to breach the colliery fence and a party of police officers, including myself, were fed into the colliery to drive out the intruders. An organised baton charge was enough to see them off, but bloody noses and other cuts and bruises were inflicted on both sides.

It was frequently commented upon by police officers that the press and other media always ensured their own safety by maintaining a position behind the police lines. I didn't blame them really because there were many nasty moments. It was a long, unpleasant struggle, and I for one was pleased when it was over. I can honestly say that I never saw an officer behave unlawfully or use excessive force in all the time I spent at Bilston Glen. A whole book could be written on the event, taking into account the efforts of miners from other areas (including England) to reach the colliery and back up their colleagues – usually foiled by police tactics resulting from good information.

Demonstration marches were a regular interruption to normal policing. They were invariably held on Princes Street, the best 'stage' in Scotland. Usually these went off without any trouble, and the police would escort the march throughout. On occasions, I saw someone I knew from the folk-music scene taking part and would have a chat. It relieved tensions between the police and marchers. I never felt it was 'us against them' anyway. I was all for 'saving the whale' and supported other causes. One regular marcher was a friend, Christine Kydd, and a couple of times I walked alongside her during the march, chatting. However, on one march Christine quietly said to me, 'Ian, you are a good friend, but please don't talk to me when I am on a march. I'm losing my street credibility.' This had never occurred to me.

One day I was in charge at an Orange Lodge demonstration at The

Mound and had police officers ringing the moderate gathering. This was to prevent the 'opposition' from getting at the throats of the Orangemen. As I walked round the outside of the fairly well behaved crowd, I spotted the late great folksinger Danny Kyle standing nearby observing proceedings. He had not noticed me, so I briefed a constable and without warning we grabbed him by either arm, lifted him off his feet and bundled him into the nearby police box. We then had a good laugh and Danny recounted the story many times afterwards.

Another incident involving Danny occurred when I was on night shift at Gayfield Square Police Station. A call came to me from the station sergeant at Braid Place Police Station where one, Danny Kyle, was 'locked up' and pleading to speak to me. Apparently a 999 call had been received from a resident in a south-side street concerning a man acting suspiciously, going from door to door on both sides of the street. The police arrived and arrested Danny who explained he'd been invited to a party and could not remember the number of the common stair, although he knew the surname of the occupant. The police were fairly sure his story was genuine, but wanted confirmation that I knew Danny and could vouch for him before release. For sheer devilment, I asked the station sergeant to hold him for another hour or two. When Danny was finally released, the sergeant explained that I was responsible for him being detained longer than necessary. I don't think he ever completely forgave me.

Occasionally, a group of demonstrators (usually students) would suddenly descend on a major junction (Princes Street at the North Bridge was a favourite) totally blocking all movement of traffic in any direction. To gain press coverage at their demonstration, the organisers would invariably call a newspaper editor to inform him of their intentions. In turn, thankfully, the newspapers always gave us the lowdown, so on these occasions we were actually waiting for them. The usual procedure was to have a chat with the leaders once they were in position and reach a compromise as to how long they could disrupt the traffic. Usually, they would keep their word and, after the agreed time, would get up and disperse. Rarely was there any need for arrests. I knew many of the press people and it was always a game with them to try to take a photo of me negotiating with the demonstrators.

I was in charge of an event which took place in Princes Street Gardens one morning when a wreath was being laid at one of the monuments. An American tourist took my photo and spoke to me briefly. A few weeks later, the photograph arrived at police headquarters, addressed to 'Chief

'Chief Constable' Green in Princes Street gardens.

Constable Green'. Not sure what the real chief constable thought about that, but the photo was passed on to me, marked 'for the attention of **Inspector** Green'!

I was in my final year in the police when I was instructed to attend an inspectors' course at Tulliallan Police College. I suggested to Chief Superintendent Miller, who had replaced Alastair Hood (on secondment to Tulliallan), that my attendance at this stage was unnecessary. He explained I should attend because further promotion – to Chief Inspector – was a possibility if I chose to extend my police service beyond 30 years. The course would be most beneficial in those circumstances. I took the line of least resistance and went to Tulliallan, giving it my best shot. In the event I really enjoyed the course which proved to be extremely interesting and varied in content – but also very testing.

There were many exercises in which all officers had to take command of simulated major disasters – aircraft crashes, large outbreaks of fire, chemical spillage, public disorder etc. There were also lectures by industry experts. I recall one from one of the world's foremost air-crash investigators, who demonstrated his talk with the most horrific photos I had ever seen. His words were harrowing, leaving nothing to the imagination. He 'said it as it was'. I was fearful of flying for some time afterwards, and then foolishly made a study of air disasters by reading the 'Black Box' and other similar gory writings.

Speaking in public and undertaking interviews with a real TV interviewer – BBC's Reevel Alderson – were important elements of the course. These mock interviews were recorded on video, and then played back in the presence of all the class and the interviewer. He then made his criticism and suggestions for improved TV technique. This was great fun. Most evenings were taken up with study and research of subjects which required either a written paper or a practical exercise. As on previous police college visits, I found I had to devote more time to research and preparation than some of my fellow students, but my usual determination to do well prevailed on this, my final visit to Tulliallan.

Towards the end of the course we were informed that Tulliallan was hosting one of its formal College Dinner Evenings, to which a number of VIPs are always invited, along with the entire college (from the first and second year students to the sergeants', inspectors' and superintendents' courses, plus college staff). As I recall, a couple of chief constables, an MP, a local councillor and other dignitaries were invited. The inspectors' course was given 'the honour' of providing the main speaker of the evening. Some of my fellow students were prepared to give their right hand to make the speech, believing this was a way to 'be seen'. Me? Well, I didn't want any part of it but, from the moment the dining night was announced to our course, I had that sinking feeling I was going to be the 'fall guy'. A week or two before the big night, the training team advised our class that, as far as they were concerned, there could only be one choice – the most senior inspector on the course. My worst fears had become a horrifying reality – Ian Green was to be the principal speaker of the night. I tried to wriggle out of it but failed miserably.

The speech had to be written and presented to the director of the college who looked at my first effort and covered it with red ink – it was too humorous (me a comedian? I ask you), it was politically incorrect in many places and wasn't nearly long enough. I was told it had to be about 30 minutes long. Well, I tell you, I spent my every waking moment writing and rewriting that dammed speech until, finally, the director of the college accepted it. I then had to rehearse it. I was allocated a deserted classroom each evening where I read this speech to the walls, and occasionally to one of our course instructors, until it seemed to flow – but that was without the inevitable nerves. I even took it home at the weekend and had a 'dress rehearsal' with June as my audience.

The day arrived and I was like a 'hen on a hot griddle'. I wandered around the college grounds all afternoon (sports day) doing deep-breathing exercises, in an effort to compose myself. I was petrified.

The dreaded evening was suddenly upon me and the huge dining room filled to capacity, with a top table of 'big guns'. I sat with the course members and ate my dinner. It was a great meal, but I might just as well have been eating cardboard.

Finally, the lectern was brought to me, and I stood up with my knees knocking. I could hear whispered good-luck messages from my fellow inspectors as the lights were thankfully dimmed slightly. Then the strangest thing I have ever experienced occurred. After welcoming the principal guests by name, plus the college staff and students, I suddenly felt totally calm and found myself able to make the speech flow, with the occasional humorous anecdote thrown in. I sat down to applause. It was an astonishing experience. After congratulations from my classmates, the first person to approach was Chief Superintendent Alastair Hood, who rushed up and pumped my hand enthusiastically as he congratulated me, saying, 'I knew you were the man for the job. I told your instructors it had to be you.' I knew then who had been responsible. I also received congratulations from the director of the training college and various dignitaries. Drinking too much at the college is frowned upon, but I can tell you I had a few drams that night, many from colleagues.

The course ended and we all departed for our various forces. We had been through a tough course, and a real bond existed between us. Parting in such circumstances is therefore tinged with some sadness.

Back in B Division, my college report arrived and Mr Miller went over it with me. It was a very good one and, while the college was aware that the course had 'tested me', I had apparently been seen to have 'worked extremely hard and achieved a high standard'. I was also complimented on my speech.

My final move occurred shortly after. I was informed that my remaining months would see me holding down the administration inspector's duties. I would be responsible for the final checking of all police reports before the chief superintendent's signature and onward transmission to the court, plus various other administrational duties. I also had the Traffic Enquiry Department under my wing – familiar territory for me.

I was grateful to be off shifts and with weekends to myself once again. My area of responsibility meant working closely with the various shift inspectors who shared the same room. I also had close contact with the Administration Department and all the 'bosses', and was always in on all the gossip and jokes that circulated divisional HQ. I enjoyed the heavy workload and the time passed quickly. I kept as far away from the now permanently-sited photocopier as was possible.

A new chief constable took control of the force during this time, and immediately made a request to interview all inspectors in the force. I informed the chief constable's office that I was very near retirement, but was instructed to report for the interview anyway. At the interview, in addition to the chief constable, the deputy chief constable was also present. He was a not particularly impressive character who blustered a lot. The chief constable opened the interview by asking me how I saw my future in the police. I replied that I did not see myself progressing any further as I had only a month before retirement. The deputy chief interrupted rudely and asked, 'Then what are you doing here today?' I explained that I had told his department that it seemed pointless, but had been advised that I must attend. That put the deputy's 'gas on a peep'. So I was heartened to hear the chief say, 'Not a problem, Inspector Green. It's people like you, with your vast police experience, that I want to hear from to enable me to deal with the new challenges in the police.' We then proceeded to have a most amicable chat on all manner of police matters. I frankly made my views clear to the chief on where I thought the sweeping changes were not all for the best. He, in turn, thanked me and offered his congratulations, wishing me success in the future.

It was common practice at that time for a fellow officer of the same rank to approach the retiring officer to ascertain if he was happy for a collection from fellow officers to be set in motion (with a view to a subsequent presentation). I had paid into literally hundreds of such collections over the years, but always felt it was somehow wrong and a bit demeaning, so I declined the kind offer. Nevertheless, the divisional headquarters staff at Gayfield Square Station went quietly about unofficially collecting for a presentation. On my final day, when I adjourned with divisional headquarters staff for a pint in a local pub, a surprise presentation was made. I was very moved by what was a more personal gesture. Nice people. When making the presentation, mention was made of my routine note on reports etc. Where I needed clarification on something, I would write, 'See me re this. Inspector Green.' Unbeknown to me, this comment had become my hallmark.

It was also the custom for retiring officers to have a celebration 'booze-up' to which only colleagues are invited. Quite frankly, I did not plan to follow what I saw as a rather chauvinistic tradition and, instead, I invited family, friends and some close colleagues to a private 'do' in the Press Club in Rutland Street (where I was an associate member). We had an amazing night. June conspired with Danny Kyle, one of the real characters of the folk scene, and they set me up for a 'this is your life' send-up which was hilarious. I also had a 'Fuzzfolk' reunion at the police club to which many artists and friends were invited. We had a superb evening of songs, music and further parodying of Ian Green, including several songs written for the occasion – great stuff.

At the end of service, each retiring officer is granted one free interview with a financial advisor, and I took the opportunity to have such a meeting. I opted to take the maximum portion of my pension as a lump sum, which amounted to a significant figure – resulting in a lower monthly pension, of course. 'A bird in the hand' was my motto. I was given good advice and invested half of my lump sum and, when these investments eventually matured ten years later, I was handsomely rewarded. The remaining portion I later used to invest in my business.

I retired from Lothian and Borders Police on 15 August 1985 exactly 30 years after joining Edinburgh City Police. I attended headquarters for signing off and handing in uniforms etc. I kept my inspector's cap as a small memento of 30 years, but returned everything else. I called at 'B' Division and cleared out my locker and drawers. It is amazing what you accumulate in 30 years, but all was consigned to the waste bin. I now wish I had kept copies of some of the cases I was involved in, plus other interesting material. But I had no idea I would one day write my autobiography. Finally, I called on Chief Superintendent Miller who warmly wished me luck and good health for the future, and complemented me on my 'exemplary conduct' (written words of the chief constable) and dedication to the force.

Lothian and Borders Police Certificate.

Ian a few days before retirement.

I do admit that I walked out the station door with some sadness, at the end of a significant period of my life. However, a new life in the music business beckoned, providing another new challenge for the 'country loon'. There was no time to be melancholy and anyway, I told myself that the police service had changed greatly since 1955. I was not happy with much of what was described as progress within the service. Yes, the job had certainly changed in 30 years.

PART III

PART III

the music years

he day after leaving the police I was self-employed in the traditional music business – expanding my Discount Folk Records mail order and festival stall company. The company was already well-established. It had a worldwide reputation for good service and obtaining albums which could not be readily found. Some explanation is required though as to how I reached that point.

I earlier touched on my contact with traditional music in childhood years but, like so many other teenagers, I had lost all interest in this genre of music when I became caught up in 'pop music' and 'masterpieces' of those years, such as 'How Much Is That Doggy in The Window', 'Mares Eat Oats' etc. How did they get away with it – but then what's changed on the pop scene? Anyway, pop was my only interest in music throughout my army service and into my early days in the police. I am glad to say my taste in music later broadened immensely and now includes traditional music (of course), blues, country, bluegrass, light classical, musicals, movie soundtracks and 'world' music. Never quite got the hang of jazz though.

In the early '60s, after I passed my police sergeant and inspector exams, June and I finally could afford our first black and white Bush TV. Almost everyone we knew had a TV by then, but with our meagre financial resources we were way behind the times, with only a mono radiogram to entertain us.

We were sitting watching 'the box' one night when a programme titled 'Hootenanny' appeared on the screen. We were treated to The Corrie Folk Trio and Paddy Bell, Rae and Archie Fisher, Eleanor Smith and Dolina McLennan. I was knocked out by the songs, some of which I immediately associated with my childhood years. I was hooked. I went out next day and bought my first LP – 'Hootenanny Volume 1' – and wore it out. I next added the very first Corrie Folk Trio and Paddy Bell album – 'The Promise of the Day' – and so started my love of traditional music, referred to usually as folk music, although I prefer the former. From those small beginnings my record collection grew and now includes hundreds of 78s, LPs, music cassettes, CDs, videos and DVDs. I also have a collection of comedy albums – The Goon Show and Monty Python's Flying Circus are examples – Tony Hancock is also a favourite. However, my insatiable appetite for traditional music became an obsession, or so my family assure me.

The logical next step was going to concerts, which included The Corrie Folk Trio, The Dubliners, The Clancy Brothers and Tom Paxton, followed by folk clubs and, later, folk festivals. I was introduced to the folk-club scene by my old friend Jimmy McCalman who happened to mention that The Ian McCalman Folk Group (later to change to The McCalmans because it was easier on the tongue) were doing the Triangle Folk Club. June and I went along and I was totally blown away. This led to visits to the Buffs Club, plus other venues, and because we now had 'insider' knowledge through The McCalmans, we were soon invited to a session in a 'folky' flat in Tollcross, the latest 'pad' of Hamish Bayne and Derek Moffat (of The McCalmans). Ian McCalman wisely advised us to buy a carry-out before the pub closed at 10 o'clock. (Remember those days?) Armed with some cans of beer and a quarter-bottle of vodka for June, we made our debut entrance to a 'folk pad'. It was quite basic, with only a couple of seats which we were given the honour of sharing, but when June requested a glass to pour herself a vodka, this was greeted with roars of laugher and she had to settle for the one and only cup in the flat. What a night of great singing followed. It was still going strong when we left, I know not when.

The first festival we ever attended was the Kinross Festival, organised by the Traditional Music and Song Association, one of many wonderful weekends of music, fun and good companionship – washed down with copious amounts of booze, of course. That weekend will be forever etched in my memory. It was the first time I heard the wonderful voice of Heather Heywood and some of the tradition bearers, including Belle Stewart and Willie Scott.

That wasn't enough. I needed to be part of this amazing scene. The Police Club at York Place in Edinburgh had recently opened its doors, and the committee was anxious to have functions in the club to attract members. The Police Angling Section (or Club), of which I was a member, was looking at ways to subsidise the cost of angling outings, and Davie Scougall, who also had an interest in folk music, especially Matt McGinn, and myself came up with the idea of running a folk night in the functions room. We charged a small entry fee (far too low) and, after paying the artists their expenses, some money went to the angling funds. The most amazing thing about that first evening was the interest generated within police circles. A decision was taken by the Angling Club Committee to run a weekly folk night. This was eventually reduced to a fortnightly event which became the Police Folk Club, later to be nicknamed 'Fuzzfolk'. There was a committee member from each City Division, plus Head-quarters, the CID and Traffic Department. Each was responsible for selling tickets and the running of the club every second Sunday. 'Fuzzfolk' was immediately a huge success. It was the most popular event held in the Police Club and, quite rightly, in due course was regarded by folk artists and others as one of the best folk clubs in Scotland.

I took it in turn with Davie Scougall to act as compere, and we became the principal organisers. There were some other stalwarts of course – Jean Ferrier, Peter Ash, Tom Carlyon, Tom Shaw, Willie Cockburn and others. In an effort to maintain a succession of new artists, Davie and I often spent our own time 'scouting' for new 'acts'.

I remember we went to a club in Dalkeith, at which Billy Connolly was doing an early solo gig after the break-up of The Humblebums. We invited Billy to 'do' the Police Club and he asked for the princely sum of twelve pounds. I am embarrassed to say we beat him down to eight, and I have the signed receipt to this day. Many years later, I mentioned this to Billy and he rightly commented it was probably not a bad fee in those days, but to this day I feel guilty about beating his fee down. He was to appear many more times at 'Fuzzfolk' and always attracted a full house.

A fellow policeman hosted the visit of a number of Royal Ulster Constabulary officers, on rest and recuperation from the 'troubles'. He brought them along as guests on a Connolly night. Billy did 'The Crucifixion' to the enjoyment of all, including the RUC officers, but the host was upset and reported the Angling Club to the principal committee. Davie and me were hauled over the coals, given a severe dressing down and warned not to invite him or any other 'blasphemous' artist to the club in future. We waited a year for the dust to settle before we took the big risk of being shut down by cheekily inviting Billy back. We billed it as follows – 'If you are easily offended then DO NOT attend this folk night' and sold every ticket in a day. Billy went down a storm, especially in the second half after I told him I believed he was a 'bit restrained'. He agreed. He went out and did 'The Crucifixion' to the delight of all. Nothing was said by the 'governing body', so common sense won the day.

Billy, unfairly in my opinion, got a lot of stick from the press, but he impressed me greatly in relation to his final 'Fuzzfolk' gig. As always, he was booked a year ahead and meantime had rocketed to international stardom, mainly because of an appearance on The Michael Parkinson Show. I phoned Billy and said he could call off if he wished, principally because the money we were due to pay him (thankfully significantly more than the first fee we paid him) could not possibly compare with the fees he suddenly commanded. 'No way,' said Billy, 'I accepted the booking and the fee offered and I will fulfil the promise. In any case, I like 'Fuzzfolk'. It was the only place I was ever banned from.' Good on you Billy.

The hunt to find new acts was continuous in the early days. I was on duty in the police patrol van one day when I spotted a car ahead of me exhibiting a sign advertising 'The Cotters' on the rear window. I knew of the duo and it was a rare chance to chat about a prospective booking. I followed the car for a mile or two until an opportunity occurred to flag down the driver, little realising that the occupant, Ali Watson of The Cotters, was by then 'shitting his breeks' because of the close police attention. When I explained my purpose for stopping him, the relief on his face was palpable and the incident became a Cotters' stage story. Sadly, Ali and his partner Alex Sutherland both died of cancer at an early age. The Cotters were, in their time, the most popular group of the then flourishing folk-pub scene in Edinburgh.

After a few years, I came to the conclusion that 'Fuzzfolk' rightly deserved to be a section of the Welfare Association in its own right to allow funds generated to be utilised to fund the Folk Club exclusively, as well as further folk music within police circles. There was some resistance to this notion from members of the Angling Club, but 'Fuzzfolk' had already added significantly to their funds and since less and less was being contributed by the Angling Section to 'Fuzzfolk', good sense prevailed. The Police Folk Music Section was given a vote of confidence. The folk nights were also generating funds for the Welfare Association through bar sales, so we were by then held in some regard at least by the club committee. Thankfully, some of the original organisers, including Peter Ash and Jean Ferrier in particular, plus fresh blood, joined our newly formed Police Folk Music Section.

My involvement in the folk scene and 'Fuzzfolk' was initially frowned upon by some senior police officers, but was, in my opinion, a wonderful bit of a police/public relations exercise. It was so unjust that my promotion was at least partially held back for some time because the folk scene was regarded as a very left-wing organisation by many high ranking police officers. Pathetic really, but thankfully the wind of change heralded new thinking. 'Fuzzfolk' was then to take on an air of respectability in the force, with a few high ranking officers joining the audience and sitting with lower ranks and guests – all having a ball.

There were some amazing nights. All the major folk artists of the day appeared there, including Jean Redpath (MBE), Isla St Clair, Adam McNaughtan, Bill Barclay, Eric Bogle, Tich Frier, Dick Gaughan, Matt McGinn, Hamish Imlach, Iain MacKintosh, Nic Jones, Vin Garbutt, Cilla Fisher and Artie Trezise, Gaberlunzie, The McCalmans, Ossian, The JSD Band, Silly Wizard, The Battlefield Band and The Taysiders (which included the late, great Jim Reid), plus foreign touring artists, such as the unusually named Bushwhackers and Bullockies Bush Band from Australia, who raised the roof a few inches.

'Live' recordings were made in the club, including Bill Barclay's 'Almost Live' album ('The Twelve Days of Christmas' single charted in the UK). Matt McGinn recorded 'The Two Heided Man', but how the record company salvaged an album out of it I really don't know, because it was towards the end of Matt's career, when he was drinking heavily to the detriment of his performance. Bill Hill recorded his very clever 'Police Record' album and Rankin File recorded the final track – 'Mr Sax' – for their debut album. BBC Radio Two recorded a couple of 'live' specials in the club, and TV showed an interest but felt there was insufficient space for TV cameras to operate effectively.

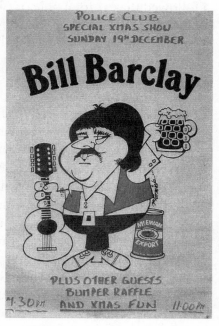

Bill Barclay appearing at 'Fuzzfolk'.

We had solid and enthusiastic floor-singers – people like Liz and Maggie Cruickshank, John Barrow, Tom Ward, Jocky Weatherstone and Jimmy Greenan. The Marshall Brothers, The Blue Lamp and the late (Detective Constable) Andy Dickson were home-grown police talent. Andy was a remarkable character. He sang mainly country and western, and self-penned songs which were usually hilarious send-ups of the police hierarchy and major policing events. He was a wonderful raconteur and

Bill Hill's 'Police Record' album poster.

a real tonic. He always went on after the interval and the 'pies'! There were many others.

John Barrow's 'Old Johnny Bugger' and 'The Lampton Worm' were always greeted with hoots of laughter and wild applause, and he became a very popular floor-singer. Sadly, only rarely is it possible to coax John into singing nowadays. I recall one very funny incident involving The Melville Folk Group who were also loved by the 'Fuzzfolk' audience and could always be called upon to help shore up nights when we were short of floor singers. Group member, Brian Clark, was late in arriving one night, and when he did get on stage to join the other three who had made a start without him, Brian apologised for being late. Quick as a flash, Stewart McDonagh, always a bit of a piss-taker, replied, 'Better if you apologised for being here at all, not for being late.' Real professionals! The other members were Jack Scott and Jimmy Neilson.

In the early days, a lad nicknamed 'Mo' came along one night to do a floor spot. Mo was always experimenting with some new fangled piece of electronic equipment and, on one occasion, he arrived with the latest bit of '60s technology. He set it up for his couple of songs, requesting to be introduced as 'Electronically Mo'd'. The equipment was supposed to provide percussion, when required, as a backing to his guitar and voice, in whatever beat or rhythm he chose. However, something went wrong with his pre-settings and each time he launched into a song or chorus, the percussion was in the wrong beat. After initial puzzlement the audience exploded in fits of laughter. Mo left the stage red-faced, but the always sympathetic 'Fuzzfolk' audience gave him a round of applause anyway. To this day some folk think it was actually a deliberate part of a comedy routine.

We usually also booked a support act, invariably artists who were just starting out on their musical careers. Some were kind enough to say we gave them their first break. Many of these supporters and other artists became close friends.

Drinkers' Drouth – the late Brian Dougan, Tony Dougan, Jack Aitken and Davie Black (before Davy Steele joined) – were great supporters of 'Fuzzfolk' and always popular with their close-harmony singing and instrumentals. When the late Davy Steele joined the group, they enjoyed enormous success and recorded two albums which I was later to become involved with. The Drouth and the Melvilles contributed in no small measure to the success of 'Fuzzfolk'.

The Melville Folk Group and wives became very good friends and we had great fun together on gigs and pub crawls, as well as at festivals and parties. The group eventually disbanded and we seemed to drift apart somehow. In 2009, Jack Scott contacted me to say the ex-group members and a couple of close friends met on the last Friday of each month in Ryrie's Bar at Haymarket, and invited me along. I had a really fine night, enjoying a few drinks while reminiscing about the 'good old days'. It was noticeable that the drinking capacity of all had fallen from ten or more pints in the 'old' days to something quite moderate. Age is a terrible thing.

It was great to meet up with the 'boys' and I intend to repeat the rendezvous in Ryrie's. It is so easy to lose contact with friends when we all move away or our circumstances change, so as we enter 2010, it is my New Year resolution to mend my ways in this respect and renew several old friendships. Life is too short.

Sadly, many of the folk artists who graced the stage of 'Fuzzfolk' have since passed away and are all greatly missed. They include such unique characters as Hamish Imlach, Matt McGinn, Iain MacKintosh, George Jackson, Danny Kyle, Derek Moffat, Bobby Eaglesham, Jackie Jennet, Jimmy Greenan, Johnny Hamilton and, more recently, Jim Reid.

Of the full-time professional musicians, some achieved TV fame, especially Billy Connolly but also Dick Gaughan, The Battlefield Band and The McCalmans, who recorded several TV series. Isla St Clair became a household name on the late Larry Grayson's Generation Game, while Bill Barclay popped up in various TV productions, often as a policeman. Cilla Fisher and Artie Trezise became national stars with their children's show 'The Singing Kettle.' From small acorns mighty oaks grow. I am often asked who the most popular artists to appear in the folk club over the ten years were and, while there were many loved by the audience, I can say that Billy Connolly, Bill Barclay and The McCalmans always drew capacity houses, and the place simply buzzed for them. 'Jamboree Nights' (when a number of top artists were invited along) were also hugely popular.

The JSD Band shot to fame after winning a national folk-group competition in Edinburgh. On their final gig at 'Fuzzfolk', their fame having spread far and wide, they arrived with a huge vanload of PA, a soundman and a manager. When they started piling huge speakers on a wooden table, I stepped in and suggested the table would never hold the weight. 'It's OK,' said the overconfident soundman, and in that instant the table gave way and the equipment crashed to the floor. The sound was loud that night – it was commented that the best place to listen to the music was in the toilets one flat above the functions room.

Des Coffield broke a banjo string and, while he was changing it, the irrepressible fiddler, Chuck Fleming, chatted a bit to the audience. Someone at the back of the room shouted, 'Get on with it.' Immediately Chuck turned to Des, who had quickly changed the string and tuned up. They nodded to each other and went into the fastest set of reels I'd ever heard. As the last note faded, Chuck turned to face the back of the hall and directed a 'v' sign at the moaner. He got the message.

In all the years, there was rarely any kind of bother in the club, although, one night, a support artist arrived with a good drink in him, and by the time he went on stage he was drunk. I let him try two songs, but he was not doing well and the audience was becoming restless, so I walked up to the front of the stage and, with my back to the audience, told him to get off. He did, but as he walked towards the exit in a fit of temper, he hurled his pint glass and contents against a wall. He was escorted very quickly and effectively out of the club and found himself in the street seconds after leaving the stage. He later apologised to me and we remain friends to this day.

I caught one artist smoking 'pot' in the cloakroom, which also served as a changing room for artists – the idiot was surprised when the joint was snatched from him and quickly sluiced down the loo. He was severely warned and wisely never returned to the club with cannabis again.

I was possibly responsible for buying Phil Cunningham his first pint. We had a policy in the club of always buying artists a couple of drinks (hospitality I think they call it nowadays) and, on one of Silly Wizard's early appearances, the band was offered the usual complimentary drinks. Phil took a pint, but I later learned he was only 15 years of age. Silly Wizard was another of the outstanding bands to appear in the club, although, as their fame rapidly spread to Europe and North America, like other bands of international fame, we could no longer afford them. The McCalmans were the exception to that rule and were very loyal.

Even after TV appearances and huge touring schedules, they continued to do their annual gig at 'Fuzzfolk', always providing great harmony singing, with hugely humorous and entertaining stage chat. What an amazing group. Ian remains a friend to this day, as do Nick and Stephen.

To facilitate the complimentary drinks, we printed tickets marked 'pint of beer', 'pint of lager', 'spirits' or 'soft drinks'. This enabled the artist to get his/her drink at the bar when it suited, and I then paid the club steward at the end of the evening. One artist once asked, 'What do I do with this?' As a leg-pull, I replied, 'You drop the ticket into a pint of water and it becomes a pint of beer.' For an instant, I think he believed me. These wee drink tickets became another hallmark of 'Fuzzfolk', and the practice was often the subject of humorous stage crack by artists. It worked though.

We were let down badly by only one artist in all the years of 'Fuzzfolk' – Johnny Silvo. I was in hospital, so I recruited Bill Barclay to compere the evening. Johnny apparently arrived drunk, did only a very short spot in the first half and was clearly not performing well. When he was reintroduced for his second spot, he went on stage, sang one song, announced he had to 'go for a pee', returned to sing another song and left the stage for good. Thankfully, Bill went on stage and did a half-hour, to the delight of his many fans. June had a row with Silvo after the gig. He offered to return his fee, but she refused to accept it and advised him that he would never receive another booking at 'Fuzzfolk'. He didn't.

I was in hospital at the time, recovering from the operation to remove haemorrhoids. This was a most humiliating operation, and the pain before and after the op was hellish. Loads of 'golden oldie' jokes helped to ease the pain, and one I was told at the time stuck with me: A man went to his doctor complaining of piles, and the doctor prescribed sup-positories. After a week or two, the sufferer returned to the doctor who asked him if there was any improvement. The man replied, 'For all the good they were, I might as well have stuck them up my arse.' The old ones are the best.

June always acted as cashier at the 'door' and was superb at shaking money out of 'chancers' who usually attached themselves to the artists, assuming that meant free entry. They rarely got past June though.

It was common practice for committee members and artists to be invited back to our home after the club, and there were many memorable late nights which sometimes lasted until daylight. The neighbours must have hated it, but never complained, with one exception. At that time, I was right into brewing beer and fermenting wine, which the guests consumed with great gusto. Often, the principal guest would stay overnight – Matt McGinn usually did. When Dick Gaughan came back to our house we were usually in for an interesting debate, and on one occasion when Dick was joined by Tich Frier, Tom Ward and John Barrow, a very stimulating discussion on the pros and cons of Communism developed. When June noticed the time was 2am, she quietly and cleverly moved the clock hands forward to 4 o'clock and then innocently announced, 'Oh my goodness. Look at the time. I have my work in the morning.' The discussion ended and our guests left in a cloud of dust, or was it flatulence from drinking my home brew? Good one, June.

Wine-making and brewing was another hobby that fascinated me, and before long my wines and beers were winning prizes at the local Corstorphine Winemaking Club of which I was a member. I was particularly good at brewing lager but my best win was from elderberries, although I once obtained a huge box of purple plums from a pub in England when our family was on holiday. This huge tree grew in the back yard of the pub and was laden with beautiful plums which were falling to the ground and rotting. I got permission to gather fresh ones from the branches and they made a cracking wine which also earned me a prize or two.

Occasionally, we'd off-load our three young 'Greenies' to Mam and Dad when musicians stayed with us at weekends. I specifically recall one weekend when the Geordie band Hedgehog Pie did a weekend of gigs in the Edinburgh area, including the police club. This was one of my first attempts as a booking agent. Hedgehog Pie could number six or as many as a dozen, and on this occasion the latter number descended upon us. They bunked down with us, John Barrow and someone else. What a weekend of music and madness we had. Amazing musicians and singers, they were also wonderful characters and really nice people. By the way guys, we still have a pair of Domino's socks – does he want them back?

When I bought my first car I paid for it with money I received from the Criminal Injuries Compensation Board (the princely sum of £150 as I recall) for injuries sustained at the hands of some villain. Owning a car placed me in the 'most wanted' category by folk-singer friends who had no transport. I remember the late Lesley Hale asked me to drive her to a folk club near Glasgow. On arrival there I found my footbrake was nonexistent and an examination revealed a burst brake pipe, from which the brake fluid had escaped. I was not a member of the AA or RAC and had no money to afford breakdown recovery either, so I had no alternative but to drive home on the handbrake and gears. It was a hair-raising journey but made a good story later.

On another occasion I was asked by Tich Frier to drive him to a gig, also in the west. The same car was by this time giving me headaches with a petrol supply problem. It was easy to do a temporary repair by banging the petrol pump with a spanner, but poor Tich sat in amazement as every few miles the engine stopped, whereupon I would leap out, whack the petrol pump and off we'd go again. At one point, he asked, 'Will we get to the gig, Ian?' What do you expect of a car that cost only £75.00 and was bought from another policeman?

Many years before he gained fame as a comedian, after-dinner speaker and actor, Bill Barclay also had a dodgy old car. John Barrow told me the story of Bill and him travelling very slowly to a gig in Fife with some fellow folkies. Everything was passing him, including a bicycle I believe, and at one point Bill asked, 'Is there anyone behind me?' A humorist in the rear replied, 'No, everything's passed you, Bill.'

I made my first foray into the recording business with a cassette of 'Fuzzfolk' floor-singers and others. A German friend, Peter Wennerhold, recorded the various tracks live on his reel-to-reel tape recorder – a Philips, I think. We then edited it down to the final selection, and I made copies on a quite professional cassette machine at home. Ken Thomson designed the cassette sleeve. The albums were sold only to 'Fuzzfolk' patrons. In the days when such albums were not easily produced, it was something of an achievement, although in retrospect it was no work of art. One of the artists commented that it was 'bloody awful', but it captured a moment in time and, to this day, I still get an occasional request for a copy of 'Fuzzfolk' Volume 1 – there never was a Volume 2. Peter was absolutely folk mad, a bit like myself really, and recorded hundreds of hours of reel-to-reel tapes during his time in Edinburgh. Many years later, he was the prime mover in setting up the Scottish Folk Festival Tour of Germany. I have lost touch with him these days.

I remained involved in 'Fuzzfolk' for ten years, but by then I was finding my involvement in so many spheres of folk music and other hobbies a bit excessive. Anyway, I felt I needed a change, and it was time to move on. A good, experienced committee was well-established, and it seemed I could bow out without seriously affecting the folk club's future. I had steered it to a healthy bank balance and a reputation second to none. Alas, after a year or so, audiences dwindled and eventually the club folded.

The finger was pointed at me, I regret to say, because I was at that time involved in a series of fund-raising concerts in an Edinburgh hotel with John Barrow and Ken Thomson, which some felt conflicted with the interests of the Police Folk Club. I didn't agree. It seemed to me, as often happens, when the driving force moves on, a vacuum is left and, if not filled by one with equal commitment and enthusiasm, the organisation collapses. A great pity, but a fact of life, and Fuzzfolk was not alone in this respect.

Sandy Bell's Broadsheet concert poster.

I was asked to return and get the club operating again but, in my opinion, it is a mistake to turn back the clock. Having made a clean break, returning would have been a retrograde step – in any case the enthusiasm for that venture was by then on the wane. I did run a hugely successful folk night in the Police Club when I retired from the police and, a few years later, I organised a Greentrax Recordings Showcase concert at the request of the Club Steward, Jan Smith, the best steward the club ever had. In addition to the passage of time, however, the layout of the functions room had been changed to the severe detriment of live performance. It was as far as I am concerned, an evening lacking in atmosphere, although the best of artists performed that night.

My work with the Police Folk Club was eventually recognised by the Police Welfare Association. I received a presentation for services to the association in general and the club at York Place in particular. Howeve, memories are short, and although I was invited many years later to the Police Club for a celebration of the life of the club, Fuzzfolk barely received a mention, which saddened me. Thankfully the patrons were more appreciative – I still meet old colleagues and friends who speak fondly of Fuzzfolk and my contribution.

I first met John and Lesley Barrow, Tom and Kate Ward, and Bill and Heather Barclay as a result of the very vibrant hotel folk scene in Royal Terrace, and we became lifelong friends. I also quickly became involved

Friends Lesley and Dr John Barrow.

Friends Kate and Tom Ward.

Friends Maxine Allely and the late
Ken Thomson.

Friends Bill Barclay and the late
Ken Thomson.

in the very active Edinburgh folk scene of the famous Sandy Bell's Bar (actually it is the Forrest Hill Bar), a recognised meeting place on the international folk scene. I have some wonderful memories of Bell's. Often great musical and singing sessions would develop, but the thing about Bell's was the craic. It was there I met the late Ken Thomson who, with his wife-to-be Maxine Allely, also became close friends.

As a serving police officer, I could well have been viewed with suspicion in such an establishment as Sandy Bell's, but I always felt at home among its many extravagant characters. On one occasion however, I dropped into Bell's in mid-evening for a pint on my way home from duty (with the usual 'civvie' jacket on top of my uniform). I had barely taken my first sip (probably a gulp in those days) when the door of the pub burst open and in strode several members of the 'Drug Squad' from Headquarters. They proceeded to search the toilets and several male drinkers, while I looked on in embarrassment. I was given a perfunctory nod as the officers left without an arrest or a seizure of drugs. For the first time ever, I became the subject of verbal accusations by a section of the customers, and only with difficulty was I able to persuade them I was not responsible for the raid. Tricky though.

Sandy Bells Forresthill Bar.

Bell's was mainly fun though – a laugh a minute, often accompanied by wonderful music and song. All and sundry from the folk-music scene of those days dropped in when gigging in Edinburgh or when passing through – The Dubliners never failed to show up when in town. Talented guitarist, the late Dennis Cairns, was often in the thick of a session, and Freddie Thompson was rarely absent. Groups formed as a result of sessions in Bell's, none better than Chuck Fleming, Tom Ward and Dennis Cairns, but the line-up was not to last unfortunately.

One of the most common faces in Bell's was that of the late and irreplaceable Dr Hamish Henderson of the nearby School of Scottish Studies, always keen to start a singing session.

Hamish was an exceptional poet, songwriter and academic. He served in the army in the Desert and Italy Campaigns during WWII, and it was Captain Hamish Henderson who accepted the surrender of Italy on the 29 April 1945. It was also Hamish who, on one of his field recording trips in Aberdeenshire, came across the legend, Jeannie Robertson. He was a wonderful crusader for the 'travelling people' and was revered by them. More of Hamish later.

There were other great characters in Sandy Bell's who seemed permanent fixtures, such as Mike Brennan, an Irishman known to all on the folk scene, Geordie Hamilton, who had a repertoire of songs running into hundreds, Jimmy Elliot, an amazing mandolin player and musician, Freddie Thompson whose fiddle seemed welded to his neck and many, many more.

John, Ken and I immediately hit it off, and the 'triumvirate' (as we were once described) were quickly editing *Sandy Bell's Broadsheet*. It was first published on 20 August 1973, a fortnightly publication. It was the only regular folk magazine in Scotland in the seventies, and our 'head office' was Sandy Bell's Bar, by the kind cooperation of the manager, the late Jimmy Cairney. Jimmy was a real character and knew exactly how to handle the many colourful characters who frequented the bar – he was never stuck for an answer. I recall him saying to me one day, 'Ian, this place is full of revolutionaries who don't want change.' I may well be struck down by lightning for saying this, but Sandy Bell's was never the same after Jimmy's passing.

Hamish Henderson during WWII.

The Broadsheet was John Barrow's brainchild. Ken Thomson was a professional journalist and features editor of the Scottish *Daily Record*, and one-time editor of the free Edinburgh Weekly. John and I learned so much from Ken about writing, layout and the use of photos. We usually met at John's house once a fortnight, after Ken returned from his work on the *Record*. Armed only with lots of good ideas, some assembled material, a pile of A4 paper, three dodgy portable typewriters, bottles of correction fluid and, needless to say, copious quantities of beer and whisky, we worked until it was put to bed in the 'wee sma' hours'. It was at the printer later that day. I was involved in the Broadsheet for ten years (seemed to be my attention span then), and in that time it was late on only two occasions, both due to the printer. That is some record.

Although we never denied it was a rag, *Sandy Bell's Broadsheet* was always informed, often quite critical and hard-hitting when necessary, and was sought throughout the folk scene and beyond. It was sold in various outlets, plus postal subscription.

Some amazing debate occurred within the pages of the Broadsheet, and sometimes became quite heated as stances were adopted and heels dug in. There was an amazing rumpus over a critical review of Dougie McLean's album, which included his song 'Caledonia'. (He and the song subsequently achieved international fame – the song was even used in a beer advert.) The review was by Hector Christie, who always called a spade a spade, and it certainly was not a good review. Friends leapt to Dougie's defence and some of the responses were 'red hot'. We were forced to call it a day after the debate persisted for three issues.

One year, June and I went on holiday in the north and west of Scotland and visited some folk clubs, including Ullapool. I was surprised to find that the committee of the club, who congregated at the rear of the room, kept up a bad-mannered chatter throughout the evening. It was so bad I wrote a scathing review of the club in SBB, particularly with respect to the committee, and while I was at it, I expressed the view that talk and other noise while an artist is performing is totally unacceptable. This launched another lively Broadsheet debate.

On another occasion I raised the question of some clubs giving the floor-singers too much of the available time, resulting in the main guest's two sets being drastically pruned. I considered this inadmissible, since most of the audience had paid good money principally to hear the guest. In other words, floor-singers are great, but not when so many are used to the detriment of the guest's stage time. One club organiser, clearly without a clue, wrote to SBB saying that, in his opinion the floor-singers were more important than the paid guest and if the main guest's time on stage was shortened or cut out altogether, so what? It is no wonder the folk-club scene had such a bad image at times. Some club organisers were just so bad they couldn't have organised 'a piss-up in a brewery'. Sorry, but true. On the other side of the coin, there were excellently managed folk clubs such as Edinburgh, Stirling, Glenfarg, Thurso and the unusual Linlithgow

Club which Nora Devine ran for so many years – each guest simply receiving what was dropped in the tray.

One disgruntled reader described us as the 'Edinburgh mafia', and eventually we earned the nicknames 'Fizz', 'Fuzz' and 'Fats" – if I tell you Ken was a wee bit overweight, does that help with identification? We gained notoriety throughout the Scottish folk scene and beyond. Jimmy Cairney was behind us all the way and donated the Sandy Bell's Broadsheet Cup for annual presentation to someone who had contributed significantly to folk music. Recipients included Alastair Clark of *The Scotsman*, the legendary Alex Campbell, the redoubtable Hamish Henderson, the entire Fisher Family and singer/songwriter extraordinaire Eric Bogle. The last recipient was Aly Bain who may still have this wee SBB tribute.

Fizz, Fuzz and Fats were invited to the launch of The Gaugers' first album in Aberdeen, but that morning it was snowing heavily. We met in Bell's around midday, and every wee while one of us would poke his head out to assess the weather. Eventually the snow stopped, glasses were emptied and off we went in my father-in-law's car. A stop for a 'comfort break' and further refreshment, was made about halfway to Aberdeen, but we arrived in time for the launch in a rather swanky university building. We were later invited back to Peter Hall's home for further refreshments in celebration of the album, but drink had taken its toll – a wonderful photo showed Fizz, Fuzz and Fats sound asleep on Peter's couch. We never lived that one down.

Presentation of The Sandy Bell's Cup to Alex Campbell.

Sandy Bell's Broadsheet.

Sandy Bell's Ceilidh CD Poster.

We were indebted to some very talented people who provided written material and images; Malky McCormick for his incredible sketches, Tash MacLeod for her caricatures, especially of Fizz, Fuzz and Fats, which adorned the front page of one Christmas (colour) issue. Numerous contributors made the magazine fresh and interesting. We also had amazing supporters from around the globe. We never made a penny out of SBB and occasionally F, F and F would dip into their own pockets to ensure the next issue went to print.

During one of our particularly 'broke' periods, I suggested we invite some of the Edinburgh artists to help us make an album, with profits going to SBB. The response was staggering, and soon we had tracks from Aly Bain, Dick Gaughan, Chorda, The McCalmans, Liz and Maggie Cruickshank, Bell's Chorus and Bell's Big Ceilidh Band. Bell's Chorus included all and sundry (even Fizz and Fuzz – Fats was at work!) and The Melville Folk Group. Bell's Big Ceilidh Band was a Jimmy Elliot production. He whipped a host of Bell's regulars into shape, resulting in two really big tracks. The album was recorded in the Pan Audio Studio, and to assist relaxed vocal chords we bought in a keg of beer, followed quickly by a second. This was not a wise move because several singers became 'too relaxed' and eventually recording had to be abandoned for the day. It was a lot of fun – and once again confirmed the strength of the folk scene and the willingness of artists to support what they believed to be a worthy cause. Thanks to all. The album was released in 1977.

The LP sales helped the finances of SBB, and later when I launched Greentrax, I re-released the album in cassette format with the funds going first to The Broadsheet and on its demise, to 'The Living Tradition.' It was finally re-released on CD by Greentrax in 2006 and the artists who so readily contributed tracks now earn a few pounds in royalties from sales. The album sounds as fresh today as it did in 1977.

Prior to releasing the CD I thought I would add a couple of additional tracks by the excellent Edinburgh group, Town Choice, who were part of an EMI album of runners-up in a Scottish folk-group competition from the same era. Unfortunately, like so many of the major recording companies, EMI had no understanding of folk music and I was forced to drop the idea due to the exorbitant advances and royalties they demanded.

Around nine years after its launch, Ken decided to call it a day with SBB. John and I soldiered on for another year but, having been doing it for ten years, I also pulled out and we offered the Broadsheet to any suitable, interested party. Jack Foley, a colleague of Ken's, took on the mantle of sole editor and the transition to simply 'The Broadsheet' was smooth. STV recorded and transmitted a documentary on the life of *Sandy Bell's Broadsheet* and its three editors. What fun we had over the years. It really was an amazing experience, resulting in wonderful memories. I have every single copy of SBB in a box in my loft, as does John Barrow in his.

The triumvirate, plus Sid Kiman, launched the Edinburgh Folk Club in George Square on the third of October 1973. As I was recently reminded by John Barrow, this was as a direct result of the demise of the Buffs Club which was closed after a police raid for illegal drinking. The main guest that last Buffs night was to have been bluesman Mike Whellans. It made sense, therefore, for us to open the new Edinburgh Folk Club with Mike.

Very quickly an EFC committee comprising the instigators, wives and sundry others was formed. The subsequent committee meetings were something to behold – arguments, referred to as 'discussion' in the club minute frequently went on into the night, accompanied and encouraged by more drink. This was a folk club like no other however, and some of the ideas presented at these uproarious committee meetings, usually by Ken Thomson, went on to become a Christmas pantomime, a Burns' Supper with a difference and other amazing events, including a football match. The first pantomime was pure genius. Ken (who wrote it) made us all take part, I was landed with the task of handling sound effects – a bell rang when somebody knocked on the door an example of the madness. I edited the sound effects onto a cassette, and it would surely have gone haywire but for Ken's insistence on several 'dress' rehearsals. We made a tape recording of the pantomime, but some bugger managed to lose the master. It was bloody hilarious on the night. The first Burns' supper was actually cooked by the female committee members, the haggis was 'piped' in by Ian Cruickshank's mouth organ and again we were delegated 'parts'. I had to 'address the haggis' and did so quite badly, but it was all part of the fun – well, madness really.

Edinburgh Folk Club Poster.

One rule in the club, which perhaps other folk clubs could have emulated, was that everyone paid the entry fee, including all committee members. EFC was healthy, well-organised, unique and never stagnated. John, Ken and myself all took turns of doing floor spots (another Kenny idea). I often sang at home and at parties, but had never performed on any kind of 'stage', except at Fornighty School, when I sang 'Hooray and Up She Rises' in a duet with a girl classmate at an end-of-term concert. This led me to singing in other folk clubs, sing-arounds and bizarrely, in an old folk's home on one occasion. I am unsure who were more bemused, the inmates or the motley crew of singers. In retrospect, I was not a very good singer, just enthusiastic, and I always found it stressful to stand up in front of an audience and sing. It all went horribly wrong one night when I forgot my words, perhaps more common in the music business than one might imagine, but it absolutely destroyed my confidence and I never sang in a folk club again.

One year, John and I went down to the Tynemouth Folk Festival. John's folks lived in Tynemouth and kindly invited me to stay for the weekend. Mrs Barrow looked kindly on me and felt I was probably in bad company at the festival. She said I was welcome to return to the garden if I was not enjoying myself. John and I had settled in to the afternoon open-air concert with a huge carry-out of Newcastle Brown Ale, as you do, when Mrs Barrow appeared on the horizon. The bottles were quickly hidden under our coats. I never worked out why really, not to offend John's mum I suppose. Mrs Barrow asked me if I was enjoying myself and again invited me to sit in her garden, patting me on the head in a motherly fashion. Sitting in even the loveliest of gardens during a folk festival was not what either John or I had in mind.

In need of further refreshment after the concert, we visited the local jam-packed pub where we came across Chuck Fleming – the original fiddler in The JSD Band, but replaced when he went 'walkabout' when the band was touring the USA. I suspect Chuck had spent the day in the pub. As we arrived, he was being given a final warning by the manager for bad behaviour, at which point he howled abuse at the manager, picked up his pint and downed the remains. He headed towards the exit but stopped en route, picked up the nearest pint, downed it and shouted further abuse at the manager. He did this a couple of times, to the astonishment of the deprived drinkers, and with one last roar of abuse, disappeared out the door. We, especially the Scottish contingent in the pub, breathed a sigh of relief, but then the door burst open and Chuck gave forth with further oaths, before disappearing for the last time. He was some character. One of his many stories was about the period when he worked in a car show-room. He was moving a car in the showroom, but somehow managed to drive it straight through the showroom window and into the street. I believe that was the end of his career in the motor industry – but what a fiddle player!

Another incident at Tynemouth that year was when John and I went to a hotel to hear the wonderful singer, Nic Jones. I approached the very busy bar, eventually fought my way to the front and ordered two whiskies. The harassed barman rudely told me he had no time to fiddle around with whiskies and I could only have two bottles of beer. These were passed to me, whereupon I told the barman I would pay for them when he served me my two whiskies. It worked, but it was the drink talking, I suspect.

Nic Jones was, as always, on top form, but he struggled against audience noise. When John and I spoke to him at the end of his perform-ance, he thanked us for being the only two who had paid much atten-tion to his singing. It was noisy right enough. Some years later, Nic was sadly involved in a bad motor accident which ended his singing career.

Later that night, John and I visited a Tynemouth club – by then I was somewhat beyond knowing where – and we were treated to one of the longest and best sets of session tunes I have ever heard, played by the Hedgehog Pie lads. Eventually the music had to stop, because of the neighbours, but I recall Roy Harris and me continuing in total silence to mime one song after another. How daft can you be with drink? Afterwards, John and I set a rather erratic course for the Barrow residence, but had to stop some distance from the house to regain our composure and control the giggles. What we were giggling about I haven't a clue. We sneaked in without awakening the redoubtable Mrs Barrow. Music festivals are invariably memorable, but none more so than Tynemouth that year. Thanks for inviting me along as your driver John.

June and I attended many festivals over the years, at first as general punters and later with our festival stall of LPs, cassettes and CDs, plus music books. Kinross Festival was an amazing affair and, while the music was always incredible, the mad escapades on the camp site after the pubs closed were hilarious, often accompanied by quite extraordinary singing sessions. Later I was elected onto the committee of the Traditional Music and Song Association of Scotland, responsible for Kinross and other festivals. In common with all committee members, I had to compere and perform other duties. On one occasion I was compere of a late-night concert. June was helping by controlling entry on the door, a thankless task because everyone had a tale to tell to gain entry to these concerts which were usually sold out in advance. Amongst those June refused entry to was Rab Noakes, one of the principal guests. June was doing her, 'I don't care who you are, you are not getting in here,' when I had to intervene and placate an irate Rab.

One year we managed to hire a caravan at Kinross camp site and I have never in all my life seen so many people squeeze into such a small space. The craic was great, and somehow we also managed to drink and sing in a space you could not swing a cat. Another year, we erected our 'walk-in' tent on the site – how it was not burned down I have no idea because we used candles for lighting and in those days when everyone smoked, this added another serious fire risk. I cannot remember how many people slept in the four-person tent, but it was in excess of twelve. No one seemed to mind and of course we were only asleep for an hour or two, and then back into serious drinking again. I really don't know how we maintained the pace from Friday to Monday – I certainly do not have the stamina nowadays when bed invariably beckons around 9pm.

Newcastleton Traditional Music Festival was another great festival where camping was also the order of the day. We were usually accompanied on the camp site by many friends who all turned out to view our arrival. To explain; we used our faithful Victor Vango tent over many years, for both camping holidays and festivals, but June never really got the hang of the necessary routine required in erecting it. I have a reputation, especially amongst friends, for being a bit impatient at times, and it is probably well-deserved. When the tent erection was not going well, yet again, I would shout at June to 'get a grip' (or words to that effect), to the amusement of our friends who dropped everything to watch 'the comic opera.' This only served to make me more angry and impatient with June, while the 'gallery' roared with glee. Ach well, it's good to give people a laugh and, once the bloody tent was up, it was off to the pub for a well-earned pint or ten. Later, when I had the record stall, the Newcastleton committee generously allowed me to set up in the lobby of the festival office where almost everyone passed through. I was eventually made an Honorary Member of the festival, and more recently the TMSA bestowed Honorary Life Memberships on June and me – both great honours.

Keith Traditional Music Festival, also under the auspices of the TMSA, was always a grand affair, until teenagers with absolutely no interest in the music but uncannily adept at under-age drinking, turned up in ever-increasing numbers and made the main thoroughfare of Keith a somewhat daunting place to walk down at night. That aside, it was a great opportunity to hear some of the finest tradition bearers from the 'travelling' community, including Belle Stewart, her daughter Sheila MacGregor, Lizzie Higgins and other great characters like Jane Turriff, Willie Scott, Willie MacKenzie, Tam Reid and not forgetting the always-present Jim Reid and The Foundry Bar Band. I also first saw The Vass Family at Keith. It seemed everyone in the family could play an instrument or sing. A long time afterwards, I was to meet with Mike Vass when he joined the Scottish group, Malinky.

I had a cousin, James Duncan, who for many years worked at the Black and White Distillery at Mulben near Keith. When it was mothballed for some years, James and his very generous and cheerful wife Myrtle moved into Keith itself. Having previously stayed in hotels and assorted bed and breakfast establishments in Keith, June and I were invited to stay with them at festival time. James was known affectionately by all and sundry in Keith, especially in the Football and British Legion Clubs, and his reputation for disposing of 'wee drammies' was legendary. He would sometimes waken me in the morning with a wee dram, and then sit me down to an enormous breakfast – what a start to the day. After James sadly died at a premature age, Myrtle insisted we continue to stay with her, and we did so until we gave up the festival stall.

Lona and Jim Thomson were stalwarts of the Keith Festival for years, and there was always a warm welcome from both of them when we arrived at Keith. They were ably supported by several other tireless workers. What would folk festivals be without unpaid volunteers?

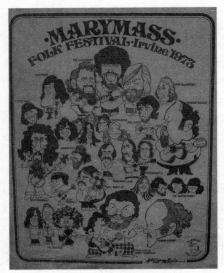

A Malky McCormick Poster.

We were late starters in attending the Tonder Music Festival in Denmark and only ventured there after the festival director, Carsten Panduro, a larger-than-life character, persisted with an open invitation. This festival has over a thousand unpaid volunteers, who do everything from manning the bars in the beer tents, cooking and serving the food, stewarding the concerts and even cleaning the loos. Apparently they have a waiting list of hundreds of people, all with a desire to become part of this amazing army of volunteers. Most of them work in the same teams each year, so there is this incredible continuity which helps to make Tonder one of the best-organised and most enjoyable music festivals in the world. It was at Tonder Festival that June met Tom Paxton and while chatting it transpired Tom was a descendent of a family who originally hailed from the Scottish Borders. By coincidence, the name Paxton, also from the Borders, appears in June's family tree so there may well be a family connection, although this has not been pursued.

Thurso Festival had its own attractions, not least of which were the short hours of darkness because of its northern location. Margie and Ian Sinclair were at the helm of this festival and were members of the wonderful Mirk group. Incidentally, Mirk was once invited by the Queen Mother to her summer home – The Castle of Mey – where they sang and played for her. As was obvious to one and all, the Queen Mother was a rather charming and gracious lady, so it is no surprise that she joined the group for drinks before and after the performance.

All festivals have their fair share of troublesome drunks, and one concert-night at Thurso I was standing at the ticket desk when a drunk approached and became a real nuisance – shouting, swearing and abusing the organisers who were, in my opinion, giving this guy far too much rope. My police instincts kicked in, and before he knew what was happening, I had snatched the pint out of his hand and unceremoniously wheeled him out the door, warning him to clear off. The festival committee who had witnessed this were most impressed and thanked me profusely, although I had really done no more than on any Saturday night in the police. Mind you, that sort of incident can backfire on you.

I recall a drunk acting up at the AAL Music Centre during the Edinburgh International Festival. Some of the organisers were getting real stick from him, so I intervened and played the 'sympathy trick', waffling on about how I fully understood his point of view, blah, blah, blah. I persuaded him gently to the main exit and was in the process of shaking his hand and saying 'Goodnight pal', when his rage again erupted and, without warning, he 'stuck the heid on me'. I was poleaxed and went down like a sack of potatoes as chummy fled the scene. I had two matching black eyes next day and had to make some excuse for not going on duty for a few days. I met the same guy, sober, a while later and raised the subject of the assault with him, but he insisted he had no recollection of the incident. The AAL Centre was a folk venue within the Student's Union premises on Chambers Street, jointly organised by John Barrow, John Allan and myself.

I was told (by a member of the band) of one group, travelling from Inverness Festival to Edinburgh. It had reached the point where relationships had broken down completely, as happens with groups who are constantly 'on the road' and often confined in a cramped, smelly van for hours on end. An argument developed between band members in the back of the van and, when it reached boiling point, and the driver could no longer concentrate on the job in hand, he pulled over to the hard shoulder. The members of the band leapt out and a punch-up ensued. After a while, they all got back into the van, bloodied but not seriously injured, and resumed the journey to Edinburgh. Now that would have been worth seeing.

John Barrow and I met often for a pint and it was not long before we were planning a folk festival in Edinburgh, drawing up lists of guests and venues. These particular plans never came to fruition, but a couple of years later things did suddenly develop in this direction. However, John and I never let the grass grow under our feet, and in addition to all

our involvement in folk music, we soon branched out into concert promotion. We first presented Clannad to an Edinburgh audience in the venue
above the Triangle Folk Club, and later The Bothy Band in Moray House
Theatre. The latter requested refreshments to be provided backstage and
put away two cases of beer before the gig even got underway – at least
one member was in danger of falling off his seat. It was one hell of a gig.

We never made a penny for ourselves out of any of these folk-related
ventures, but John was nothing if not an optimist. We were sitting in a
bar one night, discussing things folkie as always, when John turned to me
quite seriously and posed the question, 'Right Ian, what's going to be
our next money-making venture?' I went into fits of laughter, but John
could not at first see the humour in his question.

The Edinburgh Folk Club became a success, the SBB had achieved
notoriety and some acclaim, but we thought that Edinburgh still needed a
folk festival. There had never been one in a city up to that point, and it
seemed an unachievable dream until John Barrow one day broke the news
to me that the Scottish Tourist Board had invited him to be the Director
of the first Edinburgh International Folk Festival – to be presented in
March and April 1979 over ten days (including two weekends). This was
ambitious stuff. Judith Sleigh was the STB liaison person and kindly
reminded me how the STB had become involved in EFF:

'In the mid-1970s, the Scottish Tourist Board formulated a policy to
bring more visitors to Scotland out with the main season – i.e. October
to March. They considered one way to do this was to stage events, a
recognised way to attract visitors. As a government agency it wasn't the
role of the STB to organise and fund events on an ongoing basis, but they
could help kick-start them by offering funding, free publicity and mar-
keting expertise. It was envisaged that this support would be for two
years only (but it may have been extended in some cases). Examples of
these were The Burns Festival in Ayrshire, the Dumfries and Galloway
Festival, the Edinburgh Winter Festival and the Spring Festival (events
held in castles and historic houses all over Scotland). Judith's role was to
liaise with organisers, help them put together their application for funds,
see it through the submissions process okay, the actual giving of the
money and help with publicity – e.g. press releases, press visits and, in
the case of the Edinburgh Folk Festival, also help with the organisation.'

Judith understood from the outset the 100 per cent commitment of
both John and me and importantly, realized that we knew what we were
talking about (well, most of the time!).

Apparently the STB strategy did work in that (a) most of the festivals continued after the STB support was ended – although some folded and some, such as the Burns Festival, were changed; and (b) it is common now for historic houses to arrange one-off events.

John Barrow's take on his selection as Festival Director is as follows:

'STB wanted to run something to extend Edinburgh's tourist season, and they looked enviously at London's 12-month tourist season. The Winter Festival which ran in January 1977 and 1978 failed, so the STB scratched their heads and looked for the festival which Edinburgh didn't have but, if it did have, would pull in the punters. They had a steering group of about 80 to 100 people who met periodically at STB Headquarters at Ravelston Dykes – a most disparate group all with one aim – selling stuff to punters. It was this body who decided on (a) the festival 'type' and (b) the two weekends and the intervening week model of the Edinburgh Folk Festival. The weekends were there because that's 'what festivals did'! The weekdays were going to be when the punters/ tourists would stay on after the weekend and spend money in shops, hotels, restaurants and so on. STB couldn't give a toss about what sort of festival they had as long as the spin off was jinglin' tills to justify STB's investment. How Scottish can you get! So by the time I went to my first meeting at STB with the steering group, they'd already decided to have a folk festival (I don't know why), and it would be in the 'shoulder' months of March-April, coinciding with Easter, and they now needed someone to run it. I went to the meeting as a result of Alastair Moffat's suggestion. He was on the steering group because of running the Fringe then, and had been asked to run this festival but declined because he knew nowt about folk music. He knew me from EFC running Fringe gigs in the Royal British Hotel in the 1970s. John MacKinnon also turned down the invitation – I think he was just too busy with the recordings of The Corries then. So, in effect, I got the job by default.'

Personally, I would like to think John got the job because he was the right man for it. At that time I could imagine no one else entirely suitable and so it proved.

I was astonished, and of course honoured, when he invited me to act as his unpaid slave (sorry, chief steward) for the venues, and to act as stage manager of the major concerts. We were very close friends of course, and I am sure he knew he could rely on me. I immediately went about organising my winter leave to coincide with the festival dates, and was given special dispensation for this. All the fairy-tale planning John and

I had previously undertaken, I believe stood John in good stead, and now became a reality.

The task of stage manager was not a new experience to me because, after the death of Jimmy Elliot, a group of friends set up The Jimmy Elliot Memorial Trust in tribute to the great man. It was intended that funds would be raised and used for the purpose of assisting any folk musician who had fallen on hard times. A fund-raising concert was organised in the Usher Hall and the various parties involved, including Robin Morton, then of The Boys of The Lough, felt I was the right man to stage-manage the concert because I was 'bloody fuzz'. It was a memorable event and, in addition to the Boys of The Lough, the 'cast' included Mike Harding and many other artists. At the end of the evening, for probably the one and only time in his life, Robin paid me a compliment: 'You run a tight ship, Green.' I also learned a lot, including the art of keeping artists away from booze during a concert.

Anyway, back to the first Edinburgh International Folk Festival. John became a full-time employee of the newly-formed festival under the close scrutiny of a board. We all joked that this was 'the first bloody job' John ever had. He'd been a 'professional' student all his life up to that point. John threw himself into his duties as director and pulled the whole thing together in quite an astonishing manner. We met regularly and discussed the festival on an almost daily basis. I then began the enormous task of recruiting voluntary stewards and planning the actual stewarding of the numerous events. This entailed John and myself visiting the venues to get a clear picture of the layout of each and assess stewarding requirements.

We had wanted a folk festival in Edinburgh for a long time, now we had one, so it was 'all hands to the pump', 'shoulders to the wheel', 'noses to the grindstone' and 'no time for slacking'. John's contribution was enormous, of course, but we both worked our arses off. Judith encouraged us at every stage, and on occasions when things went wrong during the festival, she was the first to pull the cork out of the bottle and give us a dram.

The programme went to the printer, it was launched, and all the preparations made for the 1979 Edinburgh International Folk Festival. We thought we had covered everything, but a couple of days before the festival was due to commence, all sorts of emergencies occurred and there was a lot of running about in the evening. This included finding 50 or so straw-filled mattresses for a pipe band from Brittany!

A stewards' meeting was held, and when I spoke to them, I emphasised that we would be under the microscope. There were to be no cock-ups and, in particular, no one was to turn up for stewarding duty under the influence of booze. This was too big an event to be messed up. In the event, only one steward turned up pissed, and despite being a personal friend, was replaced immediately.

We prayed for good weather the first weekend and what happened? It bloody well snowed – heavily!

I left the police station on the afternoon of the first Friday of the first festival. On arrival at the Festival office, chaos was the name of the game and almost immediately an emergency arose – chairs had to be moved from the 'Festival Club' at Chambers Street to another venue, and bodies were needed. I went to Sandy Bell's, announced the emergency and asked for volunteers. Almost to a man, the drinkers left their pints – chairs were moved and the emergency was over – then back to the pints in Bell's. I will remember that extraordinary response for the rest of my life, mainly because many of the Bell's drinkers were quite cynical about the festival in the first place, but a fellow Bell's drinker needing help was another thing altogether. You know who you are – thanks again.

The biggest event of the first festival was an Alan Stivell concert in the Usher Hall on the second Saturday. On arrival there I immediately got stick from the caretaker who warned me that the concert had to run on time and if it didn't, then he'd pull the light switch. This guy had been in the job for too long and was just a bloody tyrant who thought he was God. An argument ensued. This was not a good omen. I then learned from the soundman, Johnny Ramsay, one of the great live soundmen around, that Stivell was taking so long to sound-check there would be little time for sound-checks by the other artists. I had to ask the theatre staff to hold the doors until all the sound-checks were completed, but the queuing audience was becoming impatient and things were going from bad to worse. The concert eventually got underway, but when Alan Stivell and his big band (not the acoustic one as some of the audience expected) got on stage, almost immediately PA problems occurred – i.e. loud cracking noises through the speakers. Stivell stormed off-stage with his band while Johnny tried to find the fault. The vision of a frantic, sweating Johnny crawling about on stage with his bum all but fully exposed is embedded in my mind for all time.

It took some time to trace the fault and the audience became restless, starting to catcall and boo. The night was getting worse – get me out of here! The problem was finally resolved by Johnny's sheer genius, and a very unhappy Stivell, plus band, returned to the stage. It was a very, very big folk-rock sound and I did not enjoy the concert, but the extraneous stuff may have been the cause of that. A number of punters who had not enjoyed the concert and were baying for blood tried to storm the back-stage to express their displeasure. This was prevented by staff and stewards, and I spoke to several seriously irate guys, explaining how to apply for a refund. They were not easily placated, although only a couple actually applied for a refund. A concert I will never forget, but for all the wrong reasons.

The rest of the festival went well that first year as I recall and the Festival Club, housed in the Students' Union premises in Chambers Street, immediately proved to be a hit for singing and instrumental sessions. The one problem was its size. Many nights the club bulged at the seams as more and more people wanted a 'piece of the action'. It was a cracking venue for a club. I remember one of the most amazing instrumental sessions in the lower bar, which went on unabated all Sunday afternoon. Late in the afternoon, just for the sheer hell of it, someone (Dick Gaughan, I think) suggested everyone play out of key and as badly as they could manage (probably for some it came easy!) and I laughed until I was sore. Bairns are easily amused!

Later, we were forced to move to the larger Students' Union premises at Teviot Row and, while it could easily accommodate the festival club needs, with a number of concert venues included, it never quite compared with Chambers Street. Continual complaints came from the singing fraternity who could not find a suitable place to sing, but on a couple of occasions the singers crammed into the stone spiral staircase of Teviot House which proved to have wonderful acoustics – the harmony singing made your hair stand on end.

The final Sunday night of that memorable first festival was a remarkable occasion. The tiredness drained away from everyone and the celebrations were incredible. John Barrow was carried shoulder high and we all sang 'For he's a Jolly Good Fellow'.

It was a very exhausting ten days. Judith Sleigh has since told me she was so physically tired that, at one concert, she fell asleep standing on her feet at the back of the hall; John Barrow was so buggered one night he was unable to hold a pen and sign a cheque and the last few days I looked like a zombie (I was told). I remember going home one night, trying to resolve a cash problem arising from one venue and being almost in tears with frustration. It worked out fine the next day.

We held a stewards' party later to thank the many volunteers for their hard work. On the whole, they had performed brilliantly, and John and myself were most grateful to them.

A review of the festival was undertaken because, although it had been a stunning success (mostly) and vast experience had been gained, it was important to be prepared for the second and following festivals. It became an annual event and, with a little more funding, seemed to have a bright future. Funding, however, is a tricky business and rarely comes with any guarantees. The first year the funding was small and mainly from the STB. When this ended, Lothian Region filled the vacuum. In 1981 Welcome Inns (Scottish and Newcastle Breweries) pitched in between £25,000 to £30,000 per annum for three years.

This was very controversial because Welcome Inns wanted their 'tuppence worth', as you can imagine, and the emphasis was on free gigs in their pubs and hotels, leaving little for underwriting ticketed gigs. Punters could go to selected pubs and hear top artists at no cost, other than a few pints (clever buggers, the Welcome Inns people). Arguments raged around the pros and cons of this, and whether it detracted from the ticketed venues. Personally, I think it did, but this was big sponsorship by any standards in those days and it was hard to refuse, despite the brewery's demands. I think Welcome Inns pushed it to the limits to get more than their fair share of publicity and goodwill, plus increased beer sales, but when they demanded the festival be renamed The Welcome Inns' Folk Festival, the board took a united stand and said, 'No.' This was a name check too far.

The financial situation became critical, and in retrospect, it was bloody ridiculous to expect a festival to be financially viable principally through 'bums on seats'. A lottery was introduced to raise funds, but that could not hope to match corporate sponsorship which was hard to find, although some moderate sums were raised. The search for sponsorship is also very time-consuming and often quite disheartening. To be honest, I am astonished John Barrow managed to have such successful artistic festivals with totally inadequate finances. When the board started to prune back directors' budgets, it was a retrograde step, albeit a necessary one, and proved to be the start of a slow decline.

Some of the possible sponsors we met were utterly clueless about something as important as Scottish traditional music, and somehow considered themselves to be above us mere folkies. I recall a concert in the Odeon Theatre. At the back-stage post-concert reception, I heard one of the principal guests, who must remain nameless, make the astonishing remark: 'It's all rather jolly and quaint, this folk music, but why do they all smell like wet sheep?' This said in an upper-class, 'bool in the moo', supercilious tone which thankfully seems less common these days. I felt like cutting him down to size, but refrained in the name of possible sponsorship. In any case, the man was a moron, although he might not have thought so, and incapable of considering the insult to our Scottish culture. Am I right in thinking that these types are now almost past their 'sell-by' date or is that just wishful thinking on my part?

The second festival director was Robin Morton, then Archie Fisher, Jack Evans and finally Dave Francis. While each gave of their very best and put their own personal stamp on the festival, it became clear to me, by then a member of the Festival Board of Directors, that there was an inevitability about the festival's future.

I remained on the Board of Directors of Edinburgh Folk Festival for a number of years, but once again I had to take stock of my involvement in so many activities. Also, as intimated earlier, I was unhappy with the way the festival was going. The experience I had gained, however, was invaluable and I think it was the same for John, who would not have missed it for the world. The volunteers of EFF clubbed together and we were presented with tankards for our services to the festival. This was an unexpected and generous gesture from these lovely folk.

The festival slowly withered and died through insufficient funding. What an appalling end to something which started with such high hopes, and presented folk or traditional music to a mainly new and much wider audience. However, many people who were introduced to traditional music through EFF continued their interest and can now be seen at Celtic Connections and other major festivals, so in many ways it was very successful.

With my resignation from the festival board and then my retiral from the police, I was able to concentrate my efforts on my flourishing Discount Folk Records business. The change from being a serving police officer to a businessman was seamless. Within a few days I was on my way to a new folk festival in Islay where I was brought crashing back to reality. I did not have the right site for selling albums and punters were scarce, so I decided to cut my losses and returned home after a few days. One of the few festivals where I was not able to show a profit at all – in fact it was a distinct loss.

For the next year I beavered away at the mail-order business, attending several festival events with our stall in between, and I believe I could have earned enough to augment my monthly police pension. I was always indebted to the main organisers of such festivals as Girvan (Peter Heywood) and Melrose (Hector Christie) who welcomed me and encouraged me to set up the stall. June was, of course, very involved with the folk festival stall side of Discount Folk Records and attended many festivals with me and spent long hours manning our stall, often when I went for a pint!

It was becoming clear to me, however, that more and more record retail chains were by then taking an interest in traditional folk music, and sections of their racks were allocated to such recordings. Most importantly, I was coming to the conclusion that I again needed a greater challenge, and slowly the idea formed in my head that I could start a record label, releasing two or three albums per year. There was an astonishing and ever-increasing array of talent on the traditional music scene in Scotland, which was to all extents and purposes being totally ignored by the record majors, based mainly in London. When major labels did sign up Scottish folk artists, the albums were invariably quickly deleted, and often options on three-record contracts were not taken up. I felt my new label would fill a void.

There were other record labels in Scotland at that time, of course: Lismor, Klub, Scotdisc, REL, Temple, Springthyme and Ross Records. Lismor and Klub were recording mainly piping, Scottish dance bands and what I would describe as music-hall artists, and not looking at folk musicians seriously. Ross Records featured mainly the very strong northeast bothy ballad culture, while Scotdisc concentrated mostly on 'country' and the very commercial end of the Scottish music market. REL were following a similar policy. Temple and Springthyme were releasing albums of artists I had more affinity with but, while Temple concentrated mainly on The Battlefield Band and Robin Morton's wife, the wonderful harpist Alison Kinnaird, Pete Shepherd of 'Springthyme Records', main emphasis was on The Foundry Bar Band and Jim Reid, and releases were spasmodic. A few other smaller labels and artist-owned labels more or less completed the Scottish music record industry output, although Fellside Records from Cumbria looked favourably on Scottish artists. I enjoy catching up with Paul Adams of Fellside from time to time because we share a similar philosophy on life.

My plans of a label came to a head when the talented fiddler and composer Ian Hardie told me that he was publishing a book of his tunes – *A Breath of Fresh Airs* – which he invited me to help promote. I suggested to him that the best way to promote the book might be to release a cassette of the tunes, whereupon Ian asked me if I would like to do it. I was immediately interested, and this was to become the first album I would release. The BBC 'Travelling Folk' programme heard of my plans for a label and Archie Fisher asked me to put up a couple of LPs as prizes for a 'Travelling Folk' competition to find a name for my company. Quite a few entries were received by BBC Scotland. I eventually settled on Greentrax Records. I felt the name had so much going for it. The name Grian was also suggested, so I used that as the name of my publishing company. A final entry arrived too late to be considered, but I thought it was very clever – Copout Records!

Hard on the heels of all this, Ian McCalman of The McCalmans contacted me and proposed an album by them to help the fledgling label get underway. This was so typical of The McCalmans: always there to give a helping hand to a fellow folkie. Having someone with their clout join the label at the outset was a real boost and I will be forever grateful to them.

I decided I would take nothing out of Greentrax for the first few years, apart from phone costs and petrol expenses, to enable me to build up a good sound financial base for the company. June and I lived off my remaining police pension and June's wages for her work as a store detective with John Lewis.

So, Greentrax Recordings was almost a going concern – just a few final details to be completed before 'Scotland's favourite record company' became a reality. Yet another chapter of my life (and my book, as it's turned out) opened up.

CHAPTER NINE

the early greentrax years

With the name of the company settled, plus a name for the publishing wing of Greentrax and two albums in the pipeline, we were ready to roll out the publicity machine. Greentrax Records and Grian Music were a reality!

Ian Hardie's fiddle album was titled 'A Breath of Fresh Airs' (TRAX 001) and consisted of Ian's own compositions. A few session friends backed him. The album will always be very special because it was the first Greentrax release – and a bloody good one. Ian went on to record further albums for us. A highly talented musician, he was always a pleasure to work with.

The McCalmans' first album for Greentrax was titled 'Peace and Plenty' (TRAX 002), and the group saw it as a wee 'leg-up' for a friend. I will be forever grateful to Ian, Derek and Nick for immediately providing a household name to the label, giving us a much-needed boost. 'Peace and Plenty' later went on to gain a Scottish Music Industry Association Gold Disc for sales achieved, and it still sells to this day. The McCalmans were so pleased with the way Greentrax handled 'Peace and Plenty' they stayed with us, and this excellent vocal harmony group went on to record ten albums for Greentrax. We also re-released two previous albums, plus one of Ian's own songs sung by friends ('McCalman Singular') and a McCalmans special '30th Anniversary Compilation Album'. We had to license some tracks for this from several major labels, and for once their attitude was reasonable. As The McCalmans prepare to retire at the end of 2010, Greentrax released a double CD album – 'The McCalmans – The Greentrax Years'. This is a remarkable selection of 46 tracks, and includes contributions from the two ex-members of the group – Hamish Bayne, a multi-instrumentalist and now a maker of fine concertinas, and the late, great

Ian Hardie.

Derek Moffat. As one of Scotland's great voices, he is sadly missed by all. Derek had many other artistic talents, and was the life and soul of every party he attended.

I decided to add a third album and go for a big splash at the launch of Greentrax Recordings. This was by a talented singer/songwriter, originally from the Western Isles, living in Aberdeenshire – Iain MacDonald. It was titled 'Beneath Still Waters' (TRAX 003) and contained some fine songs.

The launch of Greentrax and these three albums was held in late summer 1986, in the Edinburgh Press Club where I was an associate member. It was a huge success. I was subsequently interviewed for various newspapers, magazines and radio stations. The media always seem to find it an interesting angle that this crazy, retired police inspector should plough a considerable part of his pension lump sum into such an uncertain business venture. For me, it was less complicated. I simply felt that there was so much talent on the Scottish traditional music scene, which the record majors were more or less ignoring, there had to be room for an independent label such as Greentrax. Clearly album costings had to be finely budgeted, and a lot of work lay ahead in promoting the label. I was not expecting to make a 'million' (there are no millionaires on the folk scene!), but surely there was some money to be made from such a venture. I was warned I would 'lose it all' by various 'well-wishers', including a couple of Scottish record label bosses who were probably alarmed by this new upstart trying to 'muscle in' on the Scottish recording scene. However, I was not deterred and felt that where there was talent, there had to be a profit margin. The label duly flourished, to the surprise of some, although not me!

It was never my intention to own a recording studio, which would have saved considerably on studio fees, because I was not a musician or a trained studio engineer. My intention was to concentrate on promoting the label and its releases. I also made an

The McCalmans – Ian, Derek, Nick and Hamish at their 30th anniversary surprise party.

early decision not to act as an agent or to manage artists. That looked like a lot of trouble, so I left that to my old friend John Barrow who had by then established The Stoneyport Agency and signed up some of Scotland's best. This left everything neat and tidy, and I hit the ground running.

I did decide, however, that I should learn as much as possible about the recording process of those days, which consisted of recording onto multi-track tape, and then mixing down to two-track (stereo) quarter-inch tape. In retrospect, this was laborious, and mixing was a nightmare. Digital recording and editing, which revolutionised the recording industry, was in the offing. Whole sections of recordings, or even words, could be easily edited into the final mix with the use of a computer and the appropriate software. The days of splicing tape with a razor blade were gone forever. The digital recording system also allowed artists and others to set up fairly modest recording facilities within their back bedrooms. Studios proliferated as a result.

I visited a cassette duplication factory and an LP pressing plant to gain working knowledge of each process, and later, when we started CD replication, I visited the Sony DADC factory in Austria, where June and I were made welcome and introduced to the production system from start to finish. This was a most interesting visit, leading to a long and happy relationship with Sony DADC who now do all our CD manufacturing. There are companies doing pressings for less, but Sony DADC is reliable, and if there is a problem, it is rectified very quickly and to the customer's satisfaction.

Distribution in the UK was arranged when Gordon Duncan Distribution agreed to take Greentrax on board at the outset. When Gordon Duncan later threw his lot in with Dougie Stevenson of BGS, Kilsyth, my direct contact became the widely experienced Jack Scott who has spent most of his life in record distribution, including some years with Pye. Jack is always cheerful, despite health problems, and has a lot of excellent connections. Distribution in England was through the Topic Records distribution network but later that was moved to Proper Distribution, now one of the biggest independent distribution companies in Britain and winners of many awards. When Highlander Music was set up by William Crawford we felt we had finally achieved good coverage across the UK. William Crawford is a good man and someone I find easy to relate to and William has strived hard to satisfy the needs of the tourist and craft outlets in the Highlands and Islands. Other distributors have come and gone but Gordon Duncan Distribution, Highlander Music and Proper Distribution are well established. I am delighted to work with all three companies, each with something different to offer.

I was at Temple Studios in Shillinghill a few times while Ian Hardie's album was being recorded, and found the process a huge learning curve. Robin Morton, who was the engineer, did a great job on the album. The McCalmans' and Iain MacDonald's albums were recorded at Pier House Studios by one of the finest recording engineers I have had the pleasure to meet in the business – Peter Haigh. Although I was often 'told off' by Peter for anxiously rattling coins in my pocket, or nervously whistling as time seemed to run away from us, we became very good friends, and remain so today. I also learned much from him. While I will never be an engineer or record producer, I have gained a lot of recording knowledge, and feel confident enough to recognise good sound and arrangement when I hear them.

For years, I suggested Pier House Studios as the first option to artists recording for Greentrax, and thankfully many did use Peter's facility over the years. All these recordings benefited from his magical touch – the excellent quality he achieved was regularly commented on in reviews. Pier House became less popular with artists in later years when new, trendy and better-furnished studios opened their doors in Scotland. Make no mistake however, Peter always had the best of gear and knew how to use it – as well as build it. He does less recording nowadays, but is in high demand for restoration work, digital transfer and mastering. He is currently cleaning and transferring my 78s to CD.

I recall a very long session during the Iain MacDonald recording which went on all afternoon, evening and into the small hours of the following morning, because the producer, Dick Gaughan, had to complete the album before heading off on tour. That was a long slog, probably too long on reflection, but it finished up a fine debut album for Iain, well produced by Dick who went on do other fine production work for us.

Other studios of note that we have used include the very well-equipped Castle Sound Studios, owned by accordionist Freeland Barbour, which has another excellent recording engineer in Stuart Hamilton. Watercolour Studios in Ardgour, run by Nick Turner, has recorded several fine albums for us and there are other studios of note in Scotland which, for such a small nation, has a very productive recording industry.

An early album which springs to mind was Heather Heywood's 'Some Kind of Love'. Heather is a reluctant recording artist, and I only enticed her into the studio by using my charm and personality (or something like that!). Once she settled down and nerves left her, she was great. When she came to record one of the big ballads – 'The Cruel Mother' – Heather suggested she would run through it once before recording commenced, but unknown to her, I told Peter to hit the record button. Her performance was faultless and that was the one-and-only take of a nine minute (plus) ballad. Brian McNeill produced the album. I used him for many later productions and we became friends along the way.

As time went by I was not always able to spend as much time at recording sessions as I would have liked, but I do try to drop in at some point during the recording of most albums, if for no other reason than to 'show the flag' and give support – although this has backfired on occasions. I recall visiting one studio, when the excellent Sangsters were recording, whereupon the equipment blew up, and it is not uncommon for other strange happenings to occur when I drop in, including artist(s) suddenly finding great difficulty recording a song or tune. Presumably my presence is too much for them!

We recorded Sangsters for no other reason than I loved their singing. The Fifers later added a fourth member but initially they were a trio singing brilliant three part harmonies: Anne Combe, Fiona Forbes and Scott Murray, who also plays guitar. All three have won traditional singing competitions. I thought the group was just braw and Fiona's humorous introductions in her broad Fife accent are absolutely hilarious. It is wonderful to be able to sign artists you enjoy and not answer to any one. Oh the power of being boss.

My first 'discovery' was made at Dingwall Highland Festival where I was invited to set up my record stall. I loved the festival, especially in the early years, because the atmosphere was special, particularly the late-night sing-arounds. The principal organiser of the festival in those days was Rob Gibson, now a Member of the Scottish Parliament. At one Saturday concert, I popped in to hear a Gaelic singer I had not come across before – Catherine-Ann MacPhee. She was brilliant. I spoke to her after the concert and asked if she had made an album. She replied, 'I've never been asked' I said, 'I'm asking.' And that was that. Cathy-Ann went on to record four albums for Greentrax, plus some additional tracks, and I love her to bits. Cathy-Ann's ambition is to one day record a country and western album, and I do believe she could.

It was at the same festival that 'The Iain MacDonald Band', comprising three Iain MacDonalds, made their one and only appearance – Iain MacDonald (singer), Iain MacDonald (piper) and Iain MacDonald (percussionist and BBC Radio reporter) – utter madness but great fun.

Things began to happen with remarkable speed for Greentrax. I was contacted by Timothy Neat, who was about to make the film – 'The Tree of Liberty' – focusing on the arranging and recording of the songs of Robert Burns in the more classical settings of American arranger, Serge Hovey, and Scottish singer, Jean Redpath. The making of the film and its subsequent screening on STV, Grampian, Borders and Channel 4 in January, 1987 resulted in advertising for Greentrax which couldn't be bought, and led to the release of 'Volume 5' on Greentrax – to much press attention. On the date of the screening, our telephone number was shown at the end of the film. The phone started ringing and did not stop for days. The subsequent licensing of Volumes 1 to 4 and 6 by Rounder Records, USA to Greentrax followed quickly. This was certainly some coup for the fledgling label.

This excellent film was directed by Timothy Neat, and produced by the late Barbara Grigor. Shortly after the making of the film, Serge Hovey sadly died, but his son Daniel produced 'Volume 7' in due course. Jean Redpath was not able to continue her work on the series after that, and no further volumes have been released to date. Esther Hovey, widow of Serge, was a lovely lady, and both she and I looked at ways to continue the series, but without success. Sadly, Esther died early in 2010.

In 1989, I received a call from Sandy Ross of Scottish Television. He invited me to select an album from the recently televised 'Aly Bain and Friends' series – probably one of the most successful traditional music TV series of all time. I jumped at this chance and spent many enjoyable days at the STV Studios in Glasgow, selecting and mixing tracks with Aly Bain and Brian Paterson (STV) for LP, music cassette and CD release (our first CD!). The release of this album was another boost, and again put Greentrax into the public eye. It became one of our best sellers. It's a cracking album which caught the atmosphere of the 'live' series.

Phil Cunningham MBE and Aly Bain MBE who recorded 'June and Ian Green's Golden years' tune.

The furious rate of progress continued, and the launch of the Scottish Music Industry Association (SMIA) was the next exciting happening. I was elected treasurer because 'having been a cop you are bound to be honest'.

Unfortunately the SMIA was fairly short-lived and, while much was achieved in a few years, government funding was withdrawn, and we lost our office and paid administrator. I had already decided I wanted off the committee because of the continual bickering when some of the so-called 'big boys' from the pop and rock scene joined the association. The Scottish traditional music members were looked upon with some scorn by the new members, and we were referred to as the 'woolly-jumper brigade'. I soon resigned as treasurer. The loss of funding and the arrival of the pop scene in our midst made the situation untenable, for me at least.

Dressed for Midem.

In 1989, I attended Midem (the world record exhibition) and travelled to Cannes for this major event on the international recording industry calendar. On the first day I wandered around the massive exhibition centre with my jaw trailing on the floor, and with not a clue where to start. Every company in the world seemed to be there, including the majors, and I felt like a very small fish in a very large pond. I had kitted myself out with a sweatshirt bearing the Greentrax name and logo on the back and front, and this proved to be my salvation.

As I walked down one of the many passageways of the exhibition, I suddenly heard my name being called out from behind. I looked back and saw what I can only describe as an 'Aussie apparition', complete with cowboy hat adorned with wine corks, bearing down on me. It was the larger-than-life Warren Fahey of Larrikin Records, Australia. He pumped my hand for a moment and said, 'Eric Bogle (Eric was signed to Larrikin Records) tells me you are interested in licensing his albums for the UK and Europe.' 'Yes,' says I, still recovering from this unexpected meeting. 'Done,' said Warren, 'I'll send you contracts when I get back to Australia'.' And with that he was gone. That was my only 'done deal' at Midem that year, although I would have many other successes in future years as I went on to sign distribution deals in many parts of the world, and agreed licensing terms with foreign companies anxious to tap into the expanding,

Prolific songwriter Eric Bogle.

rich Greentrax catalogue. We even licensed albums to South Korea and Taiwan, actually earning some royalties, contrary to popular belief.

I eventually licensed three of Eric's albums from Larrikin who took on the distribution of the Greentrax catalogue in Australia in return. When Eric ended his contract with Larrikin and started his own 'artist label', Greentrax continued to license many more albums from him, and we have had a long and happy relationship based on mutual respect. Eric once said to me, 'Ian, you're the only fucking record company I trust.' Praise indeed.

In my mind, Eric is one of the all-time great songwriters and his anti-war songs, such as 'No Man's Land' (aka 'The Green Fields of France'); 'And the Band Played Waltzing Matilda'; plus a special favourite of mine, 'As if He Knows', are masterpieces. The first two have been covered by numerous artists. In a national newspaper Celebrity Top Fifty Anti-War Songs poll in 2003, 'And the Band Played Waltzing Matilda' and 'No Man's Land' were placed first and fifth respectively, above such international artists as Donovan, John Lennon, Bob Dylan, Elvis Costello, Leonard Cohen, John Prine and others. The Melody Maker said of Eric, 'Most of the best contemporary songs of the seventies were written by Eric Bogle.' In his adopted land of Australia, he has won many awards, including the Order of Australia Medal for services to the entertainment industry, as well as a Peace Medal from the United Nations for his efforts to promote peace and racial harmony. Even Tony Blair chose 'No Man's Land' for his personal statement as an anthem for peace in Northern Ireland.

Apart from receiving the Freedom of Peebles (his place of birth) and being recognised by the Scots Trad Awards, who placed him in their Hall of Fame, I am ashamed to say that Eric's outstanding work goes mainly unrecognised in the UK, despite his loyal fans turning out in droves when he tours here. Both BBC TV and Scottish Television have consistently refused to recognise him in any kind of concert feature or documentary, despite my persistence in trying to make them see sense. Shameful! I am also proud to call Eric and his long-time touring pal, John Munro, good friends. I have released an Eric and John album, 'The Emigrant and the Exile', and John's solo 'Plying My Trade'.

Much later we released Eric's amazing five CD box set 'Singing The Spirit Home'. The box set was another first for Greentrax and represents Eric's most requested songs, plus some of his own personal favourites and some not previously released in the UK: a total of 60 songs. A very popular purchase by his fans.

Meantime, back at my desk in the spare bedroom at Morven Street, from where I continued to operate Discount Folk Records and Greentrax Recordings, with the overflow stock in a storeroom elsewhere, I received a telephone call from Dr Peter Cooke of the School of Scottish Studies. I knew that the company, Tangent Records, had released the Scottish Tradition Series of recordings from the archives of the School but had ceased to trade. I was so surprised at what came next that I damned near fell off my chair. Peter said the School was looking for a new label to take on the Scottish Tradition Series and thought Greentrax was the very label. He asked, 'Are you interested?' I blurted out, 'Yes, if you think I can handle such an important series of recordings.' And Peter said, 'Okay, send us your contract and I will assemble all the parts for the existing 15 volumes of the series and get them to you.' I came off the phone not really sure if I had heard correctly, because this series of recordings had once been described as 'the most important series of traditional recordings ever', and here was I adding it to my ever-growing catalogue of releases. In due course, we released all 15 volumes and have since added eight more.

The Scottish Tradition Series of recordings is so important that some explanation for the reader is necessary. The audio archives at the School of Scottish Studies in Edinburgh contains an impressive and vast collection of recorded audio material from the various regions of Scotland. This was collected by members of the School staff, including the late Dr Hamish Henderson and Dr Peter Cooke to name but two, plus others. Much of the archive was collected post WWII but contributions are still being added to the archive today. Many of these recordings were made on location, often in the homes of the contributors and while some of the performances are often raw and voices shaky the performances represent the oral tradition as it has been handed down through generations. The contributors are often referred to as 'tradition bearers'.

The ongoing Scottish Tradition Series of recordings are selected and prepared from the vast tape archives at the School, the material is then edited and a master assembled. Meantime much research is undertaken at the School and extensive notes on the songs, music and the performers are assembled. Additional companion booklets accompanied the earlier albums in the series but later releases have all the information contained within CD booklets, designed to the maximum number of pages possible.

The first 15 of the Series were released on LP and music cassette formats between 1971 and 1988 by Tangent Records but when the company ceased to function all the albums were deleted. On receiving the masters and what artwork was available I immediately set about the enormous task of re-releasing the 15 albums on CD and music cassette, or cassette only in some cases, and this was accomplished between 1992 and 1995, with the generous assistance of the Scottish Arts Council and a very sympathetic bank manager at the Corstorphine Branch of the Bank of Scotland. A brief resume of all the albums in the Series follows.

'Bothy Ballads' was collected in the very fertile area, in more senses than one, of North-East Scotland where this unique music came about through the 'fairm toun bothies', where the horsemen and other workers lived and entertained themselves after long hard days. The songs were usually critical of their employers and working conditions and often had a humorous slant, such as 'The Muckin' o' Geordie's Byre'. Such songs were the first I heard being sung in rural Morayshire when I was a child.

'Music From The Western Isles' has proved to be one of the most popular albums in the Series and includes choral work songs, mouth music, canntaireachd and other Gaelic songs. Canntaireachd is often described as chanting or singing in Gaelic of classical pipe music, as a means of passing on the music and sounds very much like the bagpipe. This is now almost extinct.

'Waulking Songs From Barra' is also very popular and refers to the 'fulling' or 'waulking' of home-made cloth, often by several women pounding the cloth on a table, basically to shrink and strengthen it. The seven typical examples of these labour songs on the album captures admirably the sounds of Barra women at work – waulking the cloth. This custom has all but ended.

'Shetland Fiddle Music'. It is said that 'Shetlanders are much addicted to fiddling' and it is a well chosen phrase, describing a passion that is widely prevalent amongst both young and old who live in these northern isles, which continues to produce many capable fiddlers. The music presented on the album is a small but representative fraction of the music collected in the Shetland Islands during the years 1970–73, featuring the older unaccompanied fiddlers but also the way in which the playing is moving today.

'The Muckle Sangs' (the big songs or ballads), is a unique album of original source material, with much of the pioneering collection work having been done by the late Hamish Henderson. If anyone is serious about researching into the ballad tradition, this album is an absolute must. Forget that some of these singers are old and listen through to the style and spirit of their singing. Recording was on location, often in the singer's own homes. Singers include the legendary Jeannie Robertson and her daughter Lizzie Higgins and examples of the ballads are 'The False Knight Upon The Road' and 'Andrew Lammie'.

'Gaelic Psalms From Lewis'. 'The form of church praise featured in this album is a survival of something that existed all over Britain following the Reformation. In hearing Gaelic Psalm-singing for the first time, some who are entirely outside the culture find it an intensely moving experience' so wrote Morag MacLeod of the School. These Psalms involve the congregation and the precentor who lets the congregation hear clearly the text and melody first. Every time I listen to this remarkable album I find the hair on the back of my neck rising!

'The Fiddler and His Art' illustrates the various styles of fiddling from five different regions of Scotland and includes strathspeys, reels, marches, waltzes, slow airs and more, played by such stalwarts as Hector MacAndrew, Hugh Inkster, Pat Shearer, Andrew Poleson and Donald MacDonald. The various regional styles are evident in the playing.

The above were all released on CD and music cassette format by Greentrax but finance dictated that the remaining eight albums could initially be re-released only on music cassette, which was still a very buoyant album format in the '90s.

'Calum Ruadh The Bard of Skye' is an album of mainly stories plus some song from the last bard of Skye who died in 1978. He comes over as a fascinating character in his storytelling. This album was re-released in 2010 on CD format.

'James Campbell of Kintail' is an album of Gaelic songs by one of the most distinguished concert singers that Scotland has known. In a sense he had two repertoires. One consisted of the songs which made him famous on the concert platform, the other songs he learnt traditionally, most of them within his own family circle. It was also made available on CD in 2010.

'Calum and Annie Johnston' is a collection of songs, stories and piping from the Isle of Barra and amply demonstrates their fine singing, performed with sympathy and subtlety and with respect for the Gaelic context in which they and their songs both had their origins. Incidentally Calum died while piping the coffin of Sir Compton MacKenzie to his grave in 1973. This was re-released as a double CD in 2010.

'Pipe Major Robert Brown', 'Pipe Major Robert Nicol', 'Pipe Major William MacLean' and 'George Moss' are all recordings of pibroch (piobaireachd) and are some of the first tape recordings of what is regarded as the 'classical music of the bagpipe'. Brown and Nicol are of course the 'Bobs of Balmoral' referred to elsewhere in this book.

The last album of this group is 'Gaelic Stories by Peter Morrison', which is currently out of print but will, along with the other cassette only albums remaining, be re-released on CD as funds permit.

The albums in The Series which have been released since Greentrax became responsible are as follows:-

'William Matheson Gaelic Bards and Minstrels' is a double CD of the songs of former lecturer and reader in the Department of Celtic at the University of Edinburgh. He was regarded by the School as their most reliable consultant on questions of Gaelic oral tradition, especially songs and their melodies. Some of his vast repertoire of songs was recorded by the School during 1982 and 1983. This is a considerable body of work.

'Scottish Traditional Tales' is also a double CD release and is a unique collection of traditional tales from the School's sound archive. The storytellers include Jeannie Robertson, Davie Stewart, Stanley Robertson, Betsy White and more. Many of the stories are spellbinding. The package includes a 60 page CD booklet.

'Clo Dubh Clo Don' is an album by various renowned Gaelic singers and the CD booklet contains both Gaelic and English lyrics. The singers include Hugh MacRae, Penny Morrison, Mrs Kate MacDonald, William Matheson, Peggy Morrison and the wonderful Flora MacNeil.

'Joan MacKenzie – Seonag Niccoinnich' was a Gaelic singer extraordinaire and the album leaves the listener longing for more. She was a somewhat reluctant recording artist and the School treasure her recordings. She died a few years ago.

'The Carrying Stream' was released in 2004 as a sampler of the albums released up to that point (Volumes 1 to 20) plus some other gems not previously available. This is a wonderful starting point for someone interested in the Series but unsure where to begin.

'Orkney' consists of three distinct parts – 'The Land, The Sea and The Community' and is a rich and varied set of field recordings from the

School archives. They are mainly the work of Alan Bruford and represent a comprehensive medley of song, story, custom, belief, instrumentals and even a recipe for Beesmilk Pudding!

'Chockit on a Tattie – Children's Songs and Rhymes' is an exhilarating addition to the Series and includes material recorded between 1952 and 1981. The 54 minute CD is immaculately presented and produced. It includes a short but informative introduction from the project editor, Ewan McVicar. The album is crammed with zesty pleasures. Those recorded include Lucy Stewart, Jean Redpath MBE, Ray Fisher and Jeannie Robertson. Did you know that a 'bubbly jock' is a turkey or that a 'theevil' is a porridge stirrer? The album is full of material learned in the playground.

'Wooed and Married And Aa' is a classic series of recordings and draws together a selection of songs, tunes and customs across Scotland connected with marriage. Items from both the Scots and Gaelic are included, as are items from different occupational groups including fishers, farmers and factory workers. One reviewer of this album wrote: 'Trust Greentrax. Is there a better label in Europe? 'Wooed and Married And Aa' is a fascinating and really interesting collection of music, all centering around Scottish weddings' The praise, however, should go to the School.

There are more albums in the pipeline of course but at Number 23 this is a substantial collection already. I am very proud to have the Series on Greentrax, and will be forever indebted to the faith shown in me by the good folk at the School of Scottish Studies. In particular I would mention Maggie MacKay and Kath Campbell. I would also acknowledge the help of Kath Campbell in providing some of the album descriptions.

The label attracted many fine artists already established in the music business. Rod Paterson, who I regard as Scotland's finest male singer. He is a great exponent of the songs of Robert Burns and recorded 'Songs From The Bottom Drawer', a stylish Burns collection. Rod has also sung with such fine groups as Jock Tamson's Bairns, The Easy Club, Ceolbeg and more. He has appeared on TV so often he should be a household name and deserves far more recognition. Rod has many other talents and took time out from touring to build his house in Perthshire some years back. Quite astonishing.

Jock Tamson's Bairns was one of the most esteemed and influential Scottish folk bands. The band grew out of the vibrant session scene in 1970s Edinburgh, centred on the legendary Sandy Bell's Bar. The band released two albums in the 1980s and it was Richard Thompson who picked their second album 'The Lasses Fashion' as one of his 'Top Ten

All Time Favourites' in *Q Magazine*. In 1996 Greentrax released the two albums on one CD titled 'A' Jock Tamson's Bairns' and made a comeback which lasted until 2010 when the band finally called it a day. In their 'revival' period they made two more albums, one with the unusual title 'May Ye Never Lack a Scone'. The 'characters' in the band in recent years were Derek Hoy, Ian Hardie, Jack Evans, John Croall, Norman Chalmers and Rod Paterson, which is a powerful line-up by any standards.

Adam McNaughtan is one of the great characters of the folk revival and songs such as 'The Glasgow That I Used To Know', 'The Jeely Piece Song', 'The Yellow on The Broom', based on the experiences of traveller Betsy Whyte and 'Oor Hamlet', a hilarious send-up of the original, are classics to be found in the Greentrax album 'The Words That I Used To Know'. Adam recorded another wonderful album for Greentrax – 'Last Stand at Mount Florida' – which included the side-splitting 'Erchie Cathcairt' and 'Cholesterol', both on the theme of healthy eating. Adam also has a large repertoire of street and playground songs. All this has earned Adam a most deserved worldwide reputation. Adam's often some-what dour expression hides a very funny man and a remarkably produc-tive mind. I learned from Adam that he will retire from singing in 2010 which will be a great loss.

June and I plus a few friends were invited to a recording studio in Edinburgh, many years before I launched Greentrax, to provide a 'live' audience when Adam was recording 'The Glasow That I Used To Know'. We were singing the choruses some-what tentatively I suppose when the angry recording engineer came out of the control room and harangued us severely for not singing loud enough. We were ordered to get some (free) wine down us and all the recordings were done again, with the partially inebriated singers bawling out the choruses. Proof of this is on the album which Greentrax inherited many years later, now part of Adam's CD 'The Words That I Used to Know'. Lesley Hale played guitar for Adam that night.

Adam McNaughtan (Greentrax Artist).

Brian McNeill, who'd recently left The Battlefield Band, came to Greentrax and recorded the amazing 'Back o' The North Wind' album. It is a collection of songs and music on the subject of emigration to North America. Brian toured this as a stage show highlighted with slides. The songs include – 'Muir and The Master Builder' – a tribute to John Muir of Dunbar, one of the first effective conservationists. Brian recorded more albums for Greentrax, including a follow-up to 'Back o' The North Wind' – 'The Baltic Tae Byzantium' – which explores emigration eastwards into Europe. Brian has one of the busiest schedules I know of. He is a workaholic with boundless energy. In addition to being a fine performer and multi-instrumentalist, he is a gifted producer, tutor and an author. A visit from Brian is like a whirlwind hitting the office and when the dust settles he is probably halfway to America.

The late, great Iain Mackintosh, had one of the most impressive stage personalities I have come across. I recall him coming on stage to do the warm-up spot for the JSD Band in an Edinburgh theatre, in front of a pretty unruly audience, many of whom had been on the booze. Within a moment or two Iain had them eating out of his hand and singing choruses. Iain had the most amazing ability to seek out good songs and make them fit his own personal style, with simple banjo accompaniment. I never saw Iain do anything less than a brilliant gig. From time to time he toured with many fine artists, including Hamish Imlach and Brian McNeill. There is a story that Iain, who spoke very good Danish, bumped into The McCalmans on tour in Denmark and Ian McCalman asked him for a Danish phrase to go on stage with. Iain duly obliged and Ian McCalman used the phrase for a couple of nights but was not getting the expected response, until someone told him he was telling the audience 'he had the clap'. Iain was a lovely man with a great sense of humour of course and his death meant a great loss.

Robin Laing has made several excellent recordings for us, including his unique 'Whisky' series of three albums to date. Robin wrote the winning song for the centenary celebrations of the Forth Bridge in 1990, simply titled 'The Forth Bridge Song'. It is most descriptive and captures the scene brilliantly. 'The Man Who Slits

The final lineup of The McCalmans prior to retiral in 2010.

The Turkey's Throats at Christmas' is one of Robin's party pieces and was a natural for inclusion on our 'Bah Humbug' album. Robin is a most loyal artist and has been with Greentrax since the very early years. If you can persuade him, Robin sings another hilarious song about an inflatable doll and the results of the over-sexed owner giving it a love-bite on the neck.

Ceolbeg was one of the first bands to sign to Greentrax, and what a talented bunch they were, including the late Davy Steele who contributed several excellent self-penned songs to add to the Band's repertoire. Ceolbeg, with a full head of steam, took some beating and the excitement they generated was impressive. They made 'An Unfair Dance' as their second album for Greentrax with Dick Gaughan at the helm. Dick mixed the album while the group was on tour and there was some disagreement on how it had been mixed. I was fine with it but no way could I put out an album that the group was not 100 per cent behind so some tracks were remixed. It was a bloody good album and some of the tracks were used as the soundtrack for David Bellamy's TV series 'Crossing The Border'. The front cover of this album consists of a very unusual painting of a dancer with two left feet, dancing over two swords with the cutting edges facing upwards. The subject is 'Zito The Bubbleman' a character Gordon Duncan shared a stage with in Italy. Gordon subsequently wrote the tune of the same title which Ceolbeg made their own. After Davy Steele departed, Rod Paterson took over lead vocals with Ceolbeg

Ceolbeg was followed by the ground-breaking Shooglenifty, winners of the BBC Radio Scotland Album of The Year 1994 for their stunning 'Venus in Tweeds'. The band is very exciting and their danceable music attracts a younger audience who invariably take to their feet in wild Highland-like flings. There music was described as 'acid croft' by one reviewer. They made a second album – 'A Whisky Kiss' – but then went their own way, setting up their own label. I was very sorry to see them move on because both albums are amongst our 'best sellers'. The group then underwent some personnel changes and while they continue to record, 'Venus In Tweeds' is for me their finest piece of work. Tony Blair shared the stage with Shooglenifty for a photo call in Japan and was photographed holding their first two CDs. Good one Tony.

Folk-group competition winners Burach joined the label about the same time with their heady mix of folk-rock led by Sandy Brechin's accordion. They made three albums for Greentrax and at one album launch the Band members all entered stage left from a tent. One of Sandy's brainwaves! The band underwent various changes but they could always wind up the decibels, which was not to the liking of all. I thought they really grooved.

Deaf Shepherd was another exciting band with very talented musicians and singer John Morran who did a great version of 'Huntin' The Buntin' by Gavin Stevenson from Lanarkshire. Gavin phoned me in tears when he heard this recording of his song. He was a lovely man with great writing skills – another who sadly died at too early an age. The band moved on after two albums. They did one album on their own label but only rarely make a live appearance these days. A great shame.

Then there was Mac Umba, another band doing new and exciting things with the music, although again not to everyone's taste. I had a call from a person, who shall remain nameless, who said, 'You know, this is not the way traditional music should be going, and I think you should stop encouraging this kind of stuff.' The music sounded good to my ears, so I ignored the advice, but it proves how some people think Scottish traditional music should be kept in a fossilised state and never experimented with. Rubbish!

An interesting story on Mac Umba came about when I sent their first album – 'Don't Hold Your Breath' – to a radio station in Austin, Texas. To let you understand, Mac Umba were playing Scottish music on Highland bagpipes, and merging elements of Brazilian and Caribbean percussion,

Mac Umba in Switzerland.

which thrilled audiences worldwide. The Austin radio station immediately featured the album on a programme and at the end of it the station switchboard was jammed for hours. A local record shop, Waterloo Records, ordered the album from us and went on to sell a staggering thousand (plus) copies. I thought, right, we need to capitalise on this and tried to emulate the success in other parts of the USA, but strangely without the same success. It seemed that Mac Umba music tickled the fancy of Texans mainly. What further astonished me was that, within a few months, two or three Mac Umba band impersonators were performing there. Mac Umba were later invited to take part in pre-match celebrations in both Paris and Bordeaux during the 1998 World Cup Football Finals in France.

A very strange confrontation I had in the early days was as a result of releasing an album by the superb Irish singer, Niamh Parsons. I went over to Belfast to promote the album and seek Irish distribution, but the first distributor I saw asked me if it was my intention to release more albums of Irish artists, to which I replied, 'If the right artist comes along, yes.' This was unexpectedly followed by the almost threatening reply, 'Maybe you should stick to Scottish artists and leave Irish artists to us.' I was also refused distribution on the supposed grounds that, 'No one in Ireland is interested in Scottish music.' Has anyone ever heard such nonsense? Niamh has the unenviable reputation of running up the biggest ever phone bill during a Greentrax recording session which of course the studio owner added to our invoice. I, in turn, slapped it on to Naimh's stock invoice which led to the end of a very short relationship.

There were many more wonderful artists to be signed up to Greentrax in the following years, too many to list in this book (a Greentrax catalogue, listing all our albums, is available), but some of the Gaelic signings are worthy of special mention. I was very proud to sign up Mairi MacInnes who is one of Gaeldom's best. Mairi had the great distinction of taking part in the Edinburgh Military Tattoo, singing on the castle esplanade. Also, each year she is invited to Wales to sing with a Welsh choir. Mairi has so far made three albums for Greentrax with another at the planning stage. Our wee 'Westie', Mairi Bheg', is named after Mairi MacInnes because we bumprd into her, just before going to pick the wee puppy.

Very soon, another Gaelic stalwart, Margaret Stewart, joined us and made two ground-breaking albums with piper Allan MacDonald. She then went on to make a well-researched Gaelic song album which includes an ancient waulking song, an Ossianic ballad, a Jacobite epic and other rare gems, which won her a Scots Trad Award. Margaret is not only a very fine singer but she has an amazing knowledge of Gaelic song and in particular Jacobite songs, which she features in her lectures at the RSAMD.

We signed up another great Gael in Kathleen MacInnes who also won a Scots Trad Award for her debut album. She has an unusual, slightly husky, voice and her album is racking up good sales. She has a big TV reputation and her voice can be heard in the latest film version of Robin Hood. Along with Cathy-Ann MacPhee, this effectively means Greentrax truly has a wealth of Gaelic women singers no other label can boast. And, of course, we also recorded the amazing all-woman 'waulking' group, Bannal, who present their live performance around a large table where they do a fine imitation of waulking the cloth.

The Legendary Dick Gaughan.

Among other notable artists we attracted was the legendary Dick Gaughan. He came to Greentrax in 1996, and gosh was I proud to see him come aboard. One of the most highly regarded folk singers in the UK and beyond, Dick is another artist who was a friend from the early Fuzzfolk years. I never cease to be impressed by his concerts and his song 'Both Sides the Tweed' is now a folk classic and has been recorded by many other artists. He is also a gifted producer if you are lucky enough to find him with some free time between constant touring. It is a privilege to have this folk 'giant' on Greentrax. We have six Gaughan albums in our catalogue and I regard him as a good friend.

Tony McManus, guitarist extraordinaire and ranking amongst the best in the world, has recorded four albums for us. Tony is now based in Canada and we see less of him in Scotland, which is a great pity. Tony's music was used in the film 'Ondine', an American blockbuster apparently, but Tony is used to high profile stuff and has toured with some of the world's greatest. His most recent album – 'The Maker's Mark' – features Tony playing a different make of guitar on every track and ends with him playing several of the guitars – not at the same time, even Tony isn't that good! Make a good Guinness Book of Records entry? Tony was awarded 'Instrumental Solo Artist of the Year', at the Canadian Folk Music Awards for 'The Maker's Mark' album and has several nominations to his credit.

Alasdair Fraser and Tony McManus (Culburbie and Greentrax Artists).

One of the longest established Scottish groups is The Whistlebinkies, who first recorded with the Irish label Claddagh, then came to Greentrax in 1996 and recorded a 'Wanton Fling'. This is another loyal group that has remained with the label and recorded two later albums, with possibly a fourth to come. The driving forces behind The Whistlebinkies are Rab Wallace of the Piping College and Eddie McGuire, who enjoys playing traditional music but is a composer of classical music of some note. They are a major leading force in Scottish music.

The fine traditional singer, Sheena Wellington, has recorded two albums for Greentrax, one of which includes the soundtrack of 'A Man's a Man for A' That', as sung by her at the opening of The Scottish Parliament. This was a personal triumph for Sheena because in the final chorus the entire gathering, including The Queen, appeared to join in. Sheena is another workaholic and has done so much in the name of Scottish traditional music. At one time we thought Sheena was going to continue where Jean Redpath left off with the Serge Hovey/Robert Burns project but we just could not obtain sufficient funding to pay the high costs of the production.

Isla St Clair chose Greentrax to release an album of her mother's songs, 'Scenes of Scotland', produced by that nice man, Phil Cunningham. Isla had a few understandably emotional moments when recording this album. BBC Radio 2 then invited us to release two albums of Isla from their very popular radio series, 'Tatties and Herrin' – 'The Land' and 'The Sea'. Isla became a national celebrity through her work with Larry Grayson on 'The Generation Game'. Isla was at one time married to Hamish Bayne and I signed their Wedding Banns. That's a few years ago though.

Sheena Wellington at the Opening of the Scottish Parliament. 1 July 1999.

Other artists attracted to the label include the powerful singer, Ian Bruce; who did a great album of traditional songs. Later Ian went into partnership running a highly acclaimed restaurant in Edinburgh but still manages time to do some gigs. Jim Malcolm; joined us for two excellent song albums and then joined the Scottish band Old Blind Dogs. Rob MacKillop recorded two very unusual lute and mandour albums, which attracted a lot of attention. Rob is an amazing musician. Gill Bowman recorded a collection of Burns' songs – 'Toasting the Lassies' – a look at Burns from the female perspective as a companion to her Festival Fringe show which she presented for years in Edinburgh. Janet Russell and Christine Kydd did two excellent albums, and I thought they had a great future after attending an American Folk Alliance Conference, where they took the audiences by storm, but the partnership did not last. Wendy Stewart temporarily left her role as harpist with Ceolbeg to record 'About Time', and went on to do two more harp albums. A most unusual album released by Greentrax, and described by Neil Hedgeland in Folk Roots as 'a real gem', was Lindsay Porteous – 'Portrait of a Scottish Jew's-Harp Player'. The early years were indeed busy, and thoughts of a leisurely few albums each year went by the wayside very quickly. Soon Greentrax was releasing two albums every month, which seemed to annoy some other Scottish labels.

We entered the field of piping by first recording the 'national treasure' Gordon Duncan but more of him later. Greentrax also released other great piping albums. Hamish Moore, a leader in the revival of the Scottish small pipes (also referred to as the cauld wind pipes) not only as a player but also as a maker, recorded a cracking solo album – 'Stepping on the Bridge' – which showcased his love of Cape Breton and the musicians there.

The late and sadly missed Gordon Duncan.

This complemented the very progressive and experimental recordings in his partnership with award-winning jazz musician, Dick Lee. For a time Hamish suffered from a problem with his finger joints which curtailed his playing but in recent times he has regained his fingering touch and it is good to see Hamish playing again, especially in sessions.

An unusual and fine solo album by Dougie Pincock on the Highland bagpipe and other wind instruments prompted Dougie to name his album 'Something Blew', which preceded albums by pipers, Iain MacInnes and Gary West, both associated with BBC Radio Scotland's popular radio programme, Pipeline. A pipe band album which sold well was recorded by The Scottish Gas Caledonian Pipe Band, incorporating their ceilidh band. This was somewhat different from the usual pipe band albums but generated good sales. That was followed by an album of Jacobite music by the now defunct Drambuie Kirkliston Pipe Band. It is also a most popular album, mainly I think because of the Jacobite theme, although the Band achieved significant success under the leadership of Pipe Major Martin Wilson. In 1995, The MacNaughtons Vale of Atholl Pipe Band, then a real force to be reckoned with, recorded a concert in Motherwell Civic Centre under Pipe Major Ian Duncan and his brother Pipe Sergeant Gordon Duncan. This was a mind-blowing concert, resulting in a very fine 'live' album which was cleverly titled 'Live 'N' Well'. Gordon did a solo that night and the hundreds of pipers in the hall had their eyes glued to Gordon's fingers. Those were vintage times for the 'Vale', who also had several other stunning solo performers in their midst.

It is quite an experience to attend the World Pipe Band Championships, or 'The Worlds' as they are affectionately known, and watch these and other pipe bands in action, performing at their best. On several occasions June and I rented a stall at the Worlds and always achieved significant sales. For hours afterwards you can hear pipe bands in your head, a strange experience.

I got a crack at recording The Pipes and Drums of the 1st Battalion The Black Watch by kind invitation of Pipe Major Steven Small. Peter Haigh and I travelled up to Fort George Barracks near Inverness to record the album. We had a great time. The hospitality and kindness extended to us by Steven, the sergeants and everyone else at the barracks was heart-warming. We were guests of the sergeants' mess each evening and, as such, we were never allowed to put our hands in our pockets to return the generous hospitality. On the first morning, I was ambling my way from the barrack-room Peter and I shared, when the unmistakable roar of the regimental sergeant major came from the other side of the parade ground. I came to a dead stop, aware that I was the subject of his wrath, and automatically came to attention as he bore down on me. When I explained my reason for being in the camp, he could not have been nicer to me, and said he would join me for a drink later. This was my first contact with the army since my service, and like many, I thought the army had 'gone soft', but this meeting, along with the sight of soldiers being marched around at the double and called 'horrible little men' by NCOs, made me realise that nothing had really changed. Steven was also quite a disciplinarian, and I recall one piper, who had a hangover, getting one hell of a dressing down from him. I was to meet Steven many more times after that occasion, and was delighted to learn of his eventual promotion to Captain and Director of The Army School of Bagpipe Music and Highland Drumming at Redford Barracks. Steven and I had at least one thing in common – we both dearly loved Gordon Duncan.

When I learned of Gordon Duncan's sudden death in 2005, by which time he had made three albums for Greentrax, I broke down in tears, and have cried a lot for him since. We had built up a bit of a 'special' relationship, although I would hasten to add that I consider most Greentrax artists to be my friends – there is no 'us and them' in this company. Gordon phoned me often, always with great ideas for a new album or to tell me of his latest composition. He suffered badly from depression which led him to drink a lot, and I could always tell what sort of mood he was in. If he was 'down', he'd say, 'Hello boss.' If he was up, he'd open with, 'Hello Greenie.' We had a couple of disagreements about his drinking at gigs but, give him his due, he took it on the chin from me. On one occasion, after writing him a critical note on this theme, he phoned and said, 'Hello Greenie. Are you still pissed off with me?' I burst out laughing! I could never hold a grudge against pawky Gordon.

After his death, his dad, the great bothy ballad singer, Jock Duncan,

IAN GREEN OF GREENTRAX

HORNPIPE   GORDON DUNCAN

Ian Green of Greentrax says "Gordon recorded three albums for Greentrax, the first in 1994, and in the intervening years we became good friends. Gordon often referred to me in his pawkie way as "Greenie" or "The Boss". I was very, very proud when Gordon named one of his compositions - "Ian Green of Greentrax" - in my honour".

The photo is from Gordon's second CD with Greentrax, The Circular Breath CD.

© GORDON DUNCAN'S TUNES

told me that Gordon had once said, 'You know, Ian Green is my second dad.' When Gordon wrote a tune and named it 'Ian Green of Greentrax', I was absolutely knocked out. It's a great tune, and has already been recorded several times and played at the World Pipe Band Championships. His funeral was one of the saddest I have ever attended. When Gary West led the cortege from the church, playing Gordon's 'Sleeping Tune', there was not a dry eye amongst the multitude of people in attendance. On journeys north, I never fail to stop off at his grave in Pitlochry and stand there blethering to him (none as silly as an old fool!). The Gordon Duncan Memorial Trust, on whose committee I am proud to serve, has been set up to preserve his memory and assist up-and-coming musicians. It includes members of his loving family and friends.

The Trust seeks donations, but also instigates money-making projects, including the publishing of books, and earns profit from annual memorial concerts in Perth Concert Hall. The first of these was held in 2007 and was recorded by Jamie McLean of Butterstone Studio. The album – 'A Celebration of the Music of Gordon Duncan – A National Treasure' – was subsequently released by Greentrax, with all the profits going to the Trust. It's a fine tribute to him, and I commend it to you. Ross Ainslie and Brian McAlpine deserve special mention for their management and musical direction of the concert, but many others contributed to make this, and subsequent concerts, so successful. I have never attended a concert so charged with emotion as the first one and, when photos of Gordon were projected onto a screen at the rear of the stage during the final set, there were again many tears all round.

Gordon was a prolific composer, and many of his tunes are played around the world, but none more so than his amazing 'Andy Renwick's Ferret' which has been recorded hundreds of times and was included in a set which was a 'hit' success in Canada. His tunes are available in a book compiled by his brother Ian, simply titled *Gordon Duncan's Tunes*; another, *The Music of Ian and Gordon Duncan – A Few Tunes Mair* is also available. As a piper, Gordon bordered on genius. He was a totally innovative piper, who undoubtedly changed the face of modern piping for the better. It is just so sad that a role such as 'Scotland's Piper in Residence', or some such position, could not have been found for him. Not all agreed though. One senior piper, who had by then perhaps 'lost the plot slightly', was judging a competition in 1993, between Gordon Duncan and Gordon Walker, and in his summing up he remarked, 'If this is where piping is going, then I will take up the fiddle.'

We did one retrospective album of Gordon's piping, entitled 'Just For Gordon', which consisted of tracks from various sources, mostly 'live' performances, including Gordon playing in the competition referred to above. Gordon's music will live on through his compositions and the Trust, but oh how I miss him. Thanks are due to Murray Blair, an excellent producer, for his help with this production.

I will refer later to some of the amazing signings Greentrax attracted in the second half of its existence, including the quite remarkable crop of talent emerging from the Royal Scottish Academy of Music and Drama (RSAMD) and the Plockton School of Excellence. Brian McNeill was director of the traditional music courses at the former, and my old friend Dougie Pincock is the popular musical director at the latter.

CHAPTER TEN

the GReentRAX yeARS – family events

here were, of course, many family events of note during my early days of Greentrax. Shortly after my retirement from the police, a family holiday was planned with Linda and David and their young daughter Sarah; Andrew, his wife Tricia, plus weans Craig and Lyndsey; as well as June and myself. We went for two weeks to the island of Andros in Greece and had, on the whole, a great time. Unfortunately, towards the end of the holiday, June suffered what I recognised immediately as a heart attack, and we had to call out the local doctor in the middle of the night but he did not recognise June's symptoms. He gave her a 'water' tablet and asked us to bring June to the surgery for further examination in the morning. Andrew and I got June to the surgery, but the very effort of walking to and from a taxi set off another heart attack. We crashed into the surgery, with June in a hellish state. The doctor got the message this time, maybe because I was somewhat forcefully telling him what was wrong with her. After taking a cardiograph and comparing the reading with a medical book, he went into what can only be described as blind panic. He grabbed a kit to insert a needle for a drip, but dropped the contents on the floor. I had to help him with a second kit, open it and this time he managed get the needle into June's arm to set up a drip while he administered other injections. My police training to be calm in emergencies proved to be useful that morning. The doctor then calmed down enough to get on the phone and call for a Greek Air Force helicopter to be sent from Athens.

When the helicopter arrived, the stretcher was somehow fitted into it, with June's feet sticking out the door and me hanging on for grim death, also at the open doorway. I'm terrified of heights, and flying is an ordeal for me under perfect conditions! The helicopter lifted off in a cloud of dust. I had no time to say goodbye to the family assembled at the landing field, or even enough sense to ask one of them to go back to the apartment and get me some spare clothes or my passport or, more importantly, some money. I had a few small coins (drachma) in the pocket of my shorts, a short-sleeved shirt on my back, a pair of sandals on my feet, and not another thing in the world as we hurled helter-skelter for the airbase in Athens many miles away. I was so concerned about June's condition that I had no time to be scared of the helicopter flight. I just kept feeling for a pulse in her wrist. At one point, I lost the pulse and thought she had gone. I called to the Greek man sitting beside the pilot, assuming he was a medic, but he just shrugged his shoulders and avoided all eye contact with me. Thankfully, I found June's pulse again, but she was oblivious to all around her, and remained so until we landed.

An ambulance was waiting and, with lights flashing and siren screaming, we went at breakneck speed to the Yeniko Kratico Hospital. The name is etched in my memory for all time. On arrival at the emergency department, June regained consciousness, but was suffering yet another heart attack. The actions of the people in the emergency room saved her life, of that I have no doubt; as soon as they had her semi-stabilised, they rushed her to intensive care. After a while, a Jordanian doctor (Dr Yacob) came out and told me that June's condition was very serious and that she was unlikely to survive the day. I was allowed a quick bedside visit, and was then left again outside in the corridor where I was to remain for three days – in sandals, shirt, shorts and barely enough money to buy a couple of coffees or a bottle of water. I have to admit that I just sat down and cried when a Greek family kindly approached and comforted me. Over the following days and nights, they bought me food and drink, and took me under their wing. They were also maintaining a hospital vigil, waiting for word of the man's mother who had also suffered a heart attack. What wonderful, generous people.

I was interviewed by the hospital administration at a very early stage to establish if June's treatment could be paid for. I had, of course, holiday insurance, so this satisfied them and, in a very short while, I received a call from the insurance company's agent – Euro Care. I cannot speak highly enough of this company. They not only assured me that every need would be met, but that a representative would call to see me the following day. This visit took place, and I was told that a nearby hotel room had been booked for me. The woman wisely insisted we go there, where I quickly had a shower and shave before returning to the mosquito-infested corridor of the hospital.

One night, I looked into the intensive care room just to see if June was peaceful and, to my utter astonishment, found the nurse in charge of a battery of patient monitor screens sound asleep at her post. I made noises to waken her, and she immediately chased me out of the ward, but not before I had a quick look at June. The treatment she was given in the hospital was, I learned later, as good as it would have been in Scotland, but certainly the sleeping nurse did not inspire confidence.

I learned that arrangements were being made by the holiday company to have our family transferred to Athens, but it took a couple of days. Thankfully, I was able to receive phone calls at the hospital from the family, which was reassuring. On the third morning, I saw Dr Yacob arrive at the intensive care ward and, a few moments later, he emerged absolutely jubilant. He grabbed me, hugged me and danced me around the corridor, shouting gleefully, 'She is going to live. She is going to live. She is going to live!' What a man! He sat me down and said that June would have to recuperate before leaving the hospital, and then would have to stay in a hotel until she had the strength to make the long flight back to Scotland. He was at great pains to warn me that I could not have sex with June for some months, although clearly nothing was further from my mind!

Some years later, we were passing through Athens and had time to spare, so we visited the Yeniko Kratico Hospital in the hope that we might again meet Dr Yacob and thank him. Unfortunately, we were informed that he had returned to Jordan only a few weeks earlier. I will be forever grateful to that lovely man who worked so hard to success-fully save June's life.

In due course, the family arrived from Andros and were put up in a hotel for one night, also at the expense of the insurance company, before continuing their normal holiday flight back to Scotland the next day. After they left, I felt a bit lonely, but with a change of clothes and a hotel room, life was easier. I visited June twice a day and, in between, explored Athens, a noisy polluted city, but an interesting place. Relatives of our friend Lesley Barrow invited me to their home on the outskirts of Athens, where I had the most wonderful Greek meal with plenty of raki and wines. Really nice people.

While June recovered in a hotel in Athens, our son Stephen agreed to fly out to take care of her, and I returned home. I had to go to the air-port and hope that a seat could be found for me on a flight to Glasgow where my car was parked. I waited nervously until the gate was finally closed, with one seat to spare on the plane, whereupon my case was grabbed from me and I was told to run to the departure gate. I made it by the skin of my teeth. On the plane, I was sitting next to a lady who wanted to hear what had happened. I quickly explained the circumstances, adding that I hated flying. She was also clearly very nervous about flying.

As the plane thundered down the runway, with me in white-knuckle mode, I realised the poor woman was in tears while her husband sat unconcerned, looking out of the window!

After a couple of weeks, the insurance company flew a doctor out to Athens to accompany June all the way back to our home in Edinburgh. My claim for everything was met – the insurance covered the helicopter flight, as well as all the hospital and medical expenses. The hotel and flights home for June were also covered without question. I will be forever impressed with Euro Care and, if there is a message out of this near catastrophe, it is never go on holiday without insurance. I learned later that the helicopter alone had cost several thousand pounds.

Unfortunately, on her return to Scotland, June quickly suffered several minor heart attacks, and was eventually admitted to Edinburgh Royal Infirmary where a surgeon put it to us that she had to have immediate heart surgery as the only way to save her life. After initial resistance, June was persuaded by the surgeon (and me) that this was the only option. She eventually underwent a quadruple heart bypass operation on Monday 28 November 1989, but not before she suffered another heart attack, for which I felt responsible. The operation was planned for the Monday and, to help relax her, it was suggested that I take June out on the Saturday for lunch and a wee bit of shopping, as it was getting close to Christmas. On the way back to the hospital, June had one more heart attack.

Monday was the longest day of my life. I sat by the phone pleading with it not to ring – no news is good news. When I eventually phoned in the evening, June was in the recovery room, and I was allowed in to see her the following day. The recovery room was an astonishing place, with every conceivable piece of life-support equipment connected up, and a dedicated nurse at every bed. June's recovery was spectacular, and soon she was convalescing in the Astley Ainslie Hospital in Morningside.

The Health Service comes in for some bad press these days, but I cannot praise the Cardiology Department of the ERI enough for the way they prepared June (and myself) for what is serious, major surgery. The preparation and aftercare were impeccable. If I have one complaint about the whole episode, it is that no proper warning was provided to either of us of what the long-term effects of such an operation were likely to be, and at no time do I recall receiving a warning of the possibility of June having suffered frontal lobe damage. This was to have a traumatic effect on the family in later years.

Despite this upset in our lives, it was onwards and upwards as far as

Greentrax was concerned. The label was growing at such a rate that I rather quickly reached a crossroads; I decided to focus my attention and efforts solely on the record label and discontinue Discount Folk Records. I passed my huge list of mail-order customers on to *The Living Tradition* magazine, which had by then replaced The Broadsheet. I had outgrown the spare bedroom, and found office and warehouse accommodation to rent at Cockenzie Business Centre in East Lothian where I already had a storeroom. This proved to be a very happy move and, after a traumatic 'flitting', I quickly developed a good relationship with the owners, Mike and Barbara Shaw of Microprint, who had for some time printed catalogues for me. The move to Cockenzie having been accomplished, the next item on the agenda was to buy a house in the vicinity. Some years earlier, we had purchased our council house at Morven Street and were in the lucky position of being able to sell it on. We eventually bought a house in Longniddry, some five minutes in the car from the business centre. Hurray! No parking problems, no fighting through congestion in Edinburgh anymore, and a nice, fresh, by-the-sea environment. Wished I had done it years before.

There was one problem, however. We moved into Longniddry in May 1992 while our house at Morven Street was still on the market. The only recourse we had was to take out a bridging loan, and believe me that very quickly decimates any bank balance you may have. We had the bridging loan all through the summer, and we finally sat down one evening with some serious issues to deal with. Putting the house in Longniddry up for sale was an option both June and I could barely contemplate, so the first money-saving idea was to cancel our forthcoming Greek holiday (yes, with June fully recovered we were back holidaying in Greece) which was booked but not fully paid for. With that and other saving plans to go into immediate effect, I went to the office in the morning prepared to call the holiday company. Before I could do so, the phone rang and our estate agent asked me to be at Morven Street to show a prospective purchaser the house that evening. I put the phone down and it rang again – another prospective buyer to see the house in the evening. I went to Morven Street, showed the first party around, and the man did nothing but moan and groan about the house, while the second couple thought it was just what they wanted.

The next morning, I had a call from the estate agent to be at the house right away to let a surveyor look round. I did this and, by the time I got back to my office in Cockenzie, an offer for the house was in and accepted. Shortly afterwards, I received a second surveyor's call asking to see round the house, but I had to inform him that it had already been sold. The ironic thing is that the people who had been unhappy with the house were the ones who actually bought it, and the couple who were desperate to have it were only minutes too late in putting in their offer. We heard they were desperately disappointed.

We were absolutely elated and, when we went on the nearly-cancelled holiday, I arranged to phone my lawyer from Greece, to learn that the cheque for the house purchase had been cleared at the bank. I can tell you we celebrated that evening. We are unlikely to move again. Apart from anything else, it is just too stressful, and the added worry of a bridging loan has put me off them for life. Maybe we should have sold first and then house-hunted, but we saw the house we wanted in Longniddry. It ticked all the boxes for us. We had felt, as did the estate agent, that the sale of Morven Street would be quick. Nearly ruined us though, and the horns had to be pulled back for a while.

We were delighted with our new home, but quickly it became apparent that two of the previous owners had been bloody awful do-it-yourself freaks and had left a whole series of problems which we had to overcome

Summer in the back garden in Longniddry.

at our expense. One of these characters was apparently a gynaecologist – one wit commented to us that maybe he had done all the work through the letter box!

It's okay to joke about this, but some of the amateurish work carried out was verging on criminal. We had electric power in the garage which, in addition to our car, housed the washing machine, a spin-dryer and several light fittings. One day, when June was using all the power in the garage, there was a loud bang and all the electrics went dead. When we called in a qualified electrician, he pointed out that the power in the garage had been running off a lightweight electric cord fed from the control box in the house. Several sockets and light connections had been attached to this cable, which was not unlike the kind used on domestic equipment. The electrician was at a loss to understand how this contraption had worked for many years without us either being electrocuted or the house going up in flames.

We holidayed a few times on the island of Paxos, close to Corfu, which was then quite unspoiled by tourism. It was very basic, but there was a chance to meet the people and enjoy authentic Greek food, plus an amazing atmosphere. Changes later occurred to make Paxos more accessible to tourists, and for me it lost its appeal. I tire of fellow tourists complaining 'I want roast beef on Sunday,' etc. etc.

I recall one very funny incident when June and I were sitting in a small taverna in Paxos when a day-trip boat from Corfu came in, and two British tourists entered and sat down, complete with the knotted hanky on the head and black socks up to the knees. The man asked the Greek waiter, 'I see you do pork chops, love. Do you do 'em like we 'ave 'em at home, love?' The waiter raised his eyes to the heavens!

We shared great holidays on Paxos with Linda and David, and later with our friends Rita and Jimmy Crawford. We also had a good holiday with them on Andros, prior to the family holiday there. Rita and Jimmy were fellow members of the Edinburgh Press Club and we saw them there quite a lot until they emigrated to Australia. At that time we had a great circle of friends in the Press Club, including Bill and Heather Barclay, Gus and Anne Young and others, so you could always be sure of convivial chat and a bit of fun. The Club Steward, Davie Mowatt, was a real character and, on one occasion, convinced me to unwisely go on an all-male 'dirty dozen' trip to Tenerife. This entailed a dozen guys spending a week on the island, while making a quite determined attempt to drink the bloody place dry. It was an experience and, while I quite enjoyed the holiday, I would never tackle the like again. I was a bit disappointed with Tenerife which seemed totally geared towards British tourists, with the Spanish character lost.

I came home from that holiday needing a good rest – no alcohol for a month – but we nearly didn't get home at all. We boarded the plane for the return flight to Glasgow, the pilot got to the end of the runway, revved up a couple of times, and then we were away – or so we thought. We got to just over halfway down the runway, when suddenly the plane came to a screaming, shuddering halt, followed by total silence. We all held our breath, waiting for the crash, but the pilot announced instead that one of the engines had failed to reach full power, so he was 'going back to try again'. Now bearing in mind my comments about my fear of flying, this was not good news, and I was in a state of near collapse as we taxied back to the end of the runway. The pilot again revved up his engines several times. Thankfully, he then said that it was 'no use', and we were returning to the airport. We boarded another plane, and eventually got home via East Midlands Airport.

I have a pilot friend I chat to about flying, and I asked him once what had been the worst landing he had ever experienced. He replied, 'Ian, if you walk away from the plane, there is no such thing as a bad landing!' He told me of one occasion when he was flying in to Edinburgh Airport with the co-pilot at the controls. As they neared Edinburgh, they were warned of very high gales, whereupon the co-pilot said, 'Control back to you, Captain.' My friend said the approach was horrendous, with the aeroplane being hurled about by the wind, and he was 'scared shitless'. He landed the plane safely, but was still shaking uncontrollably when he got to his hotel an hour later. I know why I'm afraid of flying. Mind you, maybe I shouldn't read all those 'Black Box' books.

In the early years, it was a six-day-week job as I toiled to establish the business. So, one Saturday morning I was sitting in the Greentrax office, tuned in to a holiday programme on BBC Radio Scotland. The reporter had been to Crete with a company named Pure Crete, and he raved about the holiday. He said that if anyone was looking for a holiday away from tourists, this was the one. Pure Crete had individual refurbished farmhouses available in small Cretan villages, away from the tourist traps. This sounded like heaven, so I sent off for a brochure. Over the next several years, June and I holidayed in the small village of Stylos in western Crete, close to the White Mountains. We made friends with many of the villagers – our very good friends Nikos and Niki who owned the house we occupied; Demetrious and Maria; Ioannis and Sula who own the small café in the village; and the lovely old Katrina, married to a farmer and very special character, Nikos, who sadly died one year shortly before our holiday. There are other very good Greek friends in Stylos who are all the salt of the earth. They befriended us simply because we took a close interest in their village. In fact, we seldom left it for any length of time on our first visit.

When we returned a second time we were treated like long-lost friends, and since then have been invited into their homes for the most wonderful Greek meals, washed down with copious amounts of the wonderful local village wine and raki. The people of Stylos are terrific hosts, and the craic is fantastic. We do not speak a lot of Greek, and few of the villagers, apart from the younger ones, speak much or any English. You might think this makes any kind of communication impossible, but not so – one way or another we have wonderful conversations. Of course, when one of the younger villagers is present, then he can interpret for all, but I enjoy the times when we have no interpreter. Then we find other ways of communicating. Strangely, Nikos has made it known to me that these are the special moments for him also. They are wonderfully happy people, with a wicked sense of humour and no inhibitions about sex or any other subject. They have given us Greek surnames based on the Greek translation of Green which is 'Prasseeni'.

On a holiday to Stylos, the flight lands in Heraklion. With a two-hour drive to Stylos, we pick up a hired car at the airport, which is returned on our departure. On one occasion, we arrived at Heraklion at about 2am and, halfway to Stylos, the car broke down. We flagged down some passing Greeks, some of whom had no English, and tried to get messages passed to the car-hire company, but we remained stuck by the roadside for many hours. I walked to a small local bakery and asked to use their phone, which was tenuously attached to the telephone line by bare wires. I somehow managed to break the wire connection, but successfully reconnected it, more by good luck than skill, just as the baker re-entered. How I would have explained what I was up to if he had caught me in the act, I have no idea! About midday, we finally had a visit from the car-hire firm, and we were on our way again.

We travelled out one year in October, after the holiday season, and Nikos and Niki gave us the holiday house rent-free. We watched the villagers making raki – a spirit distilled from the second fermentation of the grapes – followed each night by a mighty celebration. These were wonderful nights. The generosity of the Cretan people is unmatched any-where in the world. They are a bit like the Scots. They consider them-selves to be different from the rest of Greece, as we feel ourselves to be different from the rest of the UK. We have had around 11 wonderful hol-idays in little Stylos – we even helped them to harvest the grapes one year. What dear friends we have there. Parting at the end of a holiday has become a very emotional experience for us and them.

The Cretan people are at a loss, as I am, as to why the EU wants to put a stop to them making their own village wine and distilling raki for one month of the year, and simply appalled that very soon they will be unable to slaughter a goat or a sheep in the olive groves in honour of their guests. Nikos kills one or other every time we visit, and I have to be present to witness this ritual. We later feast on the favoured bits of the animal – the boiled and roasted skull, the sweetmeats and so on. Never be afraid to try what you haven't tasted – you will be surprised. We love you Stylos, and until we visit again, you are always in our thoughts.

CHAPTER ELEVEN

the greentrax years – expansion

reentrax continued to flourish, and soon it became obvious I could no longer run the company myself, so I looked for additional help. June retired from her job with John Lewis, but the office environment at Greentrax did not suit her. She found it difficult to concentrate on more than one task at a time and the continual ringing of the phone became too much for her, so she moved on to do voluntary work. Later June returned to Greentrax and now regularly helps out with the huge mail-outs of promotional albums, catalogues and so on, which we regularly have.

Other aspects of June's condition were also showing by then, in the form of wild mood swings, very emotional periods and deterioration of her short-term memory. Of course, I was in complete ignorance of her problem, although I knew there was one, and it was to be a while before a doctor was able to give an accurate diagnosis. Apparently, general practitioners were, on the whole, still somewhat ill-informed about the problems resulting from bypass operations, and June was prescribed tablets for depression. I went to see this doctor with a view to telling her about some of the symptoms June was displaying, but she would not hear me out, and kept repeating, 'Patient confidentiality.' I left in a hell of a rage. The result was that June's problem went unattended for a long time, while I was tearing my hair out, until I finally convinced her we should pay for a consultation with a specialist. One of our friends talked to a doctor she worked with, and he kindly referred us to a top psychiatrist.

The specialist spent only a couple of minutes with June and me when he advised that, although scans and tests were necessary, he was certain she was suffering from frontal lobe brain damage, caused by the irregular supply of oxygen during the bypass operation. I am reliably informed that improved equipment and techniques have all but eliminated this problem today, but June was one of the unlucky ones.

The consultant considered that we had been badly let down by the NHS and would take no fee for the consultation. He made it clear June would undergo appropriate assessment and receive the necessary medication very quickly. Within a couple of weeks, June had her brain scanned, was assessed by other professionals and, in a very short time, she was on the medication to control her difficulties. She was then regularly seen by Dr Colin Rodgers at Roodlands Hospital in Haddington and, while she would forever have to take considerable medication, the quality of our lives improved dramatically. June was soon to develop a good relationship with Dr Rodgers, and he proved to be a very caring psychiatrist who did his all for both of us. He eventually he left the NHS, and to date we have sadly not met his like again.

During the uncertain period before June was diagnosed, I suffered terribly. I seemed unable to communicate effectively about my concerns for June and was unable to gain close family cooperation, to the extent that family relationships were affected. Our daughter Linda was the first to grasp the real significance and seriousness of June's condition and its effect on us, resulting in a really strong bond between Linda and myself. Several good friends also helped me through this difficult time.

Apparently alcohol exacerbates frontal lobe problems so a medical ban on drinking alcohol was immediately placed on June. She was advised that it was okay to have a moderate amount of white wine mixed with soda water and, to her credit, she immediately adhered to this. Medication and regular visits to various doctors, psychiatrists and psychologists are the order of the day for June (and I always go along to lend support) but, apart from the necessity for her to be given a change of medication from time to time, our circumstances have improved.

During the darkest periods, my obsessive interest in traditional music and Greentrax Recordings proved to be my saviour. Had I previously opted for full retirement, I feel sure I could not have coped as well.

By then, Greentrax had taken on board two members of the family to help me run the business – first, our son Stephen, and then Andrew. Stephen accepted responsibility for our accounts, despite having no previous experience, and did a good job, while completing his studies at Stirling University as a mature student. Andrew, who had experience in sales with several companies, came on board as our sales and warehouse person. He also proved to be effective. This worked well for a time, and Greentrax appeared to have a future as a 'family concern'.

Around this time, my accountant, the excellent Forbes Fordyce, recommended that, because of rising turnover, I should change the company from two proprietors – June and myself – to the status of a limited company. Forbes could not take on this responsibility as he was not a chartered accountant, and I was sorry to move on. On the advice of my solicitor, musician and friend Ian Hardie of R & R Urquhart WS in Nairn, I began a very happy relationship with Ritson Chartered Accountants, also in Nairn (now Ritson Young CA). I received excellent advice from Bill Young who has a real depth of knowledge in accountancy. I imagine he has saved Greentrax a lot of money. Bill and Ian moved things forward quickly, and very soon Greentrax was a registered limited company. Ian Hardie then made a decision to leave the profession to concentrate his efforts as a full-time musician and so I found myself in the caring hands of Will Cowie, a partner in R & R Urquhart.

On becoming a limited company, I issued shares to all members of our family as an incentive to each of them to be personally involved in the success of the company. For a time, this seemed to work, and we settled into a happy routine. Stephen graduated and was persuaded by me to bring his studies to a conclusion by applying for a place at a teacher-training college. We supported him by retaining him on his full wage, while he maintained our accounts in his spare time at home. I hoped Stephen would remain with the company when he qualified but he felt his future lay elsewhere and he joined the teaching profession. Andrew continued at Greentrax after Stephen's departure but in due course it became clear that his time at Greentrax was over and he also went his own way.

I always strive to ensure a happy team relationship exists within Greentrax, which leads to a convivial working environment for the staff, and despite the changes, we settled back into a close knit team.

June and I suffered very badly at the time of all these changes. It affected my sleeping pattern, and I turned to alcohol to help see me through. This happened when I was still trying to recover from the trauma of June's diagnosis, and at a time when June needed a lot of support. The toll on my health was significant, and my doctor, the very caring Dr Bremner, who saw signs of increasing stress and related depression in me, finally convinced me I should accept medication to control this. The medication proved effective and I came through my bad patch a happier and more relaxed person (and also a much wiser one).

Remembering this period of my life, which I intentionally did not go into in depth, has been quite painful but at the same time it has also been cathartic. It is necessary to get on with life and be thankful for the good things that remain. Life is full of surprises but one always has to move on.

Greentrax continued to grow and the catalogue expanded substantially. At this time I worked very hard to expand our distribution and retail

Ian and employee Pat at the Highland Trade Fair.

outlets. Annually we attended the Aviemore Scottish Trade Fair where we added many new US, Canadian and Australian retail accounts. There appeared to be many shops across these countries which specialise in Scottish goods, including music. Our stand at Aviemore attracted many visitors who always spoke highly of our quality recordings and talented artists. When the Trade Fair moved to Glasgow we continued to exhibit for a while but we saw a decline in the number of visitors and eventually we opted out of the Trade Fair. By then we had established a solid core of regular buyers from North America and 'downunder'.

Simultaneously and as previously stated, Greentrax annually attended Midem, the World Record Exhibition, held in sunny Cannes in the south of France. This is a lovely little jaunt in late January each year, when the weather in Cannes is Spring-like, although one year it actually snowed during Midem. Every Midem is a hard slog during the day, when I usually have a full diary of appointments, but there is still time for 'play'. Most companies have a strict schedule of only half hour meetings so on occasions you have to do some swift talking to get your spiel across. Meetings can be in the Exhibition Centre or outside at a café or restaurant. These are the most enjoyable. Lunches and long dinners in the evening are the order of the day, often the best opportunities for so called 'networking'. I struck many deals at Midem with distributors and record labels from across the world. French food is of course world renowned and it was in Cannes I developed a taste for frogs' legs.

At Midem I always presented a miniature of malt whisky to all my established contacts which seemed to take a trick. That plus a friendly approach rather than the hard-nosed business style meetings in my opinion developed good personal relationships. I have tried to apply this approach to all business meetings and many friendships have developed. Franco Ratti of IRD, our Italian distributor, always used to recount our meetings to his mother and she always passed on her regards through Franco to me, although I have never met the lady. I particularly enjoy the social occasions with Dougie Stevenson of BGS and Thomas Fenn of Fenn Music Services, Germany. Both are really nice people.

Invitations to Trade events and the Celtic Colours Festival in Canada, were accepted gratefully, providing further opportunities to meet 'World Music' entrepreneurs in Halifax, Nova Scotia, Regina in Saskatchewan and Cape Breton. These were wonderful events where June and I were treated almost like royalty. Another trip I had was at the invitation of the BBC World Service to Budapest, Hungary. The airline lost my suitcase on the outward journey and I finally got it two days later. I had to attend the airport to collect it but first it had to go through customs. A customs officer, bristling with side arms, asked me to open the suitcase whereupon my sample CDs spilled out on to the floor. For a second I thought he was going to lose the plot with me but he then said in broken English, 'You too much trouble, go, leave here', and I scuttled off before he changed his mind, thanking him profusely as I went. Budapest is the only place in the world I have been serenaded at dinner by a gypsy band. You are expected to place paper money in their pockets.

These and other visits broadened my traditional music outlook considerably and I met some wonderful people, all with a similar love of traditional music. I was successful in promoting Greentrax in all these foreign parts. They were heady times.

Our advertising budget was extended and full page colour adverts could be seen in all the traditional and world magazines, including *fRoots*, *Living Tradition*, *Songlines*, *Irish Music*, *Rock 'n' Reel* and more on home soil, but also abroad, especially *Sing Out* and *Dirty Linen* in USA and the unusually named Penguin Eggs in Canada. Many artists, distributors and mail order customers commented on seeing our adverts 'everywhere' at that time.

Success breeds success of course and at the time there was always some spare cash in the 'piggy bank' to allow interesting projects to be slotted in at short notice. Greentrax was seldom out of the 'news' for long, with numerous articles on me and the company in magazines and even national press, while radio interviews were frequent. Greentrax and traditional music was certainly on the crest of a wave and I was enjoying every moment of it. So much for the pessimists who had said, 'Don't do it, Ian.'

One cloud hanging over us at that time was when our USA distributor, Distribution North America (or DNA), went bust owing us £11,000.00 (Sterling!). We never received a penny of that debt but it could have been much worse. A few months earlier DNA regularly owed us at any moment in time in the region of £20,000.00. DNA must have known for a while what was coming because they reduced their weekly orders considerably in the final weeks. It was a shock and left us reeling for a while. We had suffered losses before when distributors and retailers went down but never before on that scale. It is of course a trading hazard but we got a bloody fright. We shook off that loss, however, and it was soon onwards and upwards again.

CHAPTER TWELVE

the GReentRAX yeARS – 15th and 20th anniveRSARIeS

G reentrax celebrated first its 15th, and later its 20th anniversaries in the Queen's Hall in Edinburgh, with a galaxy of Greentrax talent who agreed to appear for expenses only. These celebratory concerts were quite stunning events, and the Greentrax artists rose to the occasion, egged on the first time by comperes Sheena Wellington and Adam McNaughtan. On the second occasion, Adam compered alone, delivering his introductions in hilarious rhyme. A lot of people gave their time towards these concerts, but special mention has to be made of Brian McNeill, Jack Evans, Dave Francis and Ian McQueen, house manager of The Queen's Hall. Some tickets were sold for these events, but invitations mainly went out to the media (in all its forms), Greentrax artists and business associates. Greentrax-sponsored parties followed both concerts and, at the 20th anniversary concert, The Occasionals Ceilidh Band provided an after-concert ceilidh. On this occasion, June and I also celebrated our Golden Wedding, as a follow-up to a small dinner and sing-around with family and friends at the wonderful Rocks Hotel in Dunbar. Phil Cunningham generously composed a tune in our honour – 'June and Ian Green's Golden Years' – which Pil and Aly Bain recorded for us. Who knows what the 25th anniversary will bring.

June and Ian - our Golden Wedding.

Greentrax continued its very fertile period, and new releases continued apace. By this time more outstanding artists had joined the label, including the amazing Cape Breton fiddle player, Natalie MacMaster.

Natalie is an amazing fiddler with a stage presentation to match. She is a mega star in North America. June and I attended a concert at Carnegie Hall in Dunfermline on one tour and the packed house gave her a standing ovation. We went backstage for a chat at the end of the concert and found her surrounded by adoring fans. She spotted me and burst through the crowd to give me a huge hug. I love hugs, especially from attractive young women, and Natalie certainly is. I also went to see her doing a gig at Celtic Colours and met her lovely Mum. For a time we released all Natalie's albums, including her back-catalogue. I always felt really proud of this signing because another Scottish label, plus some of the majors in London were after her signature. A real feather in the cap of Ian Green. We followed up by later releasing an album of her equally famous uncle, fiddler Buddy MacMaster.

We also released albums by two very exciting bands from Canada – Slainte Mhath and the very young Cottars. These were also very special signings and once again I was chuffed to bits to obtain their signatures ahead of other companies. Slainte Mhath toured the UK a couple of times which raised their profile immensely but it was hard for them to make good money from the tours because they were still 'rising stars' as it were. They really were a very special outfit to watch, with pipes, fiddle, piano and bodhran driving the music along. Step-dancing was also a feature of their act. Unfortunately, The Cottars never managed across the 'pond' to the UK but when they twice won awards at the East Coast Music Awards of Canada everything seemed to be set for them going big-time. Fiona MacGillivray was only twelve when the band recorded their first album but she had a voice that made most folk go weak at the knees. The other three were equally talented on fiddle, guitar piano and more. A while later, as so often happens, the band broke up and although I have heard the band has reformed, changes have been made and I think the chemistry of the original line-up is going to be hard to attain.

The ever-changing but very popular Poozies came to Greentrax after two of the band, harpists and singers Patsy Seddon and Mary MacMaster, known as Sileas, recorded their Greentrax 'Play on Light' album. The first Poozies album (for Greentrax) was 'Changed Days, Same Roots' which reflected changes in a line-up which did not include Sally Barker but did include Eilidh Shaw, who plays a pretty mean fiddle and has a bubbly personality. Eilidh recorded a rather tasty album for Greentrax but she never found time to promote it and as a consequence it struggled to break even. The second Poozies album saw Sally Barker return to the fold and

her strong vocals and songwriting talents added zest to the latest creation of the group. I returned after many years to the Police Club (now
with a hotel licence) at 28 York Place, in the first half of 2010, to enjoy
a great evening with The Poozies. Mairearad Green, accordion and vocals,
is a comparatively new member of what is now a formidable outfit.

The hugely popular Occasionals have recorded four albums of their
special blend of ceilidh dance music for us. Fronted by accordionist
Freeland Barbour and fiddler Ian Hardie, plus Kevin Macleod adding a
quite different sound to other Scottish dance bands with his various stringed
instruments, and Gus Millar on drums this is a ceilidh band that takes
some beating. Kevin has recorded three solo albums with Greentrax. In
2010 The Occasionals produced for us a most unusual gem; a CD with
12 dance sets, plus bonus tracks, an extensive booklet with full dance
instructions and a DVD demonstrating the 12 dances plus some extra
footage of the band. There is some rare footage of the band members in
far flung places. A remarkable package and a first as far as we are aware.

The Glencraig Scottish Dance Band, with Nicol McLaren on lead
accordion, is away ahead of most other Scottish dance bands presenting
the standard line-up of lead and second accordion, fiddle, piano, double
bass and drums. So far the band has released three albums in a series: 'The
Ceilidh – Are Ye Dancin?'; 'The Reel Party – Are Ye Askin'?'; 'Scottish
Country Dances – Ah'm Askin', while the fourth 'Old Time – Ah'm
Dancin' is to be released later. The band won the National Association
of Accordion and Fiddle Club Award for 'CD of the Year 2007' and has
twice been nominated for the Scottish Dance Band category at the Scots
Trad Awards. The band travels far and wide, and in recent times went
to Tbilisi, Munich, Brisbane and Melbourne. In 2009 they were invited
to play at a Ceilidh at the British Grand Prix in Silverstone.

The storming Fiddlers' Bid have recorded three albums for us and
band members Chris Stout and Catriona McKay have recorded with us
– Chris as a soloist, Chris and Catriona as a duo. This is serious talent
we are talking here with the other members of the band well up to it also.
Fiddlers' Bid play in Shetland style as you might imagine since they hail
from those islands, where almost everyone picks up a fiddle at one time
or another. Of all the multi-fiddle bands in Scotland I think the 'Bid' lead
the way. I am left breathless on occasions by Chris Stout's enthusiasm.
He almost missed a gig in The Queen's Hall because of a delayed flight. He
arrived breathless and without further ado bounded on stage with the
band. Chris and Catriona regularly tour Japan.

Gaelic Mod and Scots Trad Award winner, Fiona J MacKenzie joined us with her popular 'Duan Nollaig' Christmas song album in 2007, followed quickly by 'A Good Suit of Clothes – Songs of The Emigrant Gael', as her contribution to 'Homecoming Scotland 2009'. Fiona adds yet another 'string to the Gaelic bow' of Greentrax. She has such a great personality and is another Greentrax artist with a constant stream of new ideas.

The most unique band name on the label is Ceilidh Minogue (I kid you not) and when the album was released I waited in some trepidation for the lawyer's letters, which fortunately did not materialise! Their music, as the name suggests, is for ceilidh dancing but the band also play sets just for sheer listening pleasure. An exciting outfit.

The late Willie Hunter, a most excellent fiddler from Shetland, bravely phoned all his friends, including myself, just before his untimely death due to cancer. He wished me good luck and goodbye. Willie had finished his hugely popular album, 'Leaving Lerwick Harbour', only a few days earlier. What a loss. In the short time I knew him I found Willie to be an absolute gentleman and what a fiddler, and composer. June and I attended the following Shetland Fiddle and Accordion Festival to launch the album and were guests of Willie's widow Pat and family. The generous hospitality made both of us feel quite humble. We were later to be guests of the Shetland Folk Festival, when we were again treated right grandly. In all we released three Willie Hunter albums, including one with The Cullivoe Band.

I was to make a third trip to Shetland for the funeral of 'Peerie' Willie Johnson, the legendary Shetland guitarist. Although steeped in jazz music, he was also a wonderful accompanist of folk musicians, including fellow Shetlander, Aly Bain. The celebration of Willie's life at both the funeral and the musical session that night made his send-off all the more remarkable. We subsequently released an album titled 'Willie's World' which was gleaned from many sources, including the tape archive of Billy Kay of Shetland, in association with Willie's sister, Evelyn Leask. Billy Kay is a very generous man and provided tracks for both the Willie Hunter and 'Peerie' Willie albums from his vast collection of recordings from the small studio in his Lerwick home.

In recent years, the steady flow of talented musicians and singers from the RSAMD and Plockton School of Excellence has been impressive, resulting in young bands emerging each year. Greentrax has been at the forefront in supporting these bands, and has signed up some crackers, including GiveWay, Bodega, The Paul McKenna Band, Jeana Leslie and Siobhan Miller – all award winners.

GiveWay consist of the four beautiful Johnson sisters who have recorded three albums for Greentrax, each under the guiding hand of their buddy Phil Cunningham, who thinks the band is 'pure dead brilliant'. Fiona (fiddle and guitars), Kirsty (accordions and vocals) and twins Amy (drums) and Mairi (keyboards) are a real tonic to an old codger like me and we have had some great laughs. They won a 'Danny Kyle Award' at Celtic Connections and later added the 'BBC Radio 2 Young Folk Award' to their tally. They've had very successful USA tours plus they were support for Run Rig on a UK and European tour in 2009. Phil, always up to some mischief or fun, ordered a 'stretch limousine' to convey the girls in luxury to the launch of their first album. They came to the label as very young girls and are now beautiful young women.

The members of Bodega met at Plockton School of Excellence and enjoying each other's company and music, quickly formed the band. Greentrax, on the recommendation of Jack Evans, one of the School tutors, was equally quick to sign these talented young folk. Their debut album, simply titled 'Bodega' and produced by Jack, immediately gained them wide recognition and tours of the USA. The band won a 'BBC Radio 2 Young Folk Award' and were nominated for a Scots Trad Award when

The 'GiveWay' sisters sign to Greentrax.

they released their second album 'Under The Counter'. Singer Norrie MacIver has also been nominated for 'Best Gaelic Singer'. They are such nice young folk to work with and their music hits the spot for me.

The Paul McKenna Band came to my notice after I released an album by the fine Irish singer Mary Burke. Paul worked on Mary's album and he passed a band demo on to me. At first I did not think we could fit the band into our release schedule but I had second thoughts and am I really glad because their debut album was stunning and won a Scots Trad Award immediately. Paul has a very unusual and interesting voice and the members of the band are very skilled musicians. I am privileged to have them on Greentrax. They are to release a new album in 2011 and band member Rua (Ruairaidh) Macmillan has already produced an exciting fiddle album after winning the 2009 'BBC Radio Scotland Young Musician of The Year Award'.

Jeana Leslie and Siobhan Miller are two lovely young girls and both graduates of the RSAMD Traditional music course. They won the 'BBC Radio Two Young Folk Award' of 2008 and followed that up with a Scots Trad Award with their debut album 'In A Bleeze'. Siobhan has a voice to die for but both girls combine beautifully in song and in addition Jeana plays fiddle and piano. A new album – 'Shadows Tall' – was almost complete at the time this book was being published. Siobhan is the daughter of Brian Miller who has had a lifetime involvement in folk music, including spells with The Laggan, The Vindscreen Vipers and as a duo with Charlie Soane. Singing seems to be passed down from generation to generation in the Miller family. While both girls are beautiful singers, Siobhan's ballad singing sends the hairs on the back of my neck tingling.

You may well ask why Greentrax attracts all these lovely young people to the label? I really don't know, except that we have always tried to maintain a high level of debut albums of talented young singers and musicians and I am prepared to take a risk on artists who do not yet have any profile. Nevertheless, I feel very fortunate that so many join the happy family that is Greentrax, and long may it continue.

We also released an excellent album of various RSAMD traditional music students – 'No 1 Scottish'– produced by Brian McNeill and this close relationship with the RSAMD has led to me being invited on occasions to speak to the Third Year Traditional Music Course on the subject of the recording industry. A second RSAMD album – 'Forward With Our Past' – is due for release as I write this. It is produced by Phil Cunningham.

It's not all 'new kids on the block' of course. Some fine recordings have been made by the 'older school', such as Archie Fisher, who for many years was the presenter of BBC Radio Scotland's 'Travelling Folk'. Archie has a great radio voice and I had the honour to do many interviews with him over the years. I never quite knew what Archie was going to ask me and I was often left scrambling for an answer. Archie's stint on 'Travelling Folk' sadly came to an end in 2010. He is not a prolific recording artist but his recent work has all come to Greentrax for release on licence in the UK and Europe: 'Sunsets I have Galloped Into' was licensed to us by Snowgoose Songs, as was 'Off The Map' (with Garnet Rogers). More recently we released Archie's long awaited 'Windward Away', an album recorded over many years and licensed to us by Red House Records, USA. I love Archie's laid back and almost understated presentation on stage. He was in on the folk revival at the very beginning and it is great to see him fit and still gigging. When not doing so he is riding his beloved horse through the Border countryside.

Winner of 'Singer of the Year' at the Scots Trad Awards in 2006, Sylvia Barnes recorded the most excellent 'The Colour of Amber' shortly after. This added yet another fine traditional album to the Greentrax catalogue, sitting comfortably alongside Aileen Carr, Gordeanna McCulloch, Jack Beck, Mick West and of course Alison McMorland and Geordie McIntyre, all steeped in traditional song and outstanding exponents. An unusual and good selling album is 'Cave of Gold – Celtic Lullabies' by Lynn Morrison. The mail order company Cygnus has sold a lot of this one. Strangely, instrumental bands have been at the forefront of Scottish traditional music for a while and traditional song has been less popular. I am assured traditional song will again have its day but I do hope it is soon because song is so important to our culture.

We released a retrospective album of the late, great fiddle player Hector MacAndrew from tapes unearthed by his son Pat and then edited and selected by another great North-East talent Paul Anderson, who later released his own 'best of 'compilation on Greentrax from several albums he released himself.

One of those weird circumstances came to light with Hector MacAndrew's album. When his son Pat came to see me it transpired that his father had been head gardener on Lethen Estate prior to my father taking on that role which meant we had both lived in the same cottage many years before.

Fergie MacDonald, a real character, came to us when Phil Cunningham persuaded him it was time to make a new album. It was duly produced by Phil and was titled 'The 21st Album', meaning of course that it was the 21st album of Fergie's career. It was a great experience working with Fergie and Phil. The latter has, as you have read, produced many albums for Greentrax. He is such good fun to be around, and a very talented musician and producer. I hope he won't mind me telling one of his 'Fergie stories' which are many. Fergie was playing at a dance, wearing his kilt and the legendary red socks. He was seated and each time he pulled up the accordion the kilt lifted a bit higher. At the interval a dancer approached him and said, 'Fergie, do you know your willy's showing?' Fergie is reputed to have immediately replied, 'No, but that will be a Phil Cunningham tune.'

Malinky is a band that signed and has remained with us since 2000. They're super people to work with and multi-talented. They've recorded four albums with us, the first two of which included Karine Polwart, who went on to carve a very successful solo career for herself. The lovely Fiona Hunter replaced Karine and one or two other changes have taken place over the years. The backbone of the band and ever constant are Steve Byrne (vocals, bouzouki, guitars and more) and Mark Dunlop (vocals, bodhran and whistles). Both have made very excellent solo albums for Greentrax. Mike Vass, from the very talented Morayshire family I mentioned earlier, and Dave Wood are more recent members but they managed to fit in a duo album along the way. The band has toured far and wide, including the USA, and been nominated for the Scots Trad Awards a couple of times. I am at a loss to know why they have never won their category. As far as we know Malinky was our only band to get stranded in Denmark at the time of the volcanic ash crisis and eventually had to hire a minibus to get back to Scotland. The hire and hotel bills resulted in the tour being a total loss for the band so they returned home tired and penniless.

Jean Redpath MBE.

Some of our signings have been of very high-profile artists – Isla St Clair, Jean Redpath, Archie Fisher, Dick Gaughan, Eric Bogle, The McCalmans, all already mentioned, are just some examples but the list also includes the several-times World Pipe Band Champions, The Simon

Ex-Runrig front-man Donnie Munro.

Fraser University Pipe Band of Canada. We released two albums of this legendary concert and competition band, who have won The Worlds many times. One album included my tune 'Ian Green of Greentrax' which gave me a real kick.

Greentrax continues to attract 'big name' artists. In 2007, I was honoured when former Runrig front-man Donnie Munro joined the label. His first album won 'Best Album of The Year' at the Scots Trad Awards that year. Donnie went on to release an album from a really memorable concert at Celtic Connections, 'An Turas – The Journey'. It is a real pleasure to have established and internationally acclaimed artists like Donnie on the label because, in addition to enjoying his music on Greentrax, it introduces our music to a new and wider audience. I love Runrig but I believe he was the voice of the Band.

As I was completing my book, Barbara Dickson signed a contract to record her new album with Greentrax. It is due for release early in 2011. This was yet another circle completed, because Barbara was around the folk scene in Edinburgh when I was first involved in it. Barbara is a charismatic performer and I was knocked out by her performance in front of a full house when I attended her concert in the Glasgow Royal Concert Hall in 2010. The audience was with her on every song and she received a well-earned standing ovation at the end. Barbara's small but tightly

The stunning Barbara Dickson OBE.

knit band led by Troy Donockley were fabulous. By the way, give yourself a treat and buy Barbara's autobiography – *A Shirt Box Full of Songs*. It is bloody brilliant.

It is necessary to continue to maintain a balance of 'big' names on the label, but be assured I am equally proud of the many artists to whom we have given the opportunity to make debut albums. Although disappointed to lose some of them, I feel a sense of pride that they were able to go on and produce their own.

After the death of Davy Steele, the remaining members of Drinkers' Drouth suggested I re-release on CD the two Drinkers' Drouth albums, which included Davy Steele. They asked that all royalties go to Marie Curie Cancer Care, who cared for him in his final days. This was a most generous act. Brian Dougan sadly died a few years later and is also greatly missed.

Following in the footsteps of the late Davy Steele (of Prestonpans), another great singer/songwriter emerged from the 'Pans' and came to my notice in 2009 as a 'Burnsong' winner. Alex Hodgson has been singing his songs for years but somehow our paths never crossed and it was only when Alex's wife Isobelle passed me a demo and I immediately sat up and took notice. With a voice uncannily like Davy's and many of his songs based on Prestonpans also, Alex recorded a brilliant album, 'Jeely Jars and Coalie Backies' for me. He had an absolute host of great session musicians, a 'who's who' of the Scottish music scene in fact, including rock musicians. At the album launch in the Gothenburg Pub in Prestonpans, Alex took the place by storm and I was transfixed by his stage performance. Alex's Mum did her promotional bit and could be seen making the rounds of the Pans with her tartan trolley, selling CDs to all her friends and neighbours. I wish a few more artists' Mums would do this. By coincidence, Isobelle Hodgson plays piano in The Glencraig Scottish Dance Band. Keep the music in the family eh?

I have worked hard to get Greentrax involved in the local community where possible. There are the recordings of Davy Steele and now Alex

Hodgson, plus a compilation album of East Lothian songs; then there is another compilation, 'People and Songs of The Sea' (mentioned later), in which we involved local singers and a choir for three tracks; and more recently yet another compilation album, 'The Battle of Prestonpans 1745'. This compilation has eight of the local women stitchers singing 'Sound the Pibroch'. The album is a companion to the 'The Prestonpans Tapestry' which is a project dreamed up by the Baron of Prestoungrange and put into effect by designer Andrew Crummy. The Tapestry is the longest in the world at 104 metres and involved 200 women stitchers, plus two men. It is a remarkable piece of work to be exhibited throughout Scotland and elsewhere, before finally finding a permanent exhibition home in Prestonpans.

In 1996, I was approached by piper Rab Wallace of the Piping College in Glasgow, and Norman Matheson, former piobaireachd competitor and judge. Their proposal was that a series of recordings, to be named 'Masters of Piobaireachd', should be released by Greentrax. The series was to be edited from the many recordings made by Norman in the 1970s, plus others, who, armed with analogue recorders, were welcomed into the homes of Robert Brown and Robert Nicol (affectionately known as 'The Bobs of Balmoral'). Norman had a substantial quantity of reel-to-reel recordings of 'The Bobs', passing on their piobaireachd knowledge. Both Rab and Norman are acknowledged piobaireachd experts, but I seriously doubted the commercial viability of their project. Reluctantly I agreed to take it on, and was subsequently taught another lesson in life.

Offers of recordings from other sources were forthcoming. The enthusiasm of Norman and Rab carried me along, and in 1997, 'Volume 1' was released, although I was still unconvinced that worthwhile sales could be achieved. In a very short time, my estimated couple of hundred albums was greatly exceeded. Well, how wrong I had been. While such album sales are never likely to compare with 'pop' stuff, they are very respectable for this genre of music. Eventually, ten volumes of 'Masters of Piobaireachd' were released by Greentrax, igniting in me an interest in this unique music. Do not underestimate the classical music of the Highland bagpipe – it is neither 'boring' nor does it 'all sound the same', as I have so often heard it described.

In 2001 I signed a deal with Scottish fiddler Alasdair Fraser, owner of Culburnie USA, and re-released on licence the entire Culburnie catalogue in the UK and Europe, plus other countries around the world. This added another string to the Greentrax bow. It is a pleasure to work closely with

The dynamic Alasdair Fraser.

Culburnie and to be associated with Alasdair, now living in the USA, one of the world's great fiddle players. We continue to release his prolific recording output and it has proved to be another excellent collaboration. Alasdair and cellist Natalie Haas won the 'Best Traditional Album' at the 2004 Scots Trad Awards. Alasdair and I have a similar vision for Scottish traditional music and it is a great honour to work with Alasdair, who always presents his music both professionally and with dynamism. Mention must be made of the exciting Skyedance group Alasdair formed and which included the internationally acclaimed piper Eric Rigler, whose music can be heard on many box office blockbusters including 'The Titanic'. This was an absolutely stunning band overflowing with talent.

Other projects, giving the label even more credibility and a wider profile, occured when the Edinburgh International Festival embarked on a series of traditional music concerts, inviting Greentrax to release compilation albums to coincide with each in the series. The first was 'Folk Songs of North-East Scotland', the second, 'Scottish Harps', the third, 'Orain Nan Gaidheal' (Gaelic song and music) and the fourth and final one was 'Ceol Na Pioba – Piob Mhor' (a piobaireachd recital by Scotland's best). There was also 'Scottish Fiddle' in the series, but no album came out of that. All were hugely successful concerts for the Edinburgh Festival, and all the resulting albums proved to be solid sellers. The 'Orain Nan Gaidheal' and 'Ceol Na Piob' albums were recorded 'live' at festival venues in which the atmosphere created by the very enthusiastic and informed audiences was captured.

Some other interesting compilations we have released include an album in association with the Scottish Trades Union Council's Centenary Celebrations – 'If it Wisnae for the Union'. This album included tracks by Run Rig, The Dubliners, Arthur Johnstone, Christy Moore, Matt McGinn and even Victor Jarra, the Chilean singer/songwriter who dedicated his life to creating a just society, and died for his ideals in 1973. 'The Nineties

Collection', in two volumes and consisting of new tunes by some of Scotland's most prominent composers, were completed in association with the Traditional Music and Song Association of Scotland. There were also 'The Captain's Collection', Gaelic song and music, and 'Songhunter', contemporary songs composed by songwriters in Scotland. These projects were in association with the Highland Festival. Some of these collaborations were more successful than others, but they were all a challenge and great fun to be involved with.

One stunning compilation album gave me a great deal of satisfaction when it was concluded three years after the idea had been put to me by Mairi MacInnes and Cathy-Ann MacPhee. The title was quite simply 'Gaelic Women' ('Ar Canan 'S Ar Ceol') which consisted of one track from each of the fine Gaelic women singers whose albums abounded in 1999. Malcolm Jones of Run Rig produced a number of tracks, as did musician and producer, William Jackson. Jim Sutherland, producer, musician and composer, produced one track. The reason that it took three years to complete was due to the geographic spread of the singers, together with getting them to studios at the same time as the session musicians and producers. I have to admit there were times when I almost gave up. Fortunately, Mairi was always there to encourage me when delays occurred. When the album was released, the reviewers were ecstatic; the positive feedback we received was phenomenal.

Praise was heaped upon the singers, musicians, producers and me for making this 'dream' come true. I got a real buzz out of that album.

I have to thank the Scottish Arts Council (SAC) for helping to fund it, and some of the Scottish Tradition Series albums, because 'Gaelic Women' was a very expensive production. It cost Greentrax a lot, but the help from SAC was crucial. Thankfully, it has sold well. Strange to relate, the SAC would not give me the final but smaller part of the funding because I succeeded in bringing it in a little below my original budget.

Almost immediately after the

Ian presenting 'Gaelic Women' at Celtic Connections.

Ian with his 'Gaelic Women'.

Ian, June and artists at the 20th Anniversary Concert of Greentrax.

release of the album, I was approached by Colin Hynd, then musical director of Celtic Connections, who proposed to feature many of the singers in a 'Gaelic Women' concert in the Glasgow Royal Concert Hall. It subsequently pulled in the largest audience ever for a Gaelic concert, and I was given the honour of being compere for the evening. It was a fabulous success. The girls were like daughters to me and insisted I have my photo taken with them and it was hugs all round, again.

This led to another Colin Hynd idea – a 'Scots Women' concert at the following Celtic Connections. It was recorded 'live', resulting in a double album 'Scots Women' which, in Colin's words, 'redressed the balance'. This was also a cracking concert, produced by musical 'magician' Brian McNeill. The following year, a cast of many of the 'Gaelic Women' and 'Scots Women' amalgamated, and went on tour around Scotland as 'Scottish Women'. Shows were recorded, and yet another great album resulted. Heady times for 'Gaelic Women', 'Scots Women' and 'Scottish Women'.

Many other fine compilations were released by Greentrax over the years, including 'The Music and Song of Scotland' in 1989. It had no particular theme, but is a fine album. It was gleaned from the rapidly expanding Greentrax catalogue, plus tracks specially recorded for this compilation. It included a hugely popular version of 'Dumbarton's Drums', recorded for me by Jean Redpath. We released special compilations for the 10th, 15th and 20th anniversaries of Greentrax, which all looked retrospectively at the Greentrax back catalogue.

The 20th anniversary album – 'Scotland – The Music and The Song' (subtitled '20 Year Profile of Greentrax') was a three-CD digipak set, selling eventually for the price of one CD. This consisted of 56 tracks chosen by me from what was by then a huge storehouse of all facets of Scottish music in the Greentrax catalogue. It was put together with a lot of love and affection; it's a collection I am extremely proud of. It was received enthusiastically from every quarter – some of the reviews had a very emotional effect on me. It made all the trouble, strife and hard work worthwhile.

The reviewer, Dr Alan Murray, wrote of 'Scotland – The Music and the Song':

'This landmark recording does a number of things. It marks the achievements outlined earlier in terms of recording, presenting, stimulating and influencing the Scottish musical tradition. Through initiatives like the 'Gaelic Women' concert and CD, Greentrax has gone beyond the normal call of duty for a record label and has actually lent a firm, gentle and entirely principled guiding hand. The CD also clearly offers a mammoth 'sampler' to enthusiasts unfamiliar with the Greentrax stable of musicians. It is, with its sensibly tourist-friendly packaging, a very affordable souvenir of real Scottish music. It is a fine alternative to the shortbread-tin sentimentality or bastardised country-and-western in tartan trews that generally graces the stalls of the Edinburgh Woollen Mill. I make no apologies for the purple prose and no, I have not abandoned the 2008 'Bechhofer' rules of fair, critical and reasonable reviewing! This set really is that good. Greentrax's achievement really is that important. Ian Green really is one of the nicest, most honourable men you're likely to meet, whose influence on Scottish music will outlive him and all the rest of us. Happy Anniversary, Ian, June and all at Greentrax. We owe you a drink or many.'

Well what can I say to such kind words except, I'll drink to that, Alan.

Other compilations which deserve mention are 'Gentle Giants', a celebration in song of the majestic and gentle Clydesdale horse, produced by Robin Laing, and forged out of love for an animal and country way of life missed by both Robin and myself; and 'Guitar Music from Scotland and Beyond' ('The Clear Stream'), which included tracks by such guitar geniuses as the late Tony Cuffe, Dick Gaughan, Jack Evans, Tony McManus and others, and was slowly 'distilled' over a number of years from an idea by Brian McNeill. 'The King Has Landed' (an album of Jacobite songs) arose from an idea submitted by Torcull Kennedy, who at that time worked in the Coda Music Shop on The Mound in Edinburgh. This was the first Greentrax album featuring a licensed track by my old friends, The Corries. Torcull also wrote the very informative sleeve notes.

On the sad passing of Dr Hamish Henderson of the School of Scottish Studies, who was responsible for collecting considerable material which is now in the extensive school archive, it was suggested to me by Dr Fred Freeman on the day of the funeral that a tribute album to the great man was a must. I agreed. Fred immediately set about producing 'A' the Bairns O' Adam'. Classic versions of Hamish's songs were licensed by Greentrax, including 'The John McLean March' by the legendary group The Laggan, and 'The Song of the Gillie Mor' by Dick Gaughan, but many tracks were recorded specially for the album, including a stunning version of 'The Freedom Come All Ye' by Jim Reid and Rod Paterson. Hamish's own recording of 'The 51st Highland Division's Farewell to Sicily' was uncovered in the school's archive. Thanks are due to many people for their contributions to this album, including Tony Engle of Topic Records, Jim McLean of Nevis Records, The Corries and the School of Scottish Studies, as well as the various artists. It is a wonderful tribute to a great man who once said very generously of me on television: 'Every now and again there comes along someone like Ian Green who is sorely needed at that time.'

One track on this album has a great story to it. Hamish was a staunch supporter of the struggle against apartheid in South Africa, led by Nelson Mandela, and during Mandela's imprisonment on Robben Island, Hamish wrote the song 'Rivonia' (aka 'Free Nelson Mandela'). On meeting The Corries in Sandy Bell's one evening in 1968, Hamish persuaded them to go to the nearby School of Scottish Studies. While they learned and rehearsed the song, Hamish set up his tape recorder. They then recorded 'Rivonia' for Hamish who duplicated a copy and sent it to Mandela. It was smuggled into the Robben Island prison and he was able to listen to it. He subsequently wrote to Hamish, thanking him for his 'time, effort and concern', but this letter has sadly been lost. After being freed, Mandela visited Scotland to be given the Freedom of the City of Glasgow. He specifically requested that Hamish be invited to the event, and the two hugged each other on the platform in front of thousands of people. After Hamish's death his wife Katzel came across a box of tapes, and amongst them was the original recording of 'Rivonia'.

Katzel, Ronnie Browne, Bill Smith and the trustees of the late Roy Williamson all kindly agreed to allow the track to be included on 'A' the Bairns O' Adam'. I sent a copy of the album to Nelson Mandela, and the circle was complete. I received a very nice reply from him.

Ian with the parcel sent to Nelson Mandella.

I have quite a collection of letters of appreciation from VIPs, MPs, MSPs and others to whom we have sent copies of various albums. It includes a letter from Prince Charles about Adam McNaughtan's album, 'Words, Words, Words', which I sent him after he recited two verses of 'Where is the Glasgow That I Used to Know?' at the opening of the Glasgow Garden Festival in 1988. I also received a letter from the Queen after sending her

Volume I of 'The Masters of Piobaireachd', recordings by 'The Bobs of Balmoral', who had both been employed on the Balmoral Estate at one time. The Queen thanked me and said she had 'fond memories' of 'The Bobs'. I also sent copies of 'Far, Far From Ypres' ('Songs, Poems and Music of WWI') to both the Queen and Prince Charles, and again received letters of thanks.

For some years, Ian McCalman has been writing bloody good songs, which have been recorded by The McCalmans and others. It occurred to me that Ian's songs were worthy of a solo album. When I approached him, he was very pleased, but went away to think about the project. What he came up with was really interesting. Apart from a couple of songs which he would sing himself, he suggested that he would call on his many singing friends to record one song each. The result was a cracking album, with such fine artists as Barbara Dickson, Isla St Clair, Sheena Wellington, Dick Gaughan, Allan Taylor and Mike Whellans, each taking on one of Ian's songs and giving it their own interpretation. In addition, Aly Bain and Phil Cunningham recorded a set of his tunes. This is another fine compilation addition to our growing list. It's titled 'McCalman Singular'.

On the occasion of the release of our 20th anniversary compilation, 'Scotland – The Music and the Song', I sent numerous copies to Members of the Scottish Parliament with a view to stirring up what I saw as a waning enthusiasm for Scottish traditional music. I also wrote to every MSP urging them to do everything to further Scottish culture and, in particular, traditional music. While I did receive some letters of thanks for the album and some replies to my letter, the majority failed to respond at all. One MSP who had clearly not bothered to listen properly to the three-album set, complained that there were no Scottish dance-band or accordion tracks included, when in fact there were several. Ach well, what do you expect from politicians who rarely listen to anyone but themselves, and rarely get their facts right.

I was greatly honoured, however, when Linda Fabiani, MSP, generously raised a motion (S2M – 4460) in the Scottish Parliament:

That the Parliament congratulates Greentrax Recordings, 'Scotland's Favourite Record Company', on its 20th anniversary; welcomes the recognition of founder, Ian Green by the Royal Scottish Academy of Music and Drama in its award to him of the honorary degree of Doctor of Music; thanks Ian Green and all at

Greentrax Recordings for their work in the preservation and promotion of Scottish traditional music and contribution to our nation's culture; and looks forward to many more years of great music.
Supported by Michael Matheson.

That sort of stuff makes the head spin a bit. More on the honorary doctorate later.

CHAPTER THIRTEEN

the GReentRAX yeARS – the wwi project

n 2004, another milestone project was suggested to me by Des Brogan of Mercat Tours International, and an ex-police colleague of mine, Jim Paris, a part-time tour guide. Amongst other things, this company arranges coach tours of the cemeteries and battlefields of wwi in Belgium and France. Des and Jim had the notion that an album of wwi Songs, with more of a Scottish perspective, would be a really worthwhile addition to music already recorded. Des also emphasised that he would sell such albums on his coach tours, using the music to illustrate the tour. Incidentally, many of these tours are exclusively for secondary school pupils, who apparently return visibly moved by what they have seen and heard. This seemed like a project I could get my teeth into. However, it sat on the 'back burner' for a couple of years because of lack of funds, until Des decided to shake me out of my lethargy, and invited June and myself as guests on the tour.

It consists of a coach journey from Waterloo Place in Edinburgh to Hull, followed by an overnight ferry crossing to Zeebrugge. Three days are then spent visiting many wwi cemeteries, large and small, and all immaculately maintained by the War Graves Commission, plus battlefield museums, indoor and outdoor. It also includes a visit to Ypres, and the very moving 'last post' ceremony at the Menin Gate monument, which contains the names of 54,416 British and Imperial soldiers with no known grave on the Ypres Salient. The local fire brigade provides the buglers every day, of every week, of every month, of every year for the ceremony. No one leaves the Menin Gate ceremony without being seriously emotionally affected. June was given the honour of laying a wreath on behalf of our coach party, and Des went 'beyond the call of duty' when he had the coach driver go many miles off the usual tour route to allow June to visit her grandfather's grave in the small Villiers Station Cemetery. Our fellow passengers accompanied us to the grave. Des said a few words, and then played 'The Flowers of the Forest' on his tape machine. This was a very moving occasion. June is only the second family descendant to visit the grave. There were many other emotional moments when, for example, we visited the grave of one of the youngest volunteer soldiers, and another where father and son lie buried together. The Tyne Cot Cemetery is a scene which remains imprinted in the mind. Here, there is row, upon row of gravestones, and a memorial, commemorating 35,000 servicemen from the UK and New Zealand, who died in the Ypres Salient after 16 August 1917, and whose graves are unknown.

I have read many, many books on WWI (and also WWII, plus the seemingly never-ending struggles in every corner of the world) – not because I am a warmonger, but because I am in awe of the bravery of all these (mainly) young men who give their lives for the cause of freedom. Unfortunately, in recent times, for less clear-cut reasons. WWI was promoted as 'the war to end all wars' – we know better now.

Nothing, however, had prepared me for what I saw and heard on the WWI trip, and it had a profound effect on me. I was emotionally drained, but in a strange way exhilarated by the experience, and unable to focus on anything else for days on end. When it did start to crystallize in my mind, I realised the recording project should receive priority status. I set in motion the recording and compiling of an album of the many songs, poems and music resulting from this bloody conflict. It was intended to be a single-CD project, but gradually it became clear that a double CD would be required to accommodate the many soldiers' 'marching and trench songs', the music-hall songs of the time, and also the songs, poems and music written mostly after the war. I am indebted to Des and Jim for their valuable help, and also for firing me up to become as focused on the project as they were. It became a labour of love.

In my mind, there was only one man to produce and record this album, and that was Ian McCalman. Here was the right man, a singer's singer, to pull together the voices and instruments for the task. When I described the project to him, he was enthusiastic, and immersed himself in it. I just cannot thank him enough for his untiring efforts, his stream of ideas and a determination to get it just right. In the end, the quality of the product speaks for itself, but reviewers were generous in their praise of the album which we titled 'Far, Far From Ypres' ('Songs, Poems and Music of World War One'), and it received massive airplay. On Armistice Day, 2008, it featured on almost every radio station in the UK, including a long 'special' on BBC Scotland's Reel Blend, when Ian and I were interviewed at length by Robbie Shepherd. On air Ian humorously

The WWI Tynecot Cemetery.

John Macrae in Flanders Fields.

warned, 'If Ian Green approaches you with the words, 'I have a wee project in mind for you', run for cover.'

My special thanks go to all who took part in the project; Iain Anderson, BBC Scotland's well-loved presenter, for his beautiful readings of the poems, Captain Steven Small (yes, my old pal) of The Army School of Bagpipe Music and Highland Drumming at Redford Barracks, who organised an Army School Pipe Band to record sets of tunes for the album, and of course all those who willingly licensed tracks for CD 2 to Greentrax – Eric Bogle, Dick Gaughan, Ronnie Browne and Jim Malcolm, who all feature on CD 2. We named the singers who performed on CD 1 'The Scottish Pals Singers', in WWI volunteers from the same town or even the same workplace were called 'Pals Battalions', so that seemed appropriate. 'The Scottish Pals Singers' were Ian Bruce, Stephen Quigg, Ian McCalman, Tich Frier, Nick Keir and Hamish Bayne, and all gave a first-class performance. Fiona Forbes took the lead where appropriate in the music-hall songs, and was superb. The sympathetic instrumental backing was by Hamish Bayne, Nick Keir, Ian McCalman and Martin Allcock (who played a variety of instruments, and used a synthesiser to produce all sorts of additional sounds). The youngest singer on the album is Stevie Palmer, who sang his own award-winning song, 'Black is the Sun', which I find spine-chilling and quite awesome. Watch out for a debut solo album on Greentrax by this fine songwriter in 2010.

I must also commend John Slavin of Design Folk, who does a lot of magnificent sleeves for Greentrax, but excelled himself with this one. The front cover is stunning. It is a real pleasure to work with John, who is not only artistic but quite dedicated and is one of the best.

The album was appropriately launched in Edinburgh Castle, when a night of speeches, songs and music was washed down with much alcohol and a tasty buffet enjoyed by the many guests.

I have never quite experienced the kind of feedback we got on this release. Many customers wrote to say

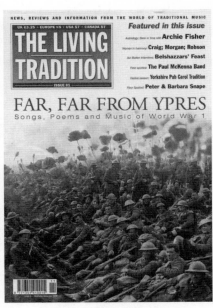

Living Tradition Cover.

that they were moved to tears by the album. One said she was listening to it in her car, but was forced to pull over while she regained her composure. Personally, I cannot listen to the album without a tear or two.

One surprising disappointment was the attitude of a member of the administration of the Royal British Legion Scotland, who suggested that none of the members of the British Legion would be interested in such an album, which he dismissed out of hand. Fortunately, a more senior member at the Edinburgh headquarters was more sympathetic, and somewhat embarrassed by his subordinate's attitude. In the following issue of the British Legion Scotland magazine there was a free advert which was greatly appreciated by me. We have also sold a considerable number of albums to British Legion Scotland members through our own efforts by circulating the individual Legion Clubs around Scotland.

I am desperately proud of what we achieved with this album and, while it has a more Scottish perspective than any of its predecessors, you must consider the inordinate proportion of Scottish soldiers who fought (and died) in WWI. Maybe this album was long overdue. It is, however, intended as a tribute to all the soldiers from Scotland, England, Ireland and Wales, and also their Commonwealth brothers in arms from all corners of the globe, who fought and suffered together in the so-called 'Great War', and in particular all those who died.

The album sells well, especially in most of the WWI museums and visitor centres in both France and Belgium. In addition to being played on every WWI Mercat Coach Tour, it also sells like 'hot-cakes' to those on the tour. I honestly believe that everyone should go on this trip. It is a must-do one, and I am sure Mercat Tours International, who have won several awards, will be pleased to accommodate you. You could also buy the CD!

I am greatly indebted to Ian McCalman who put his heart and soul into this album and like me was greatly affected by it. A very special album this one.

CHAPTER FOURTEEN

the GReentRax yeaRs – otheR majoR pRojects

have worked on several projects with Jack Evans, an ex-member of Jock Tamson's Bairns and The Easy Club. He is a very talented guitarist and multi-instrumentalist. In addition to producing several fine albums for Greentrax, he also worked on a project which was initially an idea only and had no name. My brief was an album which should include many of the Scottish favourites, such as 'Amazing Grace', 'Flower of Scotland and 'Auld Lang Syne', arranged with a 'clubbie' beat, which I hoped would be popular with the younger generation in particular, but include Scottish traditional instruments, such as the fiddle and Highland bagpipe. There had to be a balance between instrumental music, jigs and reels, with some vocal tracks included. Jack went enthusiastically to work and, in due course, came up with the very album I was looking for, which we named 'Keltik Elektrik' ('Edinburgh Hogmanay Party Mix'). We did a massive promotional mail-out of the album to all the usual media people, but also to nightclub proprietors and disco presenters, and received really good feedback. One DJ said that the 'Auld Lang Syne' track was the one thing he'd always needed for a party because, usually after playing that song, everyone sat down and the party ended. But our version had a set of reels added to the song, and apparently 'the dancers went into a wild, demented Highland Fling'. Pleased to help!

It was quite strange, but Jack was unable to find a singer for 'Flower of Scotland', so it became an instrumental. I was aware that in some quarters there is a resistance to the song because it is considered to be anti-English, and many are concerned that it is becoming generally accepted as the Scottish National Anthem. I think it is a good song in the right hands, but certainly not a contender as a Scottish National Anthem. It should never be sung in a challenging manner, which it so often is. I believe that 'The Freedom Come All Ye' is a far better contender for a national anthem, by a long chalk.

The album sold very well, especially after we did some TV advertising

– a damned expensive exercise. Jack went on to produce two more 'Keltik Elektrik' albums – 'Keltik Elektrik 2' and 'Hotel Kaledonia' – using the very best musicians and singers from the traditional music scene. The first is the best seller of the three.

He also recorded an album with Mairi Campbell and Jenny Gardner – 'Once Upon a Time in the North' – which was a stunning album, but suffered from the fact that the three artists did not tour with it. In addition, Jack compiled a Greentrax album – 'A Clear Day's Dawnin'', which was released to mark the beginning of the new Scottish Parliament. It was a good album, consisting of some remixed Greentrax items, plus specially recorded tracks, but it did not hit the mark.

Another album, which came from my own eccentric mind, is 'Bah! Humbug', ('The Alternative Christmas Album'), which is a collection of songs poking fun at the commercial aspects of the modern-day Christmas. The songs include: 'Santa Bloody Claus' (Eric Bogle); 'There are no Lights on our Christmas Tree' (Cyril Tawney); 'The Man Who Slits the Turkeys' Throats at Christmas' (Robin Laing); and 'The Twelve Days of Christmas' (Bill Barclay), plus a fairly serious version of 'We Wish You a Merry Christmas'. My old buddies Drinkers' Drouth played a big part on that track. The royalties on the track go to cancer research. We also send a cheque to the same charity each Christmas as a more appropriate alternative to sending out business Christmas cards. 'Bah! Humbug' was also advertised on TV and has sold very well. No accounting for the bad taste of some, including the deranged Greentrax MD! I must admit that I'm not much of a lover of the big 'Christmas thing', but I suppose the finger can be pointed at me for adding a further degree of commercialism to this religious festival.

The legendary Scottish cartoonist, Malky McCormick, designed the brilliant front cover of 'Bah! Humbug'. His cartoons are world famous, but what is not so widely-known is that Malky was also the banjo-playing member of the hugely entertaining Vindscreen Vipers group, which also included the so sadly missed Danny Kyle, plus Mike Whellans, Tich Frier and others. I booked the Vindscreen Vipers many times into Fuzzfolk, and they always brought the house down. It was Danny who initiated The Danny Kyle Awards competition at Celtic Connections.

The Keltik Elektrik albums and Bah Humbug! were released on a new label I introduced in 1998: G2. Richard Branson introduced a label for his Virgin Records named V2 so G2 seemed entirely appropriate. The G2 label was to accommodate artists and albums which were within the broad stream of traditional music but only just. The first release was by the Edinburgh 'country' band The Felsons. The singer, Dean Owens, wrote all the songs which was the aspect of the band that interested me. The band toured the UK with The Mavericks (USA) but shortly after that the band broke up. Sales immediately died, as always happens with band albums. We also released a 'live' album by the late Tam White and his Shoestring Band. This came about when Tam's sound engineer recorded one of the band's concerts on to a music cassette. When he later listened to it Tam realised it was a very special gig and a master was pro-

Bah Humbug Poster.

duced from the music cassette. An album from a cassette is a first as far as I am aware, certainly it is for Greentrax. Tam died in 2010 and hundreds turned out for his funeral.

The most successful band on our G2 label is Salsa Celtica. The Band is a mix of Celtic and Latino musicians who fuse South American and Cuban song, salsa rhythms, improvisation, Scottish reels, and ceilidh tunes to create a 'Caledonian Caribbean Salsa paradise', as one reviewer wrote. The Band create a big buzz wherever they go, which includes music festivals all over the UK and beyond. They even had a successful trip to Cuba and several tours of the USA. The two Salsa Celtica albums have sold well and are now challenging our 'all-time best sellers'. We have licensed several tracks of Salsa Celtica to Salsa specialist labels around the world and invariably the Salsa Celtica track is placed number one. You just have to get on your feet and dance when this band plays – in my case it is more a flailing of arms and legs!

In 2009, we compiled an album, titled 'People and Songs of the Sea' – songs and music reflecting the rich cultural heritage of Scotland's fishing, with 21 tracks of Celtic music's finest artists and fisher folk of the Forth. This was released in association with a photographic exhibition by Shona McMillan, staged in various libraries on the east coast of Scotland, from Edinburgh to Eyemouth, and elsewhere. This was Shona's bid to stage something in the Scottish Year of Homecoming 2009. The compilation is again a mix of music from the Greentrax catalogue, specially recorded material and some licensed tracks. Once again, Ronnie Browne let us have a Corries' track, and others came from Kettle Records (Cilla Fisher), guitarist John Carnie, and The Harbour Lights, a group of singers who are mainly from Musselburgh down to Port Seton. The CD ends with a huge vocal track of 'Will Your Anchor Hold', sung by the Fisher Folk Choir (again consisting of people living along the east coast of Scotland) in the Old Parish Hall in Cockenzie, conducted by William Watt and recorded by Ian McCalman. Another unique project from Greentrax. Sales at the exhibition were disappointing, but the album created a big buzz, and has sold well through other sources.

We also released a couple of other albums as our contribution to the Scottish Year of Homecoming: Jean Redpath's wonderful 'Will Ye No Come Back Again', released by Rounder Records in the USA in 1986, and licensed by Greentrax for release in 2009; Fiona J. MacKenzie's 'A Good Suit of Clothes'; The McCalmans' 'Coming Home', a cracking 'live' album; and 'The Music and Song of Edinburgh', remastered and with some new tracks.

They are all doing fine, but I have to admit that, despite what the

The Fisher Folk Choir in Cockenzie Church recording 'Will Your Anchor Hold'.

politicians say, the Scottish Year of Homecoming was a bit of a damp squib. I was not able to attend the big 'Homecoming' event centred in Holyrood Park in Edinburgh, which was apparently well-attended. The word that has come back to me from all parts is that it was poorly advertised.

The Celtic Collections Series arose from my perceived need to introduce a series of quality recordings from the Greentrax back catalogue to compete in the very competitive mid-priced, tourist-based CD market. We decided to go for a splurge of albums to launch the series in 2000, and released 'Songs of Scotland', 'Songs of Robert Burns', 'Ceilidh Band Music of Scotland', 'Bagpipes of Scotland', 'Fiddles of Scotland' and a modern sounding 'Celtic Sounds of Scotland'. These all retail at a suggested price of £6.99 and sold reasonably well, but it became clear that my idea of using a different famous Scottish castle on each front cover did not appeal as much as I had imagined. I changed some of the front covers, and immediately we witnessed increased sales. Some items in the series have sold exceptionally well, with the bagpipes, ceilidh and Burns albums leading the field, until we released 'Celtic Women from Scotland'.

The idea for this one came from the ever-increasing number of 'Celtic Women from Ireland' albums (or some similar title), and to use Colin Hynd's words, 'I felt a need to redress the balance'. Once again, the Irish astonished me when a company advised me that they had a series of recordings titled 'Celtic Collections' and would I 'care to stop using this title'? When I explained that each album in our series contained Scotland in the title, and that I had no intention of releasing any Irish albums in my series, only then did they back off. 'Celtic Women from Scotland' has been very successful, as has another Jack Evans production which travels around Scotland, using tunes composed about particular places – for example, 'The Eriskay Love Lilt', 'Loch Lomond' and 'The Skye Boat Song'. More recently, we have added The McCalmans' award-winning

Bill Barclay (Greentrax Artist).

album, 'Peace and Plenty', 'Sandy Bell's Ceilidh', 'The Music and Song of Edinburgh' and old friend Bill Barclay's 'The Very Best Of'. All these had previously been on the Greentrax label, and others will be added to this popular series.

The Classics from Scotland Series are albums previously released by Topic Records. However, the MD Tony Engle, thought they were more suited for the Greentrax label, and we subsequently licensed albums by the great traditional singers Belle Stewart, Davie Stewart (both 'travellers'); John MacDonald (known as 'The Singing Molecatcher From Morayshire') and Willie Scott, (shepherd and singer of many Border ballads); plus the album, 'Cilla and Artie', (Cilla Fisher and Artie Trezise who have achieved great fame as 'The Singing Kettle) and an instrumental album, 'The Caledonian Companion'. These are all worthy collector's items and store-houses of traditional song. I have a good working relationship with Tony Engle and he has, in turn, licensed tracks from Greentrax for his projects.

We also tested the water in the video market some years ago – an Eric Bogle Australian TV Show; Natalie MacMaster's 'Fiddle Lesson' and fellow Cape Bretoner, Tracey Dares' piano-based 'A' Chording to the Tunes'. Eric's video did fine, but neither of the other two did well for us at all, although they are both very fine instructional videos. Later, we released on DVD 'Piping Live! Masters' from the Glasgow's Piping Live competition. Stunning competition piping as you would expect. Next, came The Occasionals' 'The Full Set of Basic Scottish Ceilidh Dances', already referred to. Finally, in 2009, we released 'Eric Bogle – Live at Stoneyfell Winery' (Australia), containing 21 tracks of his most requested songs. He sold this DVD, along with several CDs, on his mammoth tour of 2009, from mid-May to mid-September, and attained remarkable tour sales. Thanks Eric. You might make me a rich man yet. Eric retired from international touring late in 2009 and will be greatly missed on the UK touring circuit.

Greentrax Recordings, June and myself have received some amazing awards, of which we are most proud. The first of these was the 'Album of The Year 1994' award, nominated by BBC Radio Scotland for the ground-breaking Shooglenifty album, 'Venus in Tweeds' (their best album to date, in my opinion). In 1997, Greentrax unexpectedly, and against very stiff competition, won the Annual Achievement Award from East Lothian Business Association for good business practices and export achievements. In 2006, June and I were made Honorary Life Members of The Traditional Music and Song Association of Scotland, and in 2005, I was very proud to be presented with the 'Hamish Henderson Award for Services to Scottish

John Munro and Eric Bogle with their Greentrax awards for exceptional touring sales.

Ian, June and Brian McNeill on an unforgettable day.

Traditional Music' at the Scots Trad Awards, which automatically placed me in The Scottish Traditional Music Hall of Fame, annually displayed in various Scottish theatres. In 2006, I was stunned, but very proud, to accept an Honorary Doctorate of Music from the Royal Scottish Academy of Music and Drama in Glasgow – alongside the great Scottish comedian, Billy Connolly, singer Annie Lennox, and actress Tilda Swinton. June and I had a memorable day as guests of the RSAMD, and I was moved to tears by Brian McNeill's presentation speech, this time in front of hundreds of people (see addendum). I felt most humble I have to say.

June and I have had two tunes written for us: Ian Hardie composed 'The Green Ruby Waltz' for our Ruby Anniversary and Phil Cunningham composed 'June and Ian Green's Golden Years' for our Golden Wedding. In addition to Gordon Duncan's 'Ian Green of Greentrax', I also had the tune 'Ian D. Green' composed by the late Arthur Scott Robertson of Shetland, while Davy Steele named an unknown traditional tune 'Ian Green's Appendix' for a Ceolbeg album. It is wonderful to have a tune composed for you, but to have several is quite something!

I have been interviewed many times on BBC Radio Scotland – by Archie Fisher for 'Travelling Folk' and Robbie Shepherd for 'The Reel Blend' (so sadly missed), but also other radio stations both in the UK and abroad. I am able to relax more these days, but I was a very nervous interviewee in the early days and, being very self critical, I gave myself a lot of grief after a bad interview. I am usually more confident these days,

I was invited to present my own selection of music on a two-programme series on BBC Radio Scotland, produced by Rab Noakes. I chose as my theme for the first programme 'my personal favourite tracks' from my extensive record collection and, for my second programme, I chose the theme of 'favourite singer/songwriters', which is a subject that really intrigues me. I was reasonably satisfied by my performances on both, but the latter proved to be the better one, and was subsequently broadcast on other BBC Radio stations in England. It was a wonderful experience.

While the press have always been most generous in its praise of June, me and Greentrax, it was Scottish Television who featured Greentrax on their 'Artery Series'. They first interviewed such personalities as Jean Redpath, Hamish Henderson and Ian McCalman for the documentary, and then came to Cockenzie to film me chatting about my life and involvement in folk and traditional music, plus my work with Greentrax. Strangely, I was not overawed by the cameras, and in fact, felt quite relaxed. I chatted in my own 'couthy' style, as a friend was quick to point out! I'm not quite sure if that was a compliment or not. June was also interviewed for the programme which was transmitted a few weeks later and then repeated.

All these things are 'the icing on the cake', but the enjoyment I have had from the launch of Greentrax to the present time is quite enough in itself. I never get up in the morning and think, 'Hell, another day at the bloody office.' It's the opposite in fact. I enjoy my daily involvement in the music business where I work with good, loyal staff, and meet many quite special people, many of whom we refer to as artists, but in so many cases the word 'friend' applies.

Our current Greentrax team consists of June (director and part-time administrator); Elaine Sunter (full-time accounts and royalties administrator); Cath Mack (part-time promotions administrator); and Pat Clark (part-time warehouseman and packer). And if I am trying to wind-up stuffy, grey-suited people, I introduce our wee Westie, Mairi Bheg, as 'The Managing Director'. I wickedly enjoy the surprise such comments create! Oh, and of course, there's one more full-time member, myself, often laughingly referred to as The Managing Director. I am also a dab hand at making the coffee, washing the cups and cleaning the office. When I list these duties to some 'stiff shirt' from London who wants to speak to the 'Label Manager', 'The Recording Manager' or even 'The A & R Manager', the stunned silence is palpable, and it kind of brings them down to earth! What is an 'A & R' man anyway?

The small but perfectly formed Greentrax Team.

Previous employees were, of course, my two sons, Andrew and Stephen, and although that did not work out, they did contribute much to the company for a period of time. We also employed Brenda McCulloch about the time Culburnie Records (UK) came under our wing. Brenda was managing Culburnie from day to day and had a good knowledge of the recording industry, but her daily commuting from her home in Glasgow to Cockenzie eventually led to us parting company. Brenda wanted to work from home on computer most of the time, and although we gave it a try, I needed another pair of hands in the office. For a short period of time, we employed Davie Black (of Drinkers' Drouth fame) and later Torcull Kennedy, as sales managers, following the departure of Andrew. Davie brought a great deal of cheer to the office. He is a really nice guy and a good friend, but eventually resigned of his own accord. A temporary downturn in trading later forced me to dispense with Torcull.

Marina Clow, as she was known when she first came to me as our accounts administrator (later, also royalties administrator and latterly, office manager in my absence), was an employee who remained with me for seven loyal years and seemed to be the right person for taking a bigger part in the management of Greentrax. In the interim, she became Marina Wilson. She has a very bright daughter Rebecca who is destined to do well. Regrettably, Marina left the company 'to seek a change', and the parting proved to be a 'difficult' one. They say friendships and business don't mix well and that may be true!

The current worldwide recording industry is in the midst of change, and times are challenging, but, as the record retail market sorts itself out after the collapse of most of the record retail chains, things do seem to look brighter. HMV are thankfully still going strong. Also, download sales of tracks and entire albums are now showing a substantial increase. We are hopeful of better times ahead, and as I finished this chapter in 2010, annual sales for 2009 proved to be good and I am hopeful for the future of the recording industry. Great changes face us, but recorded music of some sort will always be high on the priority list of most thinking people. Greentrax and I will be in there fighting for our share of the market, and have no intention of calling it a day, as some have done, just because things are a bit difficult.

Earlier I mentioned how difficult it is to work with the major record labels. In the early days of Greentrax, I remember approaching a couple of majors with a view to licensing deleted albums by such high-profile artists as Billy Connolly, Matt McGinn and Hamish Imlach, and for each

I was asked for totally unrealistic advances (many thousands of pounds) tied to huge licensing royalties. I have to be honest, I told them to get stuffed (or words to that effect). I was able to license a couple of tracks from EMI on one occasion, but they charged Greentrax 25 per cent of the published dealer price (PPD), plus large advances. I tried to explain that we were talking folk music, but the guy couldn't have cared less – it was take it or leave it. I again felt like telling them to stuff it, but I had to have the tracks for a special project, so reluctantly agreed. PPD is the price that albums are sold to retailers, and is the standard figure on which most licensing agreements are based.

Some years later I did licence two albums for a compilation album 'Best of Matt McGinn – Volume 2' from BMG, who proved to be much easier to deal with. One other track included on the album was the 'Ibrox Disaster', the tragic account of this sad event and a very moving piece by Matt, released as a single with royalties going to the disaster fund. I was proud to release 'Volume 2' on behalf of the McGinn family.

A month or so after my unhappy dealings with EMI, I really got my own back, when EMI approached me with an application to license a couple of tracks for two different albums. They offered me 18 per cent of PPD and a very small advance. I replied along these lines: 'I think you've made a mistake. That should be 25 per cent, plus a higher advance, since that is what you charged me not so very long ago.' There was a pregnant pause, and then the EMI person said he'd get back to me. He later phoned, apologised, said there had been some kind of error, and would I accept 25 per cent and a higher advance. Have you ever come across such bloody chancers?

A few years later, when I was building up an attractive catalogue of the various strands of Scottish traditional music, I had a visit from an EMI representative who chatted away for a while and told me how excellent a label Greentrax was. I could see where the conversation was leading, so I stopped him and said that if a buyout of Greentrax was what he had in mind, then he could forget it. I also went on to make it clear what I thought of his company and their money-grabbing attitude. He was somewhat shamed, and left deflated. A few years later I learned that he had parted company with EMI. Wise man.

I have spent 24 years in the recording industry, and am still as enthusiastic today as I was when I launched the label. I am certainly not going to knock my years in the police, and if I had to start again, I probably would not change that part of my life. But I must say my years managing Greentrax have been my happiest, despite setbacks when family members

Pretending to be at work in the Greentrax Office.

left the company and of course June's health. The Greentrax years have also been the most challenging in some ways, but immensely satisfying. I have met some of the most talented and amazing people in the music business, and am proud to call many of them friends. I have travelled far and wide promoting Greentrax – Denmark, France, Hungary, the USA, Canada and Hong Kong. I have also been fortunate to enjoy many wonderful festivals, concerts and performances through Greentrax. I am proud to acknowledge that Greentrax has gone a long way to present quality music to a far wider audience than the music had ever reached before, and I feel in some small way, to have changed, for the better, the face of 'Scottish music'. I often look at the walls of the Greentrax office which are adorned with covers of over 400 albums that the company has released, and I cannot quite grasp the enormity of the achievement. While I have been the (obsessive) driving force behind Greentrax, there are many others who have contributed to the success of the company. I thank them all and in particular the many Greentrax artists. So many are the worthy recipients of various awards and have gone on to achieve considerable success. I am proud of you all.

I mentioned earlier that there are no millionaires in Scottish traditional music, and after 24 years, I have not earned a fortune from the company, but that is quite irrelevant as far as I am concerned. For me, it is the music that is most important, and if I make a bob or two along the way, then that's a bonus.

part IV

CHAPTER FIFTEEN

A REVIEW AT 76 YEARS

The most frequent question I am asked nowadays is: 'When will you retire, Ian?' However I am very happy doing what I do, and see no need to consider retiring. Quite frankly, the thought of sitting at home watching 'white paint drying' is just not on my agenda. It's not in my nature to sit around doing nothing, so a rocking chair is out. I don't like shopping, while June does, so the alternative to working could be trailing around shops day after day. Perish that thought. All my life I have been constantly active and involved in all sorts of activities, as you have read, so I think it would be my undoing to stop now. My answer therefore is always the same, 'As long as my health will allow, I will be actively involved in Greentrax Recordings on a daily basis.' When the time comes, I think I will know and bow out, but certainly not yet.

This brings me to the subject of my health at 76. Like many ex-police officers I suffer from indigestion, but I take the wonder drug Omeprazole – and the indigestion ended (more or less) since the day my doctor prescribed it for me. I also have to take a daily tablet to control an enlarged prostate gland, but that causes me no serious problems, although I do have to 'pee' more often these days. I also take a tablet a day to control occasional high blood pressure, but regular tests appear to confirm it is under control. My most serious problem is one which has haunted my mother's side of the family for many generations – weak chests, resulting in asthma and chronic bronchitis. My mother died as a result of the latter. I also suffer from the complaint, and Linda appears to be developing even worse symptoms than me. Linda's son

At work in the warehouse.

Jamie and some other family members also suffer. It is a terrible affliction and, although I have two inhalers and take a daily tablet to assist my breathing, I get a bout of bronchitis two or three times a year. Unfortunately, the only way to get rid of a lung infection and a barking cough is to take a course of antibiotics, which I keep at home for emergencies. Seems I take a lot of tablets, but poor June is on about 25 tablets per day for her various medical conditions, so I consider myself lucky. At the time of writing, June has also been diagnosed as diabetic, although it is being controlled with tablets.

Experience has taught me that tiredness lowers my immune system, so I go to bed early most nights, and when coughs and sneezes are about, I tend to stay away from public places. This is quite inconvenient, but is something I just have to work round. It has become a way of life, although it does curtail our social life.

After a holiday in Bute in 2009, I experienced pain developing in my left hip, at first only occasionally. The pain quickly developed and became permanent – as in 24 hours a day. I saw my doctor several times, and he prescribed various painkillers, including very large doses of morphine. The morphine had several side effects but did not even take the edge off the pain, so yet another appointment was arranged. The doctor was very sympathetic and realised I was by then in severe pain. She said it was etched on my face. She wrote a letter and sent me directly to the Accident and Emergency Department of the Edinburgh Royal Infirmary, where I was examined by another female doctor and my hip was x-rayed. She diagnosed severe hip-joint wear, and recommended a hip-joint replacement immediately. However, the orthopaedic department refused to accept me that day, and arranged an appointment for the following day. And so began the biggest administrational cock-up of all time.

I went back the next day and sat for over four hours in the most overcrowded clinic you can imagine. When I was finally seen by a male doctor, he questioned my presence there and, to my amazement, told me I was in the 'broken-bones clinic'. I explained the situation, but all he could promise was an appointment some two weeks hence, which I declined emphatically because of my severe pain. After some deliberation on his part, I was 'squeezed' into the appointment system the following day. I returned and, after another four-hour wait, was again informed that I was at the wrong clinic. Honest truth!

This doctor suggested an appointment some weeks hence, but I again dug my heels in (something I would never normally do with a doctor) and forcibly expressed the view that I required immediate medical attention. I said I would not leave the department without an examination, even if it meant remaining in the waiting room all night. She became very rude, and ordered me onto an examination trolley. This was no easy matter for me. When she impatiently grabbed my left leg and swung it on to the trolley, I almost went through the roof with pain and let out a yell. She at last realised my extreme situation, advised me I needed an urgent hip replacement (which, of course, I knew) and ordered the nurse to find me a bed in the orthopaedic ward. I returned to the waiting room but, after only a few moments, the doctor came out and whispered in my ear, 'I am very sorry I have been very rude to you. I have been working for three days and have only had five hours sleep.' Apology accepted, but this was a comedy of errors by the ERI. Had I not been very determined, I would have continued to wait and suffer.

After several more hours, I was admitted to a ward, but was told the following day (Saturday) that I would probably be sent home on Monday. I again fought my corner and it seemed to work because, about midday on Monday, I was told to prepare for the operating theatre. I sat in my wee 'goony' for hours, only to be told it would be Tuesday before I went 'under the knife'.

Despite the above shambles, the theatre team were real professionals, and the operation was completed in an hour and a half. I had an epidural and was totally conscious throughout the operation, although I was lightly sedated. I could hear the team at work and was aware of 'banging' as the new joint was put in place. The anaesthetist asked me if I would like some music during the operation, and he played me a folk album (not Greentrax I'm afraid) to which I was gaily singing along! The anaesthetist was impressed and asked, 'How do you know all the songs on the CD? I replied, 'I should. It's my job.'

I was up on my feet the next day, although I nearly fainted, and was home on the Saturday. Unfortunately, the wound partially opened up at home, and I had daily visits from a district nurse for the next three weeks. I was not allowed to move until the wound healed, and became very frustrated – I wanted to be up and doing things.

The operation was a great success, the pain ended the day after the operation. I had to use a walking stick for months, but when I moaned to my doctor, he replied, 'Ian, for goodness sake, you have been through major surgery and your body has suffered major trauma, not to mention the effect of all the painkillers. Don't be so impatient.' That's me though.

One very unfortunate side effect of the painkilling drugs prescribed before, during and after my hip operation was severe constipation, resulting in the return of very painful haemorrhoids. After being prescribed treatment for these over several weeks, with absolutely no relief, my doctor made arrangements for me to be seen in hospital. Don't tell me there are no waiting lists in the NHS. I waited for months before being seen.

I'm still working at 76, an age when most folk have retired, but it is not 'all work and no play'. No fear. In addition to our many visits to Greece before and since my police retirement, we have had many wonderful holidays in other parts of the world – one holiday was to Singapore, Hong Kong, Bali, Bangkok and the resort of Pataya in Thailand. That was a fabulous holiday, full of wonderful sights, experiences and a wide variety of tasty food.

The holiday company did warn us that Pataya was a bit of a 'sex hot spot', but even I was taken aback at how blatant it was. I was accosted several times by males as I waited for June outside shops. I thought I might be safer if I went into a bar for a drink, but was immediately propositioned by a very attractive barmaid, who grabbed my hand and tickled my palm (what could she mean?) while making sexy suggestions. When I explained I was waiting for 'Mamma', she was not the least bit phased, continuing to 'chat me up' even when June arrived! I didn't feel so bad about being chatted up by a female prostitute, I have to say. Men of all ages, some quite old, were to be seen with Thai girls, some of whom could have been no more than 14 or 15.

One bar owner recommended a less 'sleazy' pole-dancing/strip club to me, and I thought it would be 'interesting' and educational (!!!) to attend. At first I was to go on my own, but eventually curiosity got the better of June, her sister Betty and her husband John and we all trooped along to the club. It was an eye-opener right enough, but even more interesting was that the girls were pole-dancing and stripping to a Dire Straits' track. This is my favourite rock band of all time. I gave the disc jockey some cash, and he happily played Dire Straits for the half hour or so we spent drinking in the club. The girls were all young teenagers, but what stunningly beautiful girls they were. Some of our fellow travellers went to see the 'Lady Boys of Bangkok', but that was a 'sex-change' too far for me!

While in Bangkok, I had a fall-out with a Tuk Tuk driver. A Tuk Tuk is a small, three-wheeled, motorised rickshaw and carries only two passengers. We left the hotel one evening to go to a restaurant that was recommended in our guidebook. I showed the driver the address and off we went. Eventually, we pulled up at a huge and very touristy restaurant, from which I assume the driver got a backhander every time he brought a new customer. I gave him hell, and told him to get me to the correct restaurant. He drove for miles, muttering all the while. June began to think we were being kidnapped, or about to be mugged, or even murdered. At last, the driver pulled up in a street, with no sign of the restaurant I was looking for. I was really pissed off and told him to bugger off when he asked for the fare. He drove off shouting oaths in English at me. I looked around to see what to do next and spotted the restaurant I was looking for in a nearby side street. The driver had actually followed my instructions the second time round, and I felt really bad about sending him off unpaid.

An interesting dish I tasted in Bangkok was deep-fried grasshoppers from a street vendor. They were absolutely delicious. My ambition was to taste cooked snake, even if I am scared to bloody death of live ones, but snake was out of season. I was very disappointed.

At every opportunity, I make an effort to mix with the ordinary people of each country we visit and always attempt to get away from the tourist traps, despite advice to the contrary from holiday couriers. On a wonderful holiday in China, we visited a highly-recommended Peking duck restaurant, well off Beijing's tourist area. The courier told me it was not advisable to go to such an area, but off we went in a taxi and didn't feel in any way threatened. The restaurant was wonderful and we had the tastiest Peking duck dinner ever. They specialised in this one dish, which was brought from the kitchen accompanied by a loud bang on a gong. First, we were served the crispy skin, then the flesh, and finally a soup made from the carcass. Fabulous.

We visited many interesting places and sights in Beijing, including Tiananmen Square and The Great Wall of China, which were very impressive, then on to Xi'an, one-time heart of the Chinese Empire. We were conducted around the huge excavations where the Terracotta Army of the 1st Emperor Qin Shihaung had lain buried from 200BC. The ranked statues, larger than life, each unique and many mounted on horseback, was an awe-inspiring sight. We found China fascinating, but the Chinese were not yet used to hordes of tourists. Restaurants tended not to have menus in English, so we just pointed to other diners' plates and ordered that. However, in one restaurant, a Chinese lady diner who could speak good English placed our order and we had a glorious lunch.

We then flew on to Hong Kong where we attended the Asian Record Exhibition (similar to Midem). We were warned not to hand out samples to companies unless we were certain they were bona fide, otherwise our albums would be bootlegged before we got home. Strangely, the British Embassy, responsible for briefing the British contingent, was unwilling or unable to advise us which were likely to be disreputable companies. Our attendance at the exhibition was almost a complete waste of time, apart from one minor deal which I secured. But it was lovely to return to Hong Kong, if for no other reason than the dim-sum dumpling lunches. Shortly after our visit, the handover to China took place. Hong Kong is a crazy place, but so interesting – and we had the unusual and enjoyable experience of having lunch with Merry Barrow (John and Lesley's daughter) who was on a working vacation there. Believe it or not, Merry could not recommend a really good Chinese restaurant because, in common with other backpackers, she tended to eat fast food.

Another year, we had a wonderful fortnight on the River Nile. We flew to Cairo where we visited the pyramids and other historical sites over a period of two days. We then boarded a cruise boat and the rest of the holiday was spent travelling up the Nile as far as the Aswan Dam, stopping off to see the Valley of the Kings, many other excavated tombs and other memorable sites. This is a tour I highly recommend. Our only complaint was that the food served on the boat was the same as you'd get in any international hotel, whereas I wanted to sample Egyptian dishes. When I complained, I was told 'no one would eat it' but, on a special 'Egyptian night', all the Egyptian food was scoffed in next to no time. We were supposed to dress up in Egyptian dress for that evening but, just to be contrary, I dressed up with shorts, sandals, black socks up to my knees and a knotted handkerchief on my head. Some fellow travellers didn't get it.

One day we stopped at a small village and our fellow passengers set off by bus for another tomb visit. June and I decided to stay behind and visit the village. In the wake of some acts of terrorism in Egypt, two Egyptian soldiers were stationed at the foot of the gangway and, as we passed them, I noticed their weapons were old Ex-British Army Lee Enfield rifles. I showed an interest in the rifle of one soldier and, to my utter astonishment, he casually handed me the rifle to have a closer look. This breach of security was unforgivable, but he had an ulterior motive. After I had worked the bolt action of the rifle and looked down the barrel, which was rusted beyond belief, I handed it back to the soldier who immediately demanded a tip. I gave him a few coins, but then his buddy had to get the same! So much for Egyptian security during troubled times. Oh, and the rifle was unloaded, so what they'd have done had terrorists appeared from the sand dunes I have no idea. A British soldier's rifle barrel in that state would have resulted in the 'squaddie' being in 'jankers' for weeks.

As we walked into the village, I saw a young boy pick up a stone from the dirt road and run towards us, blatantly asking for money for the stone, which he alleged came from one of the local tombs. We did not stay long because we were simply besieged by beggars of all ages, who seemed to think we were millionaires. By their standards, I suppose we were. The poverty was appalling. After buying June a bit of gold jewellery, we left.

On return to the boat, we spent a wee while 'rearranging' the sun-deck furniture as a prank. To explain: fellow passengers would daily 'book' their deck chairs very early in the morning by placing towels, books etc. on their chosen chairs, and then go off to breakfast or whatever. I understood that it was only German holiday-makers who had this reputation. In an effort to teach some of our fellow passengers the error of their ways, June and I mischievously switched towels and books etc. all around the deck chairs, and then sat back and had a quiet snigger when the owners found the chaos we had created. Some asked me who was responsible, and I innocently said we had been in the village all morning.

We revisited South Africa in the '90s to see my brother Jimmy and his family. By then they had moved out of Springs (Johannesburg), and were quite near The Kruger National Park in Boven, Waterval in Eastern Transvaal. They had moved because they could no longer suffer the violence which followed the end of apartheid and the beginning of the new South Africa. Ironically, while Jimmy was meeting us at Johannesburg Airport, the house was burgled. This subsequently persuaded Jimmy and Anne to move finally to the relative safety of Cape Town. The weakness of the rand made it quite impossible for them to return to the UK with any worthwhile funds.

We had three glorious weeks in South Africa. June and I again visited The Kruger Park, this time on our own, but in my nephew's car which he had kindly loaned me for a few days. On this occasion, we saw so many animals I am unable to list them all here, but including many lions and large herds of elephants, all at very close range. I was embarrassed to return the car to Martin with a flat battery due to excessive use of the air conditioning (and possibly because he had not been regularly checking the battery level). It was a memorable holiday that included celebrating Christmas dinner in a hotel garden. New Year was a bit strange though; there was no 'Scottishness' about it. The neighbours stayed at home, and we sat in the garden looking up at the stars. Many thanks to Jimmy and Anne for their wonderful hospitality.

There had been a bit of a catastrophe back home while we were away. Due to a sustained period of severe frost, a water pipe had burst and flooded the garage, soaking our washing machine and tumble dryer. When dried out, they both functioned okay, so I suppose we were lucky.

Other great holidays we have enjoyed are much closer to home. We visited the Western Isles twice and enjoyed good weather on each occasion, as well as wonderful hospitality from the Gaels. There are some fine eating places on the islands, including Scarista House. The beautiful and famous beaches of pure white sand on Harris were practically deserted on our visit.

We have enjoyed wonderful holidays on Mull and Bute, and in 2009 we spent a week on each in May and June respectively. The weather was superb both weeks and I walked for miles, on Bute especially. I think this may have been responsible for triggering my hip pain a few weeks later.

We have also enjoyed short-break holidays to Amsterdam (several times), Paris (twice), Venice, Seville and Barcelona. Each visit had its own special delights, and I would recommend each for different reasons. When we visited Amsterdam, I persuaded June to go with me to the Sex Museum, which was hilarious, especially some of the working models – by placing a Euro into a slot, a full-size male model in a 'dirty raincoat' appeared out of a cupboard and opened the front of his coat to 'reveal all.' I was helpless with laughter by the time I left, but some fellow customers appeared to be seeking cheap thrills and took a much more serious approach. We also visited the red-light district in Amsterdam, which was quite an eye-opener, especially to see normal retail business successfully trading, while all around scantily-clad girls sat in their 'shop windows', showing their wares and touting for business. How the other half lives, eh? The Anne Frank Museum meant a long queue, but was worthwhile.

June and I also spoil ourselves with weekend breaks in Scotland, and have a few favourite hotels we return to over and over again. Probably our favourite of all is Boath House at Auldearn in Morayshire. It is an old estate house which was occupied by the army during the WWII. When they vacated the premises at the end of the war, it was partly boarded up and, as youngsters, my cousins and I would creep through the woods to have a look at it. It was supposedly haunted and, needless to say, we'd see

Ian in Venice.

'something' moving inside the broken windows and run for our lives. We always went back, of course!

In 1992 Boath House was bought by a wonderful couple, Don and Wendy Matheson, who opened it as a hotel in 1997. They are wonderful hosts, and their staff are also lovely folk, all determined to make your stay an enjoyable experience. The food is second to none. I rate dinner at the hotel as one of the finest eating experiences in Scotland. Don and Wendy have worked very hard to restore both the house and the grounds, including a lake and walled garden, and every time we visit (at least once a year) we see and enjoy the recent improvements, the result of their labours.

I enjoy a good laugh with Don – at an early stage, we were able to break down any barriers which might have existed and enjoy some great craic. Don has many funny stories, but one, poking fun at himself, is worth repeating. One afternoon he was busy working in the garden when an American couple arrived and gave him a cursory wave. Later, he was stoking the lounge fire when they saw him again and greeted him. When they sat down in the dining room for dinner, Don waited on their table, and the astonished American male asked, 'Do you do all the work around here buddy?' Don replied 'Yes', whereupon the American said, 'I hope the owner pays you well.' Don shook his head, said, 'No' and walked away stifling a laugh.

Boath House Hotel, Auldearn.

The young chef at Boath House is Charlie Lockley, who has earned himself many awards, including a Michelin Star. By coincidence, the manager, Jonny Ross, is the grandson of my cousin, Margaret MacDonald, who lives in Nairn. Long may Don, Wendy, Charlie and the others continue to provide superb service, and long may we be able to enjoy it.

Another hotel we love is the Crinnan Hotel at the Crinnan Canal which, like Boath House, is extremely comfortable, but in addition has the most glorious West Highland scenery. We never fail to order a main dish of fresh prawns, usually landed daily at the pier across the road at about 5pm. The exact time of landing is stated on the menu of the day. The owner and staff have been there for some years, and all contribute to making every visit a wonderful weekend.

Both these hotels take dogs, which is very important to us. One morning in 2002, Marina Wilson came to work with the most gorgeous wee white West Highland terrier (or Westie as they are referred to). June and I had been talking about buying a dog, and wee Archie blew us away. Apparently, there was still one puppy left of the litter, so we phoned and asked the breeder to hold it. We travelled to a house in Plean near Stirling and bought Archie's wee sister on the spot. We had met Mairi MacInnes at Celtic Connections shortly before we left to go to see the wee pup, so

The irreplaceable Mhairi Bheg.

we named her 'Mairi Bheg'. Mairi Bheg is Gaelic for 'Little Mary'. Mairi Bheg's mother was shown twice at Crufts and must have been a wee cracker. Unfortunately, we never saw her.

Mairi Bheg is the finest wee dog in the land and we love her to bits. She has absolutely no bad traits; makes friends with everyone she meets (including a couple of friends who claim they don't like dogs); welcomes and behaves with all other dogs she meets; and is loving and loyal. We were so lucky getting such a great wee friend. When we go abroad on holiday and leave her with Linda, who also has a special relationship with her, I just cannot wait to see her again. I miss her so much, so now she tends to go everywhere we go. As a result, we only stay in hotels that allow dogs, and surprisingly there are many. She has only let us down once. We were staying in Scarista House on Harris, and she 'peed' on the sitting-room carpet in front of the owner. I was so embarrassed!

I enjoy going for walks with her, or is it her that takes me for walks? Not sure, but we have great fun. She loves hunting for rabbits and, on occasions, when I walk her on the Lammermuir Hills, she flushes out all sorts of wildlife, including a white hare on one occasion. She took off after it and I feared I might never see her again, but she is quite obedient and came back when I called her. She is also expert at flushing out grouse on moors. She loves playing hide-and-seek with me amongst the dunes at Gullane beach.

Sadly, she has one serious health problem. Like many Westies who suffer from either sensitive skins or sensitive tummies, she has a sensitive tummy. Once, she almost died and had to be kept overnight in the Royal Dick Veterinary Hospital. Since then, she has to be 'persuaded' to take tablets every day, and can only eat desensitised tinned food. All this costs a small fortune, needless to say, but I do not grudge a penny of it on my wee pal. She even features on the inside of our Greentrax catalogue. As I said earlier, there's 'no fool like an old fool'.

Talking of food, although not doggie food, we are fortunate to have many fine eating places in and around East Lothian and Edinburgh, and none better than the Rocks Hotel in Dunbar, run by Jim Findlay and his family; we visit often on Sunday afternoon for lunch. We have also had some memorable staff Christmas lunches there, and celebrated our Golden Wedding in style with close friends and family. The local Longniddry Inn serves up the best 'pub food' I know of, and the helpings are enormous. Fishers' Bistro in Leith and the Loch Fyne Restaurant at Newhaven are cracking seafood restaurants and, if we have not visited either for some time, I invariably order a starter of 12 juicy oysters. For Indian food, the

Two Sleeping Beauties.

best as far as I am concerned is the Koh-i-Noor in Glasgow – their lamb Bhuna is unsurpassable. There is also a very fine Indian restaurant in Tobermory on Mull, and quite a good one in Musselburgh. We are lucky to have a very fine Chinese restaurant locally in Port Seton, the Dragon Way. Their aromatic crispy duck and pancakes are the finest in the land. A visit to the Three Chimneys Restaurant on Skye is also a great eating experience.

Yes, we are so grateful that we are able to enjoy all these fine things, and my position in the company as MD allows June and me, plus Mairi Bheg, to 'up and off' any time we want. We have, I think, reached the point where air travel is just too daunting for us, and the interminable delays at airports detract from the enjoyment of holidays. We are perhaps particularly unlucky, but we seem seldom able to fly without delays, and I am sick of air companies, particularly British Airways, losing my luggage. On one trip to Midem (Nice Airport), BA lost my suitcase on the flight out, as well as on the flight home!

June and I are fortunate to be blessed with some really good friends. I have already mentioned Kate and Tom Ward, Lesley and John Barrow, Maxine and Ken Thomson, and Heather and Bill Barclay, all of whom we have known for many, many years. We have other good friends, but these represent the closest friendships. One of life's problems is keeping in contact with friends and, some years ago, having all moved house to various corners of Edinburgh and the Lothians, there was a real danger of bonds being broken. Someone had the good sense to realise this in time, and so began what were later to be referred to as 'G8' Sunday lunches when we regularly met at different eating establishments and whiled away the afternoons in such trivial pursuits as eating and drinking.

The G8 lunches seem less frequent these days, but the 'girls' all meet from time to time, and elements of the G8 group meet for lunch. Then there are the lovely days (usually sunny) when we visit Lesley and John at a holiday cottage they rent in the lovely sheltered spot of Canty Bay in East Lothian. The location is idyllic, and many a happy afternoon has been spent there with assorted friends and family.

June and I regularly 'first foot' Ellen and Ian McCalman on new Year's Day, when we enjoy a wonderful curry and lots of good craic with the many friends invited later in the evening. What a grand way to celebrate the New Year. In recent years, we have enjoyed their company more frequently. Maggie Cruickshank is another very good friend of many years standing, who has shared many parties, festivals and other events with us.

June has a friend Cath, from Musselburgh, who she meets regularly for shopping expeditions to Edinburgh and, if for no other reason, I will be eternally grateful to her for relieving me of this onerous task. Cath is a lovely, gentle lady who sadly lost her husband when he went down, along with many others, on *HMS Hood* during the WWII.

Peter Haigh (of Pier House Studios) and myself meet for a curry quite regularly, and occasionally we are joined by Peter's son, Thomas. These are occasions when we put the world to rights, while enjoying the good food of the Indian restaurant, Britannia Spice. Peter is a great listener, and helped me no end during some of the troubled times June and I experienced.

In 2007, my good friend, Ken Thomson (the Fatz of Fizz, Fuzz and Fatz fame) very sadly passed away after several years of poor health. Like myself, Ken had no religious beliefs, so his funeral at Mortonhall Crematorium had no religious content. Maxine did me the great honour of inviting me to conduct a 'celebration of Ken's life' at the crematorium. It was a somewhat daunting and emotional task, but Ken was a longtime friend and I have many happy memories of our friendship. I was best man at his wedding to Maxine, a day to remember and savour. Ken had a wonderful send-off from his many friends who attended Mortonhall.

Dr Ian Green Hon Doc RSAMD.

Tich Frier sang Ken's own song, 'Edinburgh Town' and bluesman, Mike Whellans, sang one of Ken's favourite blues numbers. It may surprise some that Ken wrote several fine songs. We will not forget you!

I am often asked what some of the highlights of my life have been. Well, of course, my army service and time in Korea are up there, as are my successes in cycle speedway, angling and horticulture, plus 30 years' police service and my traditional music involvement, including the 'Greentrax Years'. It is, therefore, difficult to make a choice, but probably the most significant chapter of my life has to be the Greentrax years.

My proudest day has to be the

day on which I was presented with my honorary degree of Doctor of Music by the Royal Scottish Academy of Music and Drama in Glasgow. The wonderful presentation speech was made by Brian McNeill (see appendices). This is closely followed by the presentation at the Scots Trad Awards of the Hamish Henderson Award for Services to Scottish Traditional Music and entry into their Hall of Fame. John Barrow made the presentation speech (see appendices) and was most generous in his praise. A few years later, I had to make the presentation speech when John was finally recognised in the same way. Regrettably, on the night my nerves got the better of me and I did not rise to the occasion as I should have.

There are others occasions of great pride, but these two are special. I only wish Mam and Dad had been alive and present when these great honours were bestowed on me. I am sure they would have been very proud of their 'wee mistake' – and who would have thought, least of all me, of such achievements when I set out a long time ago as a wee ragamuffin 'loon' from the backwoods of Moray?

From time to time, I am referred to as a 'grumpy old man', and comparisons are drawn with the great characters of the TV series, 'Grumpy Old Men.' I include a few examples of my grumpy old man syndrome.

As a rule, I do not vote for politicians because I believe the whole system to be corrupt, with politicians who seem intent on lining their own pockets and ensuring their future as politicians, rather than looking to the interests of those who voted for them. The political system leads to complacency when parties and members of parliament are in power too long and corruption is rife – take for example the 2009 disclosures about MPs' expenses. The most frustrating aspect of our political system is that, once elected, members of parliament seem incapable of answering a question honestly, or even answering it at all for that matter; I despise the party whip system, resulting in MPs quite often voting against their conscience. Quite clearly, much of this is because MPs, and Prime Ministers in particular, have an eye on the next election. It is, however, dishonesty in my book and I despise those who casually write it off by declaring, 'Well that's politics for you.' Sorry. That's just not good enough.

I hear the cry, 'Wasted vote' but it's not entirely wasted. I do go to the polling station, collect my ballot paper and leave with it, usually to the consternation of the presiding officer or his/her assistants. I take my voting paper home and always endorse it with the words, 'Find me an honest politician and I will vote for him/her.' I sign it, address it to the Incoming Prime Minister, The House of Commons, London, and pop it in the letter box. Unsurprisingly, I never receive a reply, but I feel better for this pathetic (??) protest. I did vote for devolution and I will vote if there is a referendum for independence but, until the present political circus is changed, I will continue to 'waste' my vote by posting it to London. Do you think it might be possible somehow to convince all the voters, just once, to stay away from the polling stations as a protest? No, I suppose not.

I quite enjoy the doorstep battles with prospective candidates though. When asked, I tell them in no uncertain terms that they cannot count on my vote, and I repeat more or less what I have said above. On one occasion, a candidate was accompanied by his polling agent and he took exception to my 'dishonesty' comments, asking, 'Are you suggesting my candidate is dishonest?' I answered that with another question (which is the norm for any politician). 'Has your candidate previously been elected?' He answered, 'No,' so my reply was along the lines of, 'Well wait until he is elected, then ask me the same question in a year or so.' They stormed off rather upset. I'm not sure why! Since I began these doorstep confrontations, I have had fewer and fewer electioneering visits, so that can't be bad.

Something that really bugs me is the daily interference caused by mobile phones and their gross misuse, often in social circumstances, including restaurants. I am probably one of the few people on earth who does not own a mobile phone. I don't want one and I will never own one. I can organise my life perfectly well without one. When I am in the office, I am readily available on my landline phone or by internet. When I'm at home, I can be contacted on my house landline, certainly by my family and friends. During out-of-office hours, a message can be left on the office answer-phone, so what do I need a bloody mobile phone for – to annoy other people perhaps?

I simply cannot stand 'cold telephone calls' (uninvited sales calls in other words) and even more so, I detest the pre-recorded calls that are becoming the norm. The former are plain bloody annoying but can be dealt with verbally (and always are!), but the latter are an absolute and utter misuse of the telephone system and a personal insult to the prospective customer. Imagine 'a bloody automatic machine' calling a human being. What next? I loved the comment made by Bob Geldof on a Grumpy Old Men programme. When asked how he deals with cold and unwanted telephone calls, he replied, 'I simply say fuck off and hang up.' Good one, Bob.

I am not a person who seeks material things. I am not in any way clothes-conscious. (Fashion was invented by clothes designers to ensure high profits, and buyers are, in my opinion, extremely gullible). CDs are my only weakness. One thing I do expect when I do make a purchase is good service.

When I reached 70 years of age, I decided I would treat myself and buy what I thought would be a rather grand motor car – a Mercedes. This was a terrible purchase. I had virtually no brakes for the first few months, despite several visits to Western Automobiles who sold me the vehicle. Their customer care and after-sale service were appalling, and I quickly found myself at odds with the managing director. They refused to accept there was a fault with the brakes, and only when I wrote to the manufacturer did I get any satisfaction. A Mercedes representative arrived, road-tested the car and agreed there was 'a problem with the brakes'.

The car went to Western Automobiles, was returned after two days and I was told that no fault had been found. Remarkably, the brakes were suddenly 100 per cent perfect. There was also a very annoying rattle behind the dashboard but, despite numerous attempts by the garage to resolve this, the rattle remained; so, on the advice of a friend, I turned up the audio system so I couldn't hear it! There were other designs aspects which I did not enjoy, and I reached a point where I hated the car. So after two years I traded it in. I was so glad to see the back of that Mercedes. I bought a BMW, and the customer care from Peter Vardy BMW Sales was in complete contrast to Western Automobiles. After two years, the car is still a real pleasure to drive.

Litter is another subject that gets me going. I travel around this beautiful country of ours and am dismayed to see so much litter in our beauty spots and, of course, our cities. I am at a loss to know why people blatantly throw down rubbish and leave it! I am equally at a loss to understand why the various councils do not make a determined effort to clear it up – after all, we do consider Scotland to be a tourist attraction. What must tourists think?

Replies to my letters of complaint to councillors usually indicate a dangerous complacency and a belief that there is not a litter problem. Litter was one of the reasons I left Edinburgh. In the area where we lived, we were exactly a 'fish-and-chip-supper-eating distance' from the local 'chippie' and, while I constantly cleaned up the mess in our immediate area, my neighbours looked upon me as some kind of nut. They frequently exclaimed, 'The council should clean that up, not you.' But, of course, the council did not.

Another thing that makes me very angry: I take exception to broadcasters and newspaper hacks claiming, 'England won another medal today...' when, in fact, they mean 'Scotland won a medal', but will quite blatantly refer to the 'Scotsman or woman' who failed to gain a medal. Bugger that for a lark. I also take great exception to those who continually refer to 'England' when they actually mean the UK.

Television! Now there is a subject a 'grumpy old man' can really get his teeth into. Is it me or have we reached an all-time low in TV programming? I frequently look at the television preview for the week and fail to find more than a handful of programmes worth viewing. I cannot abide bloody 'soap operas', which are so far from 'life as we know it Jim', and all covering the same scenarios sooner or later. I loathe police programmes because, having served 30 years in the service, I am infuriated by the never-ending and quite basic inaccuracies and other garbage. 'Reality' shows and their 'dancing' and 'skating' partners, which appear to provide platforms for people with huge egos and a need to show off, just leave me cold. Then there are cooking programmes, more cooking programmes and more cooking programmes – just how many recipes do we need? If you do attempt one of their recipes, you usually find you don't have half the ingredients. In any case, there are only two chefs worth their 'cooking salt' – Rick Stein in Padstow and Hugh Fearnley-Whittingstall of River Cottage fame. I miss Rick's wee dog.

TV adverts used to add some humour to viewing, but the majority nowadays seem obscure and, in the case of car advertising, just plain daft. Most of the adverts I have to suffer through would certainly not encourage me to buy the particular product and, if that woman tells me once more 'Because we're worth it', I will scream.

So, what's left for the more discerning viewer? Well, I enjoy the daily news, although some newsreaders leave a lot to be desired. I do enjoy wildlife and travel documentaries, good films (not the blood and guts of 'Friday the 13th' etc.), some sports (although snooker has certainly reached saturation point in my opinion), actual real-life reporting of world events, good traditional music programmes or series (although these are few and far between and anything with some educational value. One advertiser I do love is Barr's Irn-Bru, especially the school crossing lady who said, 'Stop there. Ye canny have tried the piiiineaaaaaaaaple!' (Who could make pineapple sound like that but a Glaswegian?) I also love the compare the meercat.com adverts.

BBC Radio Scotland used to be a favourite station, but first Maggie Cunningham, in my opinion, destroyed much of what was good about it, and the destruction has been continued by the present musical directors, who I will not name for fear of reprisals! They seem intent on replacing all aspects of Scottish culture, and removing Scottish music, in particular, from the airwaves. For example, BBC Radio Scotland recently ended the hugely successful and popular Sunday afternoon Reel Blend programme presented by the wonderfully 'couthy' Robbie Shepherd. This eclectic programme covered all aspects of Scottish music, with 'live' interviews of the most interesting people. It was essential listening for me, as was Jimmy McGregor's sadly-lamented programme of several years back, and also Iain Anderson's hugely-popular afternoon session of Fine Tunes. The latter was replaced by one Tom Morton, who caused a real 'stushie' when he said some years ago that he did not play much Scottish music on his show because there was not much good music coming out of Scotland. Really, where have you been these last couple of decades, Tom? I switched off from his programme because the principal content is 'Americana'. There is enough of that on both BBC and the commercial radio stations.

It gave me real pleasure to see the Reel Blend programme receive the Media Award at the 2009 Scots Trad Awards, and witness the entire audience rise to its feet to give Robbie and his producer, Jennifer Forrest, a standing and lasting ovation. I enjoyed writing to BBC Scotland the next day and sticking the knife into the Reel Blend butchers. Not that the BBC Radio pay any attention. They have their own agenda, and bugger the listeners. In the words of Maggie Cunningham when she was in power, 'The day might come when BBC Radio Scotland will be a talk-only station.' Save me from such people who seem intent on destroying Scotland's culture – you might think some of them were English politicians!

I used to listen to Radio Scotland daily at the office, but I rarely bother tuning in at all now, with the exception of the specialist traditional music programmes, such as Travelling Folk, and news bulletins. I don't wish to hear the likes of Fred MacAulay 'havering' away most of the morning, with often boring guests, or the self-indulgent Tom Morton in the afternoon.

The annual Scots Trad Awards are grand affairs, and it is Simon Thoumire we must thank because it was his brainchild. He has, however, many volunteer helpers who are also to be congratulated. I particularly mention Simon because he has even more energy than I used to have and has a way of making things happen. We should be grateful to him for raising the profile of Scottish traditional music ever higher and also integrating its many strands. Alba TV has in recent years become part of the event and screens it a week later. Should Alba TV some day become part

Ian on stage at the Scots Trad Awards.

of Freeview TV then we will be well pleased, because it seems neither BBC TV nor STV are interested in backing the awards, despite invitations to do so. If you have never attended the awards, make a special effort to do so, and you will be in for some fine music, good fun amongst friends and part of an emotionally charged evening.

I wish I could say such kind words about the BBC Radio 2 Annual Folk Awards but, with one or two exceptions, they have blatantly awarded the same group of singers and musicians time and time again. There is dangerous complacency, which seemed resolved after a group of Scottish representatives met the producer of the awards at Glasgow's Celtic Connections some years back. He appeared to take on board the many relevant points raised, in particular that the awards did not fairly represent the huge talent of Scotland, Ireland and Wales. For one year the awards net seemed to be cast wider. I regret that it did not last. Like so many in Scotland, I feel it is useless making further protest and vote with my feet by not attending the event. Anyway, we have our own awards, which seem much fairer in being voted on by the general public.

I was, however, delighted to see that good sense prevailed when Dick Gaughan was presented with the Lifetime Achievement Award at The BBC Radio 2 Folk Awards in 2010.

Enough of that though, or you may really begin to believe I am the original 'grumpy old man' and that would not be quite accurate, almost, but not quite.

So what is in store for the future? I hope I have many more years ahead of me, with the health to enjoy life to the full, apart for my 'grumpy old man' subjects. I consider myself fortunate to live in one of the finest and most beautiful countries in the world, and I am fortunate to be Scottish. I could never leave Scotland permanently! I love Scotland and am proud to be a Scot. When filling in forms, I always declare my nationality as 'Scottish' and certainly not 'UK citizen'. Whatever anyone might say to the contrary, we are a unique people, and different from our English neighbours. I'm not anti-English, but I do believe we have the right to manage our own affairs.

Dick Gaughan has got it just right when he says, 'I think England should also get home rule!' I'll drink to that.

Would I change anything if I had my life to live over again? I have had some incredible highs and of course some terrible lows, many of which are included in the book. I wish family matters had steered a happier course but my daughter Linda and her family, plus our many good friends, have compensated to a great extent. I have had the great fortune to experience the extraordinary comradeship of army life, 30 years public service in the police, plus promotion. Then of course there are the achievements in the traditional music business and the remarkable Greentrax years. Looking

Linda and family.

back on a pretty hectic life, there is not much I would change. Maybe just a slightly different emphasis on certain areas – fine tuning as they say.

Thank you for buying this book. It is no literary work of art and was never intended to be so – just a review of a very active, varied and, I think, interesting life. Anyway, it's all there, 'warts and all', for you to be the judge of that. I do believe everyone should take time to sit down and write their story. I wish Mam and Dad had. As a personal experience, I have found it to be not only cathartic, but also a fascinating journey of rediscovery. Apologies for any memory lapses.

appendix one

Scots Trad Awards Hamish Henderson Award for Services
to Traditional Music
Presented by Dr John Barrow
2005

evenin' all. As I was a-proceeding in an orderly fashion in the general direction of The Queen's Hall this evening, m'lud ... Good evening. And, hasn't this just been the best evening! Good company, great music and mebbe a wee dram or a pint. Quality stuff!

Tonight I have the inestimable nay, transcendental, honour of having been asked to speak about a very old and dear friend – Ian Green – on this occasion of him being awarded the Hamish Henderson Award for Services to Traditional Music.

Much of the background in Ian being given this accolade comes of course from his work as the boss at Greentrax Recordings which he started in 1986, almost 20 years back – and, mind you, he was then going into retirement, having left the Edinburgh polis in 1985! But, there's a lot more which went before that and which led to Greentrax.

I first met Ian and June Green and their family about 1970 or 1971. Since then Ian and I have been jointly involved (along with some other excellent and very hard-working people, several of whom are here tonight) in starting ... first: the Edinburgh Folk Club in 1973; second *Sandy Bell's Broadsheet* (also 1973); third, the Edinburgh Folk Festival (the first one was in 1978 and while we didn't really start it, we both had a bit of a hand in it); fourth, the Aal Centre which began in 1982 and which mutated into the Acoustic Music Centre a few years later (you might have noticed it resurfaced this year). But, it's often said: 'You want to get a job done, find a busy man to do it!'

So in addition to that list – and that's really quite a decent list of activities for anyone's spare time – Ian was a member of the TMSA's national committee for several years and, for 10 years until about 1980 or so, ran what was popularly known as Fuzzfolk (the Police Folk Club).

Ian is still very proud of Fuzzfolk, rightly so, and always wanted good performers there.

One day Ali Watson of the Cotters duo, who were well-known locally in the 1960s, was driving along to find a panda car on his tail. This pursuit went on for a while until Ali pulled over whereupon Ian, for 'twas he, stopped behind him and, walking up to Ali's car, indicated to Ali to wind down the driver's window. At this point Ali hadn't the faintest idea what was going on – he'd been a model driver for about three or four miles. And then Ian said, 'Are you Ali Watson of the Cotters?' Ali agreed. Ian continued, '...so, could you come and play at our folk club next week?'

Ian is known for being tenacious – as Ali Watson could demonstrate! And while all of this extra-curricular stuff was going on Ian rose through the ranks to retire from the polis as an Inspector. The years since his retirement in 1985 have seen Greentrax become a respected international name in the music business, Scotland's biggest folk music label and one of the biggest specialist labels in the UK with, at the last count, almost 400 active titles in their catalogue – over 90 per cent of which feature Scottish acts which simply reflects the remarkable amount of talent in this great wee country as we have seen tonight. This is an achievement of which everybody, without exception, in this entire country should be unreservedly proud. No mean feat really, you know, for a guy who is essentially an ordinary Jock from Forres who trained as a gardener, served in Korea as a conscript (who, by the way, dug the regimental bogs and, in fact, also played in goal for a Scottish army football team out there – is there no end to this man's talents?), and then tried to keep the peace around Edinburgh for about 30 years or so.

Ian bowed out of the Aal Centre around 1985 – I sometimes wonder if it was anything to do with getting a black eye one night from an over-enthusiastic punter who was thrown out. It seems the polis take a dim view of officers turning up for work sporting a shiner so Ian had a few days enforced leave that August. He once told me, in fact, that he'd stopped carrying a truncheon on duty years ago. An arrest had been made at Murrayfield and the culprit was being locked up in the High Street for the night. Ian asked the guy why he'd kept on scrapping while they were rolling about on the ground even though Ian had been belting him about the legs with a truncheon. The guy said, 'Nae problem pal. Ye were hitting my false leg – I couldnae feel a thing!'

Now, like the majority of people here tonight — perhaps everybody here tonight – Ian had a notion that, in some way, traditional music is simply important and then he set out to do something about it, to make it happen in some way on behalf of others in fact – organising gigs – most often with June providing essential assistance, working backstage, and on at least one occasion I know of, driving right across Edinburgh to hand-deliver one album somebody had bought from him. That, however, contains an enormous amount in a relatively few words. First, it presupposes that some thought has been given to the matter; second, that choices have been made as a result; and third, that a conscious and possibly a considerable personal decision has been made. Ian's idea behind the creation of Greentrax was that Scottish folk performers would now have a Scottish label that would record them when no other labels would cast them a second glance.

Now, I'm not going to go through the Greentrax catalogue picking out such albums but there have been some notable albums which were pure labours of love. Like, for example in 2004, 'Bah Humbug: – The Alternative Christmas Album' – don't get him started about Xmas! Or voting in the General Election. Ian claims that he writes to every Prime Minister at every election and asks whoever is in No 10 (or perhaps it's a 'Dear Jack' letter nowadays?) to tell him the name of an honest politician so that he can vote for him or her. Apocryphal? I don't know, but Ian claims he hasn't voted for years.

I think Hamish would be quite pleased to see Ian receiving this award. After all we, Ian, myself plus Kenny Thomson – editors three, as were, of *Sandy Bell's Broadsheet* – awarded Hamish the very first Sandy Bell's Cup about 30 years ago. What goes around, comes around perhaps? The recipients at award ceremonies always say that it's particularly gratifying to receive a gong or whatever, since it comes from your peers in the 'business'. This award – the Hamish Henderson Award for Services to Traditional Music – is no exception and it is equally gratifying to be asked to speak for Ian at this time.

Ian's brought much to the indigenous culture of Scotland through his different activities over the years, putting his money where his mouth is. He is a most worthy recipient of this award tonight. Please, now raise your glasses with me...

appendix two

Honorary Degree Presentation Speech by Brian McNeill
2006

ord Chairman, Principal, Governors of the Academy, Members of the Academic Board, Ladies and Gentlemen, I stand before you today to celebrate a life of service and achievement which has transformed the Scottish traditional music scene.

It's a story which is remarkable on many levels. Firstly, it's to do with the realisation of a series of personal dreams. Secondly, it's to do with patience, grit and determination, and lastly, it's to do with honesty, transparency and above all, trust.

Ian Green was born on the 29 January 1934, in Forres. His father was a head gardener, and also a piper, and Ian still remembers a house which was something of a musical centre, a place where friends and players would drop in informally, and where the practice chanter and the moothie could make companionable music with each other.

Following in his father's footsteps, when he was old enough Ian began to train as a gardener, but when the time for National Service came, he went further than his due, signing up for a three-year stint which was to let him see service in both Korea and Japan, and when it ended, he decided that gardening wasn't for him. In 1955 and soon to be married to June, with whom he's about to celebrate his golden wedding, he decided on a career in the police.

And while it was the Lothian and Borders police force which paid the bills, it was a TV programme of the early '60s, one of the Hootenanny series, which was to provide the next step in a different direction. He still remembers the artistes; Ray and Archie Fisher, The Corrie Folk Trio and Paddie Bell, and Dolina MacLennan. Within a few weeks he was buying LPs and starting to seek out live performances. Like so many of the rest of us, once that catalyst moment came, there was no holding back. He was hooked and he knew it; Ian Green had become a folkie.

But unlike many of that weird and unpredictable tribe, he wasn't content to just sit back and be a consumer of this great music. He was ready to give as well as take. He wanted to make a contribution, and being the most practical of men, it took him no time at all to work out how to do it: he started a folk club.

For a music so rooted in counterculture, the Police Club in York Place, Edinburgh, might seem an odd choice to be one of the seminal Scottish folk venues, but on a Sunday night in the early '70s, there wasn't a better place to be. I got a huge part of my musical education there. Celtic music, acoustic blues, comedy – our other honoured guest reduced me to tears of laughter there often enough – contemporary singer songwriters, the lot. It was a place where, if you were in the audience, you were given enough warmth to feel like family, and if you were lucky enough to be on the stage, you were given a sharp, critical listening by one of the most educated, knowledgeable and generous audiences in the business.

Under Ian Green's guidance it ran like clockwork. Always a firm hand, always a light touch. I know my band weren't the only ones to benefit from a generous interpretation of the fee; if a good night had been had on the door and the club looked healthy, there would be a few extra quid in your back pocket when you left. Then, as now, it was the performers who were first in his thoughts.

Now, the sheer hell of running a successful folk club – a particular kind of dogged, swimming-through-treacle slog – should have been enough for even the most dedicated enthusiast, but Ian Green didn't stop there. The almost complete lack of interest in traditional music by the Scottish media frustrated him, so along with John Barrow and Ken Thompson he founded *Sandy Bell's Broadsheet*. As with everything else he turned his deft hand to, it prospered; what began as a simple information sheet – who's on where if you're a punter, who's available on tour next if you're a promoter – quickly became the folk scene's required reading, and to be reviewed in it became a much sought-after honour. Then came another folk club, the Edinburgh Folk Club, still running today. And then came Discount Folk Records, a specialist folk and traditional retailer which both did mail order and went round the festivals to sell. In short, over a 20 year period, the amount of energy this man pumped into the Scottish traditional music scene would probably have been enough to power a mid-sized city. It was, however, nothing compared to what was to come.

During the endless round of summer festivals, Ian realised that a great deal of the talent he was seeing on stage quite simply didn't have a record company that was doing them justice.

That's not to say that there were no labels. There were, but they almost all had their own agendas. Some were hangovers from the dreadful tartan-and-haggis era, where kilt was more important than content. Some were naked commercial operations which laughably tried to bend traditional acts into what they thought was top ten shape. Some were companies which produced good music, but simply weren't big enough to take on a wide roster of artists. In some, the company owner was the only choice of producer, in some, the artist's publishing rights had to be assigned to the company as a condition of the deal, and so on and so on.

And let us not forget that in this burgeoning commercial field of music, a great deal of money was, by the mid-80s, being generated. Emerging money grows its own criminals; some of these companies were – and are – being run by thieves, rogues and con men.

And so Greentrax records began life in the back bedroom of an Edinburgh council house.

A record label dedicated to giving the artist the opportunity to make the recordings they want to make. A no-frills, no hype label, one that would never promise the moon or tell the artist they were the next big thing. A label which would respect the artist's own vision. A label which would meet its financial commitments to the artist to the letter and keep its dealings with the artist entirely transparent.

It was clear within the first few albums that it was going to be a huge success. Why? It was obvious. The one magic word: trust. This was Ian Green you were dealing with; you'd never have to watch your back. The 20-odd years of fair dealing, of knowing the man, now told in spades. Established artists flocked to the label. Names like Aly Bain and Jean Redpath appeared. Many, like myself, left other labels and came for artistic freedom and better production values. Overseas artists like Eric Bogle and Natalie McMaster knew they now had a safe base from which to licence their products in the UK.

Greentrax 001 was A Breath Of Fresh Airs, by Ian Hardie. Greentrax 291, 20 years on, is Heart Of America by ex-Runrig front man Donnie Munro. In between lies a catalogue that's a veritable Who's who of Scottish traditional music. Greentrax Recordings is now the clear leader, head and shoulders above every other label in Scotland.

But in the end, it's not the undoubted commercial success which is the best testament to Ian Green's vision. The best testimonial to him I ever heard was only three words long. It came from Gordon Duncan, the Paganini of the bagpipes, now, sadly no longer with us. It came the day after we'd had a marvellous Greentrax celebration concert in the Queen's Hall in Edinburgh. We were sitting in the bar, waiting for transport. Gordon and the barman – another piper – got talking, and the barman asked if he was down in Edinburgh for more than one gig. Gordon explained why we were there. When the barman expressed his surprise that Gordon, a big star on the piping scene, would come down to play a small part in such a concert, Gordon just shrugged his shoulders and said simply, 'It's for Ian.'

There's a piece of advice that we'd do well to pass on to the ladies and gentlemen behind me, and to anyone else who ever intends to make a career out of standing on a stage and hoping to hear the sound of hands smacking together. It goes like this:

Yes, you can make it, but you can't make it alone. So surround yourself with people you'd be happy to share your success with, people you know will support you – and give back what they give you. People you know would put their hand in the fire for you – and be prepared to put your hand in the fire for them. People like Ian Green.

It is with great pleasure that I ask the Principal to confer the degree of Doctor of Music (honoris causa) upon Ian Green and invite him to come forward and accept the degree.

Luath Press Limited

committed to publishing well written books worth reading

LUATH PRESS takes its name from Robert Burns, whose little collie Luath (*Gael.*, swift or nimble) tripped up Jean Armour at a wedding and gave him the chance to speak to the woman who was to be his wife and the abiding love of his life. Burns called one of 'The Twa Dogs' Luath after Cuchullin's hunting dog in Ossian's *Fingal*. Luath Press was established in 1981 in the heart of Burns country, and now resides a few steps up the road from Burns' first lodgings on Edinburgh's Royal Mile.
Luath offers you distinctive writing with a hint of unexpected pleasures.

Most bookshops in the UK, the US, Canada, Australia, New Zealand and parts of Europe either carry our books in stock or can order them for you. To order direct from us, please send a £sterling cheque, postal order, international money order or your credit card details (number, address of cardholder and expiry date) to us at the address below. Please add post and packing as follows: UK – £1.00 per delivery address; overseas surface mail – £2.50 per delivery address; overseas airmail – £3.50 for the first book to each delivery address, plus £1.00 for each additional book by airmail to the same address. If your order is a gift, we will happily enclose your card or message at no extra charge.

Luath Press Limited
543/2 Castlehill
The Royal Mile
Edinburgh EH1 2ND
Scotland
Telephone: 0131 225 4326 (24 hours)
Fax: 0131 225 4324
email: sales@luath.co.uk
Website: www.luath.co.uk